As worship pastor becomes a standard job title in churches across the globe, we are in dire need of a guide for this unique vocation. Zac Hicks has given us a masterpiece that is equal parts manual and manifesto. This book is pastoral theology at its very best.

> —GLENN PACKIAM, pastor, New Life Downtown;
> author, *Discover the Mystery of Faith*

This book is a welcome introduction to the multidimensional nature of worship leadership. Written for practitioners by a practitioner, Hicks brings a convincing voice to the slow-growing but much-needed plea for worship leaders to take up the pastoral duties that are so vital for successful ministry. I highly recommend it for persons in any stage of worship ministry.

> —CONSTANCE M. CHERRY, professor of worship and
> pastoral ministry, Indiana Wesleyan University

Zac Hicks educates and challenges us to carefully consider how we "do" our function as congregational leaders of prayer, all the while christening us with an elevated title that suits the role: the worship pastor.

> —CHUCK FROMM, founder, *Worship Leader Magazine*

Zac has thoughtfully and thoroughly addressed the many creative avenues in which worship can be pastored. And that's so important, because techie artists like me need a better, deeper theological understanding of the influence we have over the worship space. And how we may actually be worship pastors even though it's not in our job title.

> —STEPHEN PROCTOR, visual liturgist and projection artist, illuminate.us

Not only is this book well-written, it is deeply wise and consistently scriptural. I love this book. I wish that every worship pastor (and every pastor) would read it. Read it. You will be pleasantly surprised.

> —ELYSE M. FITZPATRICK, author; *Home: How Heaven*
> *and the New Earth Satisfy Our Deepest Longings*

Leading worship is a high and important calling, and leaders need the tools and resources to pull it off each Sunday. This book provides those resources and the inspiration that worship pastors need each week and in their own lives. There is no better guide than Zach Hicks.

> —JIM BELCHER, PhD, president, Providence Christian College

Speaking from years of personal experience, Zac Hicks offers this winsome invitation to worship leaders to think of themselves as ministers as well as musicians. Essential reading.

> —MAGGI DAWN, associate professor of theology
> and literature, Yale Divinity School

THE WORSHIP
PASTOR

THE WORSHIP PASTOR

A CALL TO MINISTRY FOR WORSHIP LEADERS AND TEAMS

ZAC HICKS

ZONDERVAN®

ZONDERVAN

The Worship Pastor
Copyright © 2016 by Zachary M. Hicks

This title is also available as a Zondervan ebook.

Requests for information should be addressed to:
Zondervan, *3900 Sparks Dr. SE, Grand Rapids, Michigan 49546*

Library of Congress Cataloging-in-Publication Data

Names: Hicks, Zac, 1980- author.
Title: The worship pastor: a call to ministry for worship leaders and teams / Zac Hicks.
Description: Grand Rapids, MI: Zondervan, 2016. | Includes bibliographical references and indexes.
Identifiers: LCCN 2016023585 | ISBN 9780310525196 (softcover)
Subjects: LCSH: Ministers of music. | Music in churches.
Classification: LCC ML3001.H53 2016 | DDC 264/.2—dc23 LC record available at https://lccn.loc.gov/2016023585

Cover design: Julie Calareso
Interior design: Kait Lamphere
Interior art: Julie Calareso, Scott Bajgrowicz

Printed in the United States of America

17 18 19 20 21 22 23 24 25 /DCI/ 15 14 13 12 11 10 9 8 7 6 5 4 3 2

For Abby

CONTENTS

ACKNOWLEDGMENTS

Many moons ago a dear friend, Dave Farmer, encouraged me to start a blog because he thought I had something to say. This book would not exist if it weren't for that providential moment over coffee on a brisk Denver afternoon. *The Worship Pastor* is a community project, from beginning to end, and I want to offer some words of thanks to those communities.

The Community That Poured into Me

To my early mentors in worship, Todd Yokotake, William Lock, and David Clemensen: Thank you for teaching me what worship from the heart and a passion for Christ's church look like. To the pastors I've worked alongside and learned from, Jim Talarico, Steve Sage, Don Sweeting, Marty Martin, Bruce Finfrock, Brad Strait, Barb Roberts, Dave Strunk, Tullian Tchividjian, Rob Pacienza, Duane Mellor, Paul Hurst, Leo Reilly, Adam Masterson, and Nick Lannon: I've learned more from you about pastoring than any book could ever teach me. To the scholars, theologians, and doxologists whose writing and reflection have shaped me deeply, Craig Blomberg, Bryan Chapell, Chuck Fromm, Douglas Groothuis, Bob Kauflin, Ashley Null, Lester Ruth, James K. A. Smith, Kevin Twit, John Witvliet: You are in these pages, and I am forever grateful.

To Jono Linebaugh: Your friendship and wisdom has made this book far different, far better, than it would have been without you in my life. Thank you for the countless conversations and for pointing me to the Reformation, to Paul, and (therefore) to the Jesus that this book is all about.

The Community That Supported and Strengthened the Crafting of This Book

To my home-base editorial team, the rock-star trio of women who made this book better than it deserves to be, Julie Anne Vargas, Brenda Hicks, and Abby Hicks: I thank you for the unique gifts you've given in this process. Julie Anne (along with Erick), you gave me the invaluable insight of my readers and intended audience. Mom, you gave me the exacting insight of a professional editor, and you gave me a writer's genetics. Abby, you gave me the honest insight of my own heart, which apart from you I often had a hard time hearing.

To my thoughtful friends Bruce Benedict, Glenn Packiam, Ryan West, Simeon Zahl: Your feedback on specific chapters made them all significantly better. To my crowd-sourced brain trust—the Liturgy Fellowship (Facebook group): Thank you for being important sounding boards, committed philosopher-practitioners, even research gophers.

To my main editor at Zondervan, Ryan Pazdur: Thank you for the theological sharpening, style smoothing, and important contributions which have made my maiden voyage feel both safe and free. To my agent, Andrew Wolgemuth: God only knows the countless mistakes I would have made without you. Your calm wisdom and reliable accessibility meant the world to me. To the two artists who made my book beautiful, Julie Calareso and Scott Bajgrowicz: The cover and all the inside diagrams (respectively) exceed all my hopes. We agonized over this, and it paid off. Thank you!

To the choir of Coral Ridge Presbyterian Church, along with Chelsea Chen and Julie Anne: Thank you for being indispensable processors of this book's ideas in devotional and conversational form. You've been my army of prayer and encouragement. To my new family at Cathedral Church of the Advent and the pastoral team I am privileged to serve alongside, Andrew Pearson, Deborah Leighton, Matt Schneider, Craig Smalley, and Gil Kracke: Thank you for joining me in this vision and for being so hospitable to me and my family in this season.

The Community That I Can't Live Without

To my parents, Leon and Brenda Hicks: Thank you for believing in me before I knew how to believe in myself and for pointing me to Jesus. Thank you for your commitment to the worship and work of the church; your love became my love. To my family, Abby, Joel, Jesse, Brody, and Bronwyn: You are my home, my joy, and my safe place. You unflinchingly supported my hours away, my stressful agonizing, and my open laptop on long car rides and late nights. I love you.

Introduction

READY OR NOT, YOU'RE A PASTOR

What the church needs most is not another hymnal, larger choirs, more technology, a revised prayer book, or another set of published scripts. What the church needs most is discerning, prayerful, joyous people who treat their work as worship planners and leaders as a holy, pastoral calling.

—John Witvliet, 2003[1]

Dear Worship Leader:

You have an extraordinary job with high stakes and grand opportunities. You aren't *just* a song leader. You aren't *just* a lead musician. Your set lists aren't *just* inspiring medleys of well-glued songs. You aren't merely on a stage, and those people out there aren't merely the audience. They are Christ's bride, God's beloved, gathered in from the four corners of the world that they might be reclaimed by and reaimed toward the Author and Perfector of their faith. They are disciples, followers. What you do and how you lead have a direct and formative impact on their journey of faith. Whether you know it or not, you are *pastoring* them.

Each and every week, you are helping people answer the question, How do I approach God? Every worship service consistently shapes the faith of God's people by training them on what relating to God looks like. And faith shaping is pastoral work. Ready or not, you're a pastor.

Each and every week, you put words into people's mouths that become the language they will use to relate to God the other six days of the week. We wish people were regularly reading their Bibles and consistently engaging in life-on-life community, but if we're honest, many aren't. The only way many learn how to talk to God is through the words, lyrics, and prayers of the services you lead. Those things all

---

1. John Witvliet, *Worship Seeking Understanding: Windows into Christian Practice* (Grand Rapids, Mich.: Baker, 2003), 248.

come together as the corporate prayers of your church that week, teaching the people how to express their private prayers. Prayer shaping is pastoral work. Ready or not, you're a pastor.

Each and every week, you shape the beliefs of the people who gather. Your songs and words don't just inspire. They teach. They help people answer their basic questions: Who is God? What is He like? Who am I? How do I look at this world? Your words and songs shape people's theology, and that kind of teaching is pastoral work. Ready or not, you're a pastor.

Each and every week, you are informing people's knowledge of what mediation between God and humanity looks like. You are answering for God's people a fundamental human question: How am I ushered into God's presence rightly?[2] Your actions and leadership (not merely your songs) answer this. Who ushers people into God's presence? Who makes their worship acceptable? Is it you, or is it Jesus by the Holy Spirit? Worship Leader, do your prayers, countenance, leadership, and song selection point people to the one Mediator between God and humanity? You see, a pastor's principal job is to point people to Jesus. Ready or not, you're a pastor.

Each and every week, you are looked up to as an example and a leader. You have a sphere of immediate influence. Because you stand in front of people and lead them in God's holy worship, you are given the status of leader. Most disciples of Christ look to mentors and leaders to lead them and help them grow. Because you are regularly up front, you are one of those people. Ready or not, you're a pastor.

If you feel underequipped and unqualified, don't take these feelings as a sign you're not called. God is in the business of pouring Himself out through weak vessels (2 Cor. 4:7), and He will give you grace for the journey. But please don't waffle any longer in the untruth that the pastoral work is all being done by the individuals with "pastor" in their title. You may not have that heading on your business card or online profile, but that doesn't change the fact that your work is inherently pastoral. You are a pastor.

My hunch is that this is surprising news to a lot of us. It was to me. When I began to see the ways that my weekly worship leadership impacted the faith journeys of the people I led, I was taken aback. I couldn't mess around anymore with my job. But before we unpack how worship leaders are pastors, we have to first ask one question: How did we get to the place where we worship leaders are surprised to hear that we are pastors?

---

2. This is the fundamental question that ignited the Protestant Reformation, probably more properly posed, How am I justified before God?

How Did We Get Here? (Historical Touchpoints)

Pastoring through worship leading is an ancient idea. The first human beings, Adam and Eve, were charged by God to be creation's worship pastors. Scholars have noted the intentional parallels between the creation account in Genesis and the descriptions of Israel's first formalized group of worship pastors, the priests. For instance, Adam's job description to work and keep the earth (Gen. 2:15) didn't use traditional farming language but terms used to describe the worship leading duties of the Levites in the sanctuary (Num. 3:7–8; 8:26; 18:5–6). The garden itself was described in both its layout and contents to show a purposeful similarity to the tabernacle and the temple—it had an eastern entry (Gen. 3:24; Ezek. 43:4), jewels and gold (Gen. 2:12; Ex. 25:11), a central "tree" (Gen. 2:9; Ex. 25:31–40), angelic guardians (Gen. 3:24; Ex. 25:18–20), and Adam and Eve's "tunics" (Gen. 3:21; Ex. 28:41).[3] In a sense, humanity's central task was to pastor all of creation's worship of God. The link between worship leading and pastoring is etched into the bedrock of creation.[4]

This inseparable relationship is fleshed out in Israel's formalized worship. The earliest records of the gathered worship of God's people show that God set aside a whole subset—the priests in the line of Levi—to oversee, administrate, and lead the worship of the people of God (Num. 3). And important for us in a day and age when *music* is (unfortunately) synonymous with *worship*,[5] we notice that, especially in David's time, music making and worship leading were consigned to the duties of priests (1 Chron. 6:31–48). There weren't priests *and* music leaders. The music leaders were priests (2 Chron. 5:11–13). In ancient Israel, leading worship (including music) was an extension of the duties of pastors.

In the New Testament era, the people of God experienced an overhaul in their theology of worship with the revelation of Jesus Christ. All the practices and duties of the past were now seen in light of His work, to such an extent that the book of Hebrews could call Him the "liturgist of the sanctuary,"[6] the one, true Worship Leader who alone is worthy to usher us into God's presence (Heb. 7:24–25; 8:2; 9:11–14). The New Testament church saw in Christ the embodiment and pinnacle of how worship leading is bound up in priestly and pastoral roles.

---

3. See Gordon Wenham, "Sanctuary Symbolism in the Garden of Eden Story," in *I Studied Inscriptions from Before the Flood: Ancient Near Eastern, Literary, and Linguistic Approaches to Genesis 1–11*, ed. Richard S. Hess and David Toshio Tsumura (Winona Lake, Ind.: Eisenbrauns, 1994), 399–404.

4. Notice, too, that it doesn't take long in Genesis before music making is mentioned with Jubal, "the father of all those who play the lyre and pipe" (Gen. 4:21 ESV). We can already observe the forming of links between pastoring, worship leading, and music.

5. Throughout this section, I will be overemphasizing music in worship leading simply because it is the water we now swim in, and I therefore want to belabor how music leading was a pastoral function for much of the history of the church.

6. In the Greek, *tōn hagiōn leiturgos*.

The unbroken lineage of our heritage of worship pastoring carried forward through the early and medieval church. Their liturgies (the earliest of which included music) were led by the priest-pastors.[7] When music developed in the church to higher levels of sophistication, just as with ancient Israel under David, priests didn't farm out musical worship to nonpastors. The church's, in fact, the Western world's, first composers, choirs, and song leaders were monks and priests. Artists were raised up from within the pastorate.[8]

Throughout the Middle Ages, we can see seeds sown which split the pastoral office from the song leader/musician. Music reached such a point of complexity with the dawn of polyphony and the advent of musical notation by the eleventh century that it became an art form to be more singularly studied and pursued, which in a sense professionalized it. In and of itself, this shift wasn't bad. It was necessary for the flourishing of the art. But with the idea of the professional musician came the notion of a nonpastoral musical figure. Musicians could conceive of their vocation outside the call of the pastorate.[9] The universities, rather than the monasteries, became the hubs of serious music making. Here we enter into the age of the church as patron to artists who composed music for liturgical texts and sacred assemblies (e.g., Gabrieli, Palestrina). Likewise, with the introduction and increasing use of the organ, church positions for choirmasters and organists emerged. These shifts introduced, or at least made more common, the idea of nonpastoral figures leading elements of worship.

If we fast-forward to the history of American evangelicalism, things look more familiar. We should pay special attention to the Second Great Awakening (1790–1840) with its westward-moving revivalism of raising tents and blazing souls. This era bequeathed to modern evangelicals a pragmatic philosophy of worship that helped not only to preserve but also to solidify the split between the pastor and the now largely musical worship leader.[10] By and large, the job of the musi-

---

7. Justin Martyr, *First Apology*, 65–67; outlined in Tim Dowley, *Christian Music: A Global History* (Minneapolis: Fortress, 2011), 51–52.

8. Because of the anonymity of monastic life, usually only the most famous figures, like Ambrose of Milan (c. 340–397) and Gregory the Great (c. 540–604), can be named as examples of musician-pastor figures in the church.

9. The problematic nature of this split of office between pastor and musician was felt, for instance, during the Reformation in England. While (for various reasons) church leaders were shrinking their music programs across the country, one set of Royal Injunctions for St. George's Chapel, Windsor (1550), sought to replace the more "professional artists" with sober-minded musician-priests who had "more regard to their virtue and learning than to excellency in music." See Peter Le Huray, *Music and the Reformation in England, 1549–1660* (New York: Oxford, 1967), 24.

10. From the Second Great Awakening on, the model that every church is marked by two leaders—a captivating preacher and an inspiring musician—has become commonplace. As one historian put it, "It was, of course, an old maxim that great preachers should keep great performers at their sides. Since the Second Great Awakening, musical performances by famous songbirds have been inseparable from the planning and orchestration of an American revival." Kate Bowler and Wen Reagan, "Bigger, Better, Louder: The Prosperity Gospel's Impact on Contemporary Christian Worship," *Religion and American*

cian in the revivalist scheme was to "warm up" the congregation for the stirring message. As this two-part liturgy, music then preaching, moved increasingly from the tent to the church, it gave credence to the idea that the church musician's job was to prepare for rather than actually do pastoral work.

Meanwhile, evangelicals had so simplified historic Christian liturgies that there were virtually no other worship elements to be led by anyone, whether they were a pastor or not, besides music and the sermon. To put it in a simplistic way, pastoral work in worship not only wasn't musical leadership, it was basically only preaching. This hurt the church in two ways. First, music leaders lost almost any sense that they were engaging in pastoral activity in their song leading. Second, pastors began believing that the only pastoral work to be done in a worship service was preaching. Both parties unwittingly participated in the erosion of the bedrock of worship leading as pastoral work.[11]

So here we are. We are living in a time of Western evangelicalism when our default assumption is that every church has two key offices—a pastor and a rock star.[12] And the current scheme of worship leadership struggles to hang on to any conviction that the work of these offices is pastoral. Worship leaders are in desperate need of a new (old) model.

The Aim of This Book

The Worship Pastor is a call to worship leaders to look to the "ancient paths" (Jer. 6:16). But because I want this book to be truly productive and edifying, it's not going to be a summons to return to antiquated forms and functions of worship leadership that can't work in the twenty-first century. I hope to offer a vision for something accessible, tangible, inspiring, and, yes, practical.

Culture: A Journal of Interpretation 24, no. 2 (2014): 195. Example pairings across history: Dwight L. Moody and Ira Sankey; Billy Sunday and Homer Rodeheaver; Billy Graham and George Beverly Shea; Brian Houston and Darlene Zschech; Louie Giglio and Chris Tomlin.

11. In fairness, I should note one tradition stemming from revivalism that might protest my generalizations here with respect to the worship leader's lack of pastoral awareness. From the late 1800s on, the Pentecostal and charismatic traditions championed an awareness among worship leaders that they perform a *very* pastoral function. It is often said by worship leaders in this tradition that they engage in the pastoral/priestly work of ushering people into the presence of God. Ironically, though, this is one pastoral responsibility (the duty of mediation between God and humanity) that is reserved for Jesus alone (1 Tim. 2:5). So, while among evangelicals our Pentecostal and charismatic brothers and sisters probably have a more developed sense of the pastoral nature of the worship leader's vocation, I would humbly submit that it's insufficiently developed if not misdirected. For more on this, see chapter 2, "The Worship Pastor as Corporate Mystic."

12. I phrase it like this for rhetorical effect, but I want readers to be aware that this issue actually cuts across traditionalist and contemporary lines. Before the dawn of contemporary/modern worship, church musicians could very much be "rock stars." The music may have been different, but the outlook was largely the same: the musicians' job was to "wow" people with great, inspiring music, with very little sense of a pastoral call in their vocation.

Each chapter will describe the worship pastor through vignettes and metaphors of how we can (and do) engage our jobs pastorally. The goal of this book isn't to load you up with a whole new set of duties that you don't have time for. It's to offer a vision of how what you're already doing is pastoral work, with the hope that your pastoral call might be strengthened toward a more robust and intentional ministry.

The status quo is already being disrupted. Some of you reading this book share my biography. You are part of a new generation of worship leaders who are dissatisfied with the model of worship leading handed down to you. Many of you are perhaps the first generation to have grown up in the purely contemporary church of the 1980s, 1990s, and 2000s. You're now coming of age and assuming positions of worship leadership in all kinds of churches, from urban church plants to suburban megachurches. You're old enough now to ask deep questions about your vocation, and you've been around the block long enough to know that church rock stardom has been weighed and found wanting. You are serious and sober, and you want to do it right.

At the same time, many churches, educational institutions, and resource hubs aren't equipped with all the tools to engage worship leading from a pastoral perspective in the twenty-first century. *The Worship Pastor* seeks to play a part in filling that void.

It should be noted that the book's title, *The Worship Pastor*, might be a bit misleading, as if a worship pastor is a special kind of office or call. The truth is that, while some like me are blessed to be able to specialize (I know that can be a dangerous word) in worship, I believe that every pastor should consider worship leadership part of their duty, and every worship leader should view their job as fulfilling a pastoral function. Every pastor and worship leader is a worship pastor. Clergy in some Christian traditions already have worship leading built into their job descriptions and training (e.g., Anglicans, Lutherans, Roman Catholics, Methodists, Eastern Orthodox).

The goal of this book is to encourage worship leaders, congregations, and their overseers to collectively up the ante on what a worship leader is. Therefore, I am speaking into the modern role of the worship leader that has emerged in recent years as a mission-critical position on church staffs, and I am pleading for us to give the worship leader's job far more weight than it is now typically given. So, though terms like *worship leader* and *worship pastor* are slippery, I choose to use them as the best touchpoints for the broadest possible connection with those who will read this book.[13]

---

13. My friend Mike Cosper says much the same thing about the liabilities of certain titles accompanying the reluctant necessity to use them. See *Rhythms of Grace: How the Church's Worship Tells the Story of the Gospel* (Wheaton, Ill.: Crossway, 2013), 21.

Who This Book Is For

This book is for worship leaders of all stripes. If you're a new worship leader, this book is for you. It will give you an inspiring vision for the road ahead. It will hopefully also provide a set of tools to help sharpen and aim your call. If you've been a worship leader for a while, *The Worship Pastor* is for you too. It will be a fresh articulation of the job you've already been doing and hopefully provide some inspiration for how to make what you do even better. So whether you're starting out or burning out or anywhere in between, there's something here for you.

This book is for pastors who want to take their oversight of worship seriously. It will be a tremendous aid to pastors for several reasons:

1. The pastor/worship leader relationship many times makes or breaks an effective ministry. Knowing your counterpart's role and call will help you both work better together.
2. If your pastoral training was like mine, chances are not much time was spent on worship. *The Worship Pastor* will not only flesh out a practical theology of worship leading, it will do so from a pastoral angle. It will speak your language.
3. This book will help you to take your call as a worship leader more seriously by giving you a tangible expression of pastoring through worship.

This book is for worship teams and volunteers. If you're in a church and care deeply about its worship, this book will energize you with a deep, inspiring vision about what you do. It will further guide you in how to make worship less of a show and more of a ministry. I'd even encourage teams to go through this book together.

This book is for colleges and seminaries. This book aims to fill a resource void in the curricula of worship programs in Christian colleges and seminaries. I am in touch with many overseers of worship departments who are eager to give up-and-coming worship leaders an inspiring, accessible, but thorough articulation of their pastoral call. It's my hope that God will use this book for that purpose and more.

This book is for a variety of Christian worship traditions. My hope is to be broad enough that the takeaways can be applied across most lines of Christian worship traditions, from free-church Pentecostal to prayer book liturgical. Whether your worship services are largely musical or based on many spoken words, free flowing or highly structured, *The Worship Pastor* should be able to relate to almost everything you do.

How to Read This Book

This book is meant to be flexible for different readers and circumstances. You can definitely read cover to cover. However, each chapter really can stand alone, and I invite you to peruse the chapter headings to see if any titles either pique some interest or expose some unexplored places. It may be that you're at a point in ministry where you want to shore up some weak spots or expand into new ministry territory. Go ahead and jump to those places.

The Worship Pastor also breaks up nicely into a roughly four-month study of a chapter per week. The chapters should be short enough to be doable for individuals, teams, or small groups, even those with busy schedules.

A Concluding Confession

A preacher and author I admire greatly, Steve Brown, once said in a sermon, "Christian authors should confess their sins in the first chapter of their book . . . and then I'll hear what they have to say."

Here's one very deep and personal confession. As I've gathered the ideas for *The Worship Pastor*, and as I've sat down to write it, many moments of self-righteous pride have welled up within me about what a successful worship pastor I must be to "write the book." I've been pretty impressed with myself at times, thinking (this is embarrassing to admit) that some of these chapters are nothing short of autobiographical sketches of my "ministry success." So I confess that I've hopelessly spilled my sin and vanity onto every page of this book, and writing it makes me want to think far more highly of myself than I ought.

But to be honest, I don't live up to what I write. In many ways these sketches are pictures of worship pastors I know whom I'm jealous that I'm not more like. So for my sake—and by God's grace, for yours—please don't miss the concluding chapter, "The Worship Pastor as Failure," for that is what we are, and, as you'll see, there's great hope in that.

Jesus, be our Worship Pastor, by the power of
Your Spirit, to the glory of the Father.

1

THE WORSHIP PASTOR
AS CHURCH LOVER

I love you dead. At this moment.

—Walker Percy, 1971[1]

Without your wound where would your power be?

—Thornton Wilder, 1928[2]

The Rarest Church-Going
Species in Modern Times

If you haven't grown up in the church, the picture I'm about to paint might look foreign, but bear with me. From before I can remember and until the day I went off to college, Waialae Baptist Church—a quaint, multicultural, evangelical gathering of the battle-worn faithful on the south side of a small Hawaiian island in the middle of the Pacific—was my church. My parents began attending there because of its vibrant worship, stirring preaching, and lively programs, but these features didn't last forever. Things happened: a minor scuffle, a major snafu, quick pastoral turnovers, cycles of financial glory and peril, and meaningful relationships occasionally torn apart—sometimes by death, sometimes by sin, always with pain. Newer, hipper churches started popping up around us, and the opportunity for my parents to abandon ship and start over seemed to be ever present.

It's only with hindsight that I can see how my parents' stubborn commitment to one church would become one of the greatest gifts they could have ever given me. I watched them serve faithfully as church members through budget crises,

---

1. Walker Percy, *Love in the Ruins* (New York: Picador, 1971), 68.
2. Thornton Wilder, *The Angel That Troubled the Waters and Other Plays* (New York: Longmans, Green, and Company, 1928), 106.

leadership conflicts, numerical growth and decline, building campaigns, mission trips, scandals, worship wars, personal attacks, and even their own son's teenage ecclesiastical wanderlust.

In an age where churches are dumped faster than middle school boyfriends, where flocks are sized up, examined, sampled, consumed, and discarded like the latest health food fad, those who commit to sticking it out with a church are becoming an endangered species. But even in times when such rare breeds were perhaps more plentiful, they were a sight to behold. The people of a bygone era once called these fanciful creatures "churchmen." For every worship leader who desires to see their job in a more pastoral light, I invite you to look with me at the churchman as a model for what loving the church can look like.

The Churchman as Church *Lover*

For several understandable reasons, *churchman* seems like a stuffy, antiquated title best left for scrapbooks and grandma's stories of the old days. First, it sounds like the worst kind of cheesy Christian nostalgia out there, on par with the sappy, waltzy, "oohm-pa-pa" hymns of the 1940s. Second, what about the church-*woman*? I encourage you that there just might be more than a kernel of timeless worth underneath this dusty, dry husk, from which both men and women who lead worship can benefit. But to avoid the PTSD some of us associate with tweed suits and warbly vibratoed hymn singing, we'll call this model the "church lover." Hopefully our examination of six characteristics of the church lover will spark a passion to cultivate these qualities in our own lives.

1. A church lover passionately loves and believes in the church. We've all seen it— that paradoxical "love is blind" relationship. The gorgeous bombshell marries the mayor of Nerdville. "What does she see in him?" we ask. "He must have a lot of money," or, "He's probably got a great personality," we say. As odd as these kinds of relationships appear, I'd submit that a simple love between a worship leader and his or her church looks a lot like this.

A worship leader who has a pastoral heart believes with desperate optimism in the church and her work in the world. As Bill Hybels has said in many places, "The local church is the hope of the world," and a worship pastor passionately believes this and loves their church for it. The local church is the hope of the world because the church is the body *of Christ*, and *Christ* is the true hope of the world. Because the Father has put all His eggs in the Son's basket, God has bet all-in on His Son's body and bride. God so delights in His people that He feels quite comfortable throwing explanation to the wind in His declaration that amounts to, "I love her because I love her" (see Deut.

7:7–8).[3] A worship pastor seeks to revel in this kind of affection, which lavishes grace on the ungraceful and love on the unlovable. Pastorally minded worship leaders attempt to grow in this "I love her warts and all" disposition exactly because it is God's disposition.

2. A church lover zealously commits to the church's vision and mission. What often distinguishes worship leaders from worship pastors is the latter's ability to place their role and work within the broader vision and mission of the local church. A church I once served had this mission: "to declare and demonstrate the liberating power of the gospel." I needed to be able to conceive of how my work in planning and leading worship services facilitated and participated in that mission. In an annual planning document submitted to my elders, I fleshed it out this way:

> The worship service is the church's "ground zero" for declaring and demonstrating the liberating power of the gospel. Because all fuel for ministry and mission is to be found in the gospel, and because the gospel is something ordained by God to be preached, heard, and received first and foremost in the worship service, our worship therefore becomes the nucleus of our vision. It is where the declaration from God, "It is finished," is most clearly heard, relieving burdens so that disciples are formed and freed to demonstrate and witness this life-changing work to others.

Most church vision or mission statements connect in some way, shape, or form with the Great Commission's call to "make disciples" (Matt. 28:18–20). A worship pastor is acutely aware of worship's role in the disciple-making process and should be able to articulate to the other church leaders and to the rest of the church body just how worship comes together with the church's vision.[4]

3. A church lover humbly submits to a church's God-ordained leadership. I firmly believe that the pastor/worship leader relationship is the most vulnerable relationship in the entire church. I can't tell you how many times I've witnessed and heard of conflicts between pastors and their worship leaders, and I can't tell you how many of those instances ended up leaving a mortal wound in the precious heart of a church. Over the years, I've found this axiom to be nearly unassailable: When my relationship with the lead pastor is solid, I can weather just about any

---

3. In a local church I once served, Rev. Dr. Marty Martin was famous for declaring to God's people at the table during Communion, "He loves you, because He loves you, because He loves you." What appears to be circular reasoning might just be the deepest, most eternal theological insight anyone could ever explore (Rom. 11:33–36).

4. For more on worship's role in the discipleship process, see chapter 4, "The Worship Pastor as Disciple Maker."

storm; when my relationship with the lead pastor is shaky, absolutely everything else feels destabilized.

We could go round and round about why pastors and worship leaders struggle to get along (left brain vs. right brain, engineer vs. artist, envy of gifts you don't have, etc.), but it no doubt gets close to the heart of the matter to simply say that a pastorally oriented worship leader should be very aware of God's choice of *ordained* leadership in a church. Regardless of your church's system for choosing and recognizing their pastor's leadership role, I am using the word *ordained* in a broad sense. I simply mean that every leader (or group of leaders) in a true church has been placed there by God, ordained by His sovereignty to be in that position. Most worship leaders in churches, however pastorally oriented they may be, *aren't* in that unique position.[5]

A worship leader who understands the pastoral calling (in both their life and the life of their other pastor[s]) takes seriously Scripture's encouragement that members of Christ's body should submit to one another in general (Eph. 5:21) and submit to their leadership in particular (Heb. 13:17; 1 Thess. 5:12–13; 1 Tim. 5:17). What does this look like on the ground? For me, it looks like building up a strong relationship of trust between my pastor and me through my faithful, easy, joyful following of their directions and, yes, orders. It means selectively choosing moments to voice disagreements and seeking to do so in gentleness and humility, and *even then* being willing to receive their no. Worship leaders like us need to think long and hard about what hills are truly worth dying on. The longer I do this, the more I find that far fewer of those hills dot the landscape of ministry than I had previously thought.[6]

4. A church lover joyfully cultivates compassion for everyone in their flock, not a select few. Just as I can't selectively love only my wife's eyes, hands, lips, and right pinky toe, so a worship pastor can't cultivate affection for a part of Christ's bride. We are called to love her wholly and completely. We worship leaders get into trouble when we start unknowingly developing rock-star-like entourages and cliques around us, complete with inside jokes and us-and-them behavior.

When Jesus gathered people to Himself, He cultivated a community that had discernible boundaries and was incredibly porous. He allowed for two-way traffic and seemed to be perpetually disrupting the status quo when the community was

---

5. It might be worth remembering here that some traditions—ranging from Eastern Orthodox to Anglican to certain Reformed and Presbyterian bodies—in their various formularies and constituting documents, actually name their ordained clergy as principal leaders in worship. Once again, as we saw in the introduction, not every stream of Christianity can make sense of how starkly we've divided the "offices" of pastor and worship leader.

6. To explore the dynamic between pastor and worship leader further, I recommend Bob Kauflin, *Worship Matters: Leading Others to Encounter the Greatness of God* (Wheaton, Ill.: Crossway, 2008), 241–48; Andi Rozier, "The Worship Leader and His Pastor," in *Doxology and Theology: How the Gospel Forms the Worship Leader*, ed. Matt Boswell (Nashville: Broadman and Holman, 2013), 161–72.

either too undefined[7] or too cliquish.[8] Similarly, when Christ is our center and the gospel's aroma of grace is wafting around, we worship leaders will notice a similar dynamic at play, which we happily encourage. A worship leader who deeply loves the church encourages and fosters relationships both inside and outside official times and places, and she constantly has her eye out to introduce new people into the "system," disrupting its tendency toward ingrown-ness.

A pastorally minded worship leader also shares God's heart for the forgotten who often reside on the margins of church (and worship) life—the unattractive, the mentally and physically disabled, the poor and homeless, and children. We see how much God cares for the marginalized in His scathing critique of Israel's hypocritically tidy worship practices alongside blatant injustices (Amos 5).[9]

5. A church lover willingly enters into their church's wounded and wounding nature. As worship leaders, we are ever tempted to wander into the temporary comforts of bitterness to cope with the perpetual pain the church inflicts on us. The criticisms are endless—from sound levels to song selection, from intolerable theology to inappropriate outfits. Our church is always wounding us.

Many a wise counselor has said, "Hurt people hurt people." The difference between a worship leader and a worship pastor is in the ability to recognize that others' propensity to wound is a symptom of being wounded. A pastoral heart builds up such a love and empathy for the church that, even in the midst of receiving wounds, he or she is able to respond in love by drawing near instead of retreating or fighting in defensiveness. How is this possible?

Insightful Catholic writer Henri Nouwen points us to a ministry model (patterned after Jesus) that he calls "The Wounded Healer." Nouwen describes our own woundedness as the very point of entry for ministry to other wounded souls. Our woundedness "is healing because it takes away the false illusion that wholeness can be given by one to another. It is healing because it does not take away the loneliness and pain of another, but invites him to recognize his loneliness on a level where it can be shared."[10]

At a church I once served, a woman wrote our elder board, criticizing my sloppy attire during an important churchwide meeting after a service. (I had untucked my shirt when the service was over.) She claimed it was just one in a series of instances that displayed my irreverent attitude toward the church, going so far as to claim

---

7. Think of Jesus' tear-filled boundary marking with the Pharisees (Matt. 23).

8. Think of His welcoming of prostitutes (Luke 7:36–50), adulterers (John 4:1–26), "social sinners" (Matt. 9:9–13; Luke 19:1–10), and children (Luke 18:15–17) when the community was trying to push them out.

9. Read more on this aspect of the worship pastor's call in chapter 8, "The Worship Pastor as Watchful Prophet."

10. Henri J. M. Nouwen, *The Wounded Healer* (New York: Doubleday, 1972), 92.

that such immature behavior was unbecoming of a minister. She requested that the elders put me under some kind of probationary discipline. Some of you are the type who can blow off such seeming absurdity with an eye roll or a shrug. Not me. To me, it struck at the heart of my vocation. It inflicted a deep wound.

I wanted to lash out. I wanted to put this woman in her place. I wanted to marshal ten billion airtight biblical arguments why God doesn't give one whip about my untucked shirt but cares greatly when false accusations are lodged against one of His beloved, ordained leaders. I was hell-bent on justifying myself. In that moment of panic, when I was on the brink of unleashing a disaster, a wise colleague and seasoned pastor gave me insight into that woman's past. She had grown up physically, emotionally, and spiritually abused by her father, a fundamentalist pastor. In a moment like this, it is amazing how knowledge of another's deep wounds transforms the way you feel and respond to the very wounds they've inflicted on you. It opened me up to hear this woman, to connect, to lean in, and to minister. Strangely, the way she hurt me became a portal of understanding the pain she had felt for so many years. The wounds that the church inflicts on you can become the very vehicle for your ministry to her woundedness. A pastorally oriented worship leader embraces this counterintuitive dynamic out of raw, Spirit-borne, gospel-rooted love for the church.

6. *A church lover faithfully reminds the church of her church-ness.* Part of loving the church well is reminding her that she is a community. In our day and age, when worship has become such a subjective experience, the church is ever prone to hyperindividualizing our faith and practice. We see this very tangibly in worship services in which we're all explicitly or implicitly encouraged to have our own private encounters with God. Sometimes we can get the impression that the most meaningful worship service looks like one in which each worshiper is having their own private devotional experience with God . . . and they just all happen to be in the same room! But as a pastor I once knew liked to say, "In worship, it's not 'Jesus and me' but 'Jesus and *we*.'"[11]

The worship pastor can remind the church of her communal nature in several ways. One of the things I like to do is balance the amount of time given to "eyes open" and "eyes closed" in my own leading of the sung portion of a worship service. I make it a point to peel open my privatized experience and look around at the saints as we sing together, as a visual demonstration to say, "Hey, church, we are all encountering God *together*."[12]

---

11. "Public worship is not private devotion, and ministers and musicians have to be clear that encouraging this kind of individualism is the enemy of corporate liturgy and community singing" (John L. Bell, *The Singing Thing: A Case for Congregational Song* [Chicago: GIA, 2000], 129).

12. Read more about leading people in the *communal* (rather than individual) experience of the presence of God in chapter 2, "The Worship Pastor as Corporate Mystic."

Another thing to think through is your community's range of physical expression. Every church is different, but there tends to be an unspoken spectrum of propriety when it comes to how physically demonstrative people are in worship. The difficulty arises when individuals stick out too far beyond the community's unspoken boundaries. From time to time I've had to approach worshipers individually who were so beyond that boundary that they were becoming a distraction to the people around them. It's my belief that we should encourage full-bodied physicality in worship and that we should stretch our congregations to increase those expressive boundaries over time. Still, a pastor will detect that worship's communal nature is in jeopardy when people are (I believe selfishly) insisting that their expressive freedom in worship trumps others' discomfort around them. Loving the church *as the church* means a willingness to step into these difficult and sensitive issues with love, grace, and a valuing of the whole body.[13]

Loving the Church by Rising to Your Call

I remember a defining moment in my new pastoral ministry years ago. A gentleman in his late sixties was dealing with his aging, dying mother and asking serious spiritual and ethical questions about whether to pull her off life support. When he called, you could tell he was in a crisis, feeling the burden of making a decision that, either way, would leave him with guilt and regret. He called me because he viewed me as a pastor.

I remember all the thoughts that went through my head for the first ten minutes of the phone call as he poured out his soul to me: Why in the world is he asking me for advice? What could I possibly offer a man nearly three times my age dealing with a problem with his mom, who was nearly four times my age? It all seemed pretty absurd to me. But before I said anything harmful, the Holy Spirit intervened and gave me a talking-to that has changed the way I've viewed my role ever since.

The Spirit's gentle lesson went something like this: "Hey, Zac: It would be extremely selfish of you and the worst kind of self-righteous, false humility to hide behind your age and inexperience and tell this man that you have nothing to offer him. You represent *Me*. Who you are in this moment is way more about

---

13. I would humbly challenge many of my charismatic brothers and sisters here, who would probably point out that stifling one's individual expression is stifling the freedom of the Holy Spirit within. Not discounting this reality, I think we need to ride this tension with prayer and pastoral sensitivity. We also need to remember that the Holy Spirit, who comes to us individually and personally, saves us *into* Christ's church *corporately and communally*. The same "wind of God" who prompts and moves us spontaneously (John 3:8) is the Spirit of *unity* who brings Christ's church *together*, working in us corporately (Eph. 4:1–6).

My call and *My conferring of a role on you* than your age, experience, and 'wisdom.' The most loving thing, for My sake and for the sake of the church I've called you to, is to rise to the call of your office and assume all the authority that this man is seeking from you. Besides, he's really seeking Me, not you. Who you are and what you're doing is way more about My call than your credentials. Speak for Me now, and comfort this man. Love My church."

The call to love Christ's church is no easy thing. But it is a must for the worship pastor. Just as we observed in the introduction, as you plan and lead worship services week in and week out, you are pastoring people whether you know it or not, and people are conferring on you a certain pastoral authority whether *they* know it or not. Loving the church well means a willingness to assume this office. But we assume it much more like a piece of clothing than a part of our identity. This pastoral call comes to us as a gift, from the Spirit, to be opened and worn. People who see this garment on you will seek you out and expect things of you even when you're not ready, even when you feel you haven't earned the right. Rise up in faith, brothers and sisters, because the same God who called you child even while you were an enemy (Rom. 5:10) is the Spirit who calls you pastor even while you're woefully underqualified.

"Worship pastor, do you love me?" Jesus asks.

"Yes, Lord, You know that I love You," we reply.

"Feed my lambs."[14]

Tender Father, help us to love Your church.

---

14. Cf. John 21:15–19.

2

THE WORSHIP PASTOR AS CORPORATE MYSTIC

"If you believe," he shouted to them, "clap your hands; don't let Tink die."
Many clapped.
Some didn't.
A few little beasts hissed.

—*J. M. Barrie, 1921[1]*

The church at worship is not only present to God; far more significantly,
the living God is present to the church.

—*Aidan Kavanagh, 1984[2]*

What kid doesn't want to be Peter Pan, the boy who never grew up? What adult isn't at least tempted to abandon the hyper-seriousness of grown-up life to take on pirates, swashbuckling, fairies, and adventure with the Lost Boys? J. M. Barrie, the author of the Peter Pan stories, knew he was giving his culture much more than entertainment during the serious and heavy times of the early 1900s. As modernism filtered down from the ivory tower into the crevices of the everyday, culture's imagination was being choked out by the answers of and proof for, well, everything. Peter Pan, the eternal boy, had something to say to the grown-ups. And he definitely has something to say to worship leaders striving to be pastors.

Reenchanting a Disenchanted World

Thinkers like Charles Taylor and James K. A. Smith have done us a service by raising Peter Pan's question afresh to us: "Do you believe?"[3] They argue persuasively

---

1. J. M. Barrie, *Peter Pan and Wendy* (New York: Charles Scribner's Sons, 1921), 140.
2. Aidan Kavanagh, *On Liturgical Theology* (Collegeville, Minn.: Liturgical Press, 1984), 8.
3. Charles Taylor, *A Secular Age* (Cambridge: Harvard University Press, 2007); James K. A. Smith, *How (Not) to Be Secular: Reading Charles Taylor* (Grand Rapids, Mich.: Eerdmans, 2014). Smith's is a helpful 152-page distillation of the thought of Taylor's massive work.

that our once enchanted world—a context in which the average person understood life to be a wondrous, fearful interaction between the natural and supernatural realms—has been ravaged by modernity's attempt to explain everything in scientific, naturalistic terms. Our frantic pursuit of understanding everything from the cellular to the cosmic has dulled our awe and muted our imagination by offering us a false sense of control over the created order. Paraphrasing Hannah Arendt, my friend Mike Cosper summarizes it well: "The telescope gave us the illusion of mastery over the stars; and the microscope gave us the illusion of mastery over minutiae."[4]

For many of us, this disenchantment has taken a toll on our worship. Anthropology and sociology have (not always unhelpfully) analyzed our practices as mere meaning-producing ritual. Psychology has explained religious experiences in worship as the projections of uneasy consciences. Science and biology have reinterpreted worship's miraculous signs and wonders as naturalistic phenomena. The constant barrage of the "explainability" of everything leaves us left with very little wonderment to bring into worship, resulting in several generations of Christians who have lost the expectation that God is *really present* in our worship.

But, then again, God raises up reenchanters from unlikely places. Orthodox theologian Alexander Schmemann gives us a fresh, enchanting vision of what it means to "go to church":

> The journey begins when Christians leave their homes and beds. They leave, indeed, their life in this present and concrete world, and whether they have to drive fifteen miles or walk a few blocks, a sacramental act is already taking place, an act which is the very condition of everything else that is to happen. For they are now on their way to constitute the Church, or to be more exact, to be transformed into the Church of God. They have been individuals, some white, some black, some poor, some rich, they have been the "natural" world and a natural community. And now they have been called to "come together in one place," to bring their lives, their very "world" with them and to be more than what they were: a new community with a new life. We are already far beyond the categories of common worship and prayer. The purpose of this "coming together" is not simply to add a religious dimension to the natural community, to make it "better"—more responsible, more Christian. The purpose is to fulfill the Church, and that means to

---

4. Mike Cosper, "Enchantment, Abundance, and the Strange World of Worship," a talk given at the Rhythms of Life Symposium, hosted by Park Church (Denver, Colo.), February 21, 2015. Cosper was referencing Hannah Arendt, *The Human Condition*, 2nd ed. (Chicago: University of Chicago Press, 1998), 262–65.

make present the One in whom all things are at their end, and all things are at their beginning.[5]

For some who have been disenchanted, the belief in God's powerful presence in worship seems like naïve hocus pocus. But I will tell you that there is a holy imagination on the other side of naiveté worth dying for.[6]

The *Corporate* Mystic

As a young Christian, I thought that the pinnacle of Christian life was a kind of baptized personal nirvana—just me and God in contemplative, intimate euphoria. Quiet times. Devotionals. Journaling. Tear-filled, hours-long prayer sessions. Ranging from the purposeful Puritans to the medieval mystics, exemplars were set before me as models of the ideal Christian life. I pursued this top-shelf virtue of personal communion with God for many years, but I never attained inwardly in myself what I saw outwardly in others. I began to discover that this holy grail of individualized mysticism wasn't the complete picture of the contemplative life, much less the Christian life.

Now hear me out. I'm not saying that these practices—the pursuit of personal experiences of the presence of and communion with God—are bad or wrong or misguided. I'm saying that they are *incomplete* when viewed as our *only* or *primary* way to experience the true and powerful presence of God in our lives. The worship leader as a pastor over the flock of God needs to reclaim the enchanted belief in the *communal* experience of the power and presence of God, particularly, and maybe chiefly, in worship.[7] The worship pastor is called to be a "corporate mystic."[8]

---

5. Alexander Schmemann, *For the Life of the World: Sacraments and Orthodoxy*, 2nd ed. (Crestwood, N.Y.: St. Vladimir's Seminary Press, 1973), 27.

6. A charismatic thinker who has served to reenchant some disenchanted places for me, especially when it comes to music, worship, and mission, is Pentecostal teacher Ray Hughes, particularly in his audio collection *The Minstrel Series* (Selah Ministries, 2012).

7. This is what is so deadly about a hyper-individualized conception of corporate worship experience. When worship becomes a place where the most prized moments are those in which it's "just me and God" in the room, we miss out on the joy and power of the *corporate* experience of God's presence. As Debra Rienstra and Ron Rienstra describe this reductionistic loss, "We wind up having personal devotions together in the same room" (*Worship Words: Discipling Language for Faithful Ministry* [Grand Rapids, Mich.: Baker, 2009], 51).

8. Just as God is in the business of resurrecting the dead, He always seems to be reenchanting the disenchanted. The charismatic and Pentecostal traditions have been God's ground zero for worship's reenchantment in modern times. While the rest of us were dying on the vine, the Spirit breathed into the church a fresh word that said, "Yes, I am really here," and waves of charismatic movements billowed forth, to the praise and glory of God. The overwhelming experiences of charismatic worship began to rebuild into the church an expectation that God was actually going to be present in a special way each

God's Presence in Worship

When you think of encountering God's presence in worship, what comes to mind? For me, I've grown up thinking of it in positive, comforting terms. And the Psalms agree, testifying that God's presence is accompanied by:

- pleasure (16:11)
- joy (21:6)
- mercy (51:11)
- love and faithfulness (61:7)
- fulfillment and ecstasy (84:1–2)

However, the Psalms present an equally terrifying picture of the divine encounter in worship. The presence of God engenders:

- humility (5:5)
- fear and judgment (9:19)
- awe and wonder (18:9–12)

At Christmas, we sometimes forget that Immanuel, the name for Jesus that means "God with us," was a terrifying idea (Isa. 7:13–17; 8:5–10) before it was a comforting one (Matt. 1:23). Scripture is full of instances where God's being with us and near to us was first for the purpose of judgment, not blessing (e.g., Gen. 11:5; Num. 12:5–9; Ps. 96:13; Isa. 51:5). This is a much-needed corrective to those of us who tend to romanticize the experience of the presence of God as a purely positive encounter.[9] The Bible actually encourages an *order* to the divine encounter, and this ordering makes the whole experience of God's presence more rich.

As God manifests His presence in worship, He draws near, as odd as it might sound, both to "kill and to make alive" (1 Sam. 2:6; Deut. 32:39).[10] God's agenda

---

and every time we gathered. And I am grateful for this precious gift. The charismatics have reminded the rest of us that worship is nothing short of divine *encounter*. As Matt Redman said, "Worship is meant to be an encounter, an exciting meeting place where love is given and received in an unscripted manner" (*The Unquenchable Worshipper: Coming Back to the Heart of Worship* [Ventura, Calif.: Regal, 2001], 51). For more on the notion of encounter as a dominant theme of charismatic worship, see Pete Ward, *Selling Worship: How What We Sing Has Changed the Church* (Waynesboro, Ga.: Paternoster, 2005), 197–210. Special thanks to Glenn Packiam for pointing me to this last insight and resource.

9. See Mark Labberton's great discussion on encountering God in *The Dangerous Act of Worship: Living God's Call to Justice* (Downers Grove, Ill.: InterVarsity, 2007), 62–69.

10. This is the fundamental and indispensable insight of the Reformation: the distinction between law and gospel, articulated well by Paul in places like Romans 3 and 7 and 2 Corinthians 3. One of the earliest, more systematic treatments of the Reformational perspective here is in Philip Melanchthon's *Loci*

is to kill the old self *in order to* make us alive in Christ. When holiness draws near to sinfulness, its first word is a word of judgment and condemnation: "You are unworthy; you must die" (Rom. 6:23; Eph. 2:1). This discomforting presence is felt in Isaiah's encounter with God, where the prophet's instinctual reaction to seeing Him was to cry out in fearful confession of sin (Isa. 6:1–5). But we notice even there how quickly God's judgment, once recognized, transitions to a relieving comfort (6:6–7). Not to be missed in this passage is the fact that the hinge on which God's presence is turned from judgment to comfort is atonement for sin. God's word of condemnation slices us open, only to have His word of forgiveness sew us back together.[11] Experiencing God's presence is very much an experience of being "born again"—death and resurrection.

So it must be for us in worship. When the Holy Spirit comes down, we cannot, as one commentator quipped, "pole vault over Calvary on the way to Pentecost,"[12] as much as we all want to. God's presence cuts both ways.[13]

Present *for What*?

If this is true, this means that the Holy Spirit has an agenda in manifesting His presence to us. We might be quick to ask the Spirit to "come have Your way among us" but slower to remember just what His way typically is. The Holy Spirit seeks to be present *to make much of Jesus.* Continuing what we said before, the Spirit is present first to convict us of our sin (John 16:8–11),[14] but as many of the Reformers would point out, this demolition of the old Adam in us is only to level the ground so that a big platform can be built to showcase the glory and wonder of the new and better Adam, Jesus Christ (1 Cor. 15:45–49).

The Holy Spirit is worship's great Enabler. His presence is what allows and propels us to cry out to the Father through the Son (Rom. 8:15).[15] Over the years, many have chimed in on what Spirit-filled worship looks like. And while we can

Communes (1521). For a marvelous, brief, and accessible treatment of the subject, see William McDavid, Ethan Richardson, and David Zahl, *Law and Gospel: A Theology for Sinners (and Saints)* (Charlottesville, Va.: Mockingbird, 2015).

11. As charismatic worship leader Matt Redman commented: "God is stripping him apart in order to put him back together as a stronger, purer worshipper" (*Unquenchable Worshipper*, 33).

12. Paul Zahl, "A Liturgical Worship Response," in *Exploring the Worship Spectrum: Six Views*, ed. Paul Basden (Grand Rapids, Mich.: Zondervan, 2004), 154.

13. How we plan and lead worship services that make room for this kind of encounter will be addressed more in chapter 14, "The Worship Pastor as Liturgical Architect."

14. Martin Luther describes this as the Spirit's preaching of the law (See "Against the Heavenly Prophets," *Luther's Works*, vol. 40, ed. Conrad Bergendoff [Philadelphia: Muhlenberg Press, 1958], 82).

15. "The Spirit is the enabler, the energizer; only in the power of the Spirit are spiritual realities actualized" (Simon Chan, "The Holy Spirit as the Fulfillment of the Liturgy," *Liturgy* 30, no. 1 [Nov. 2015]: 33).

(and I think must) affirm that it certainly means a vibrant, emotionally charged, surprising, and transformative encounter, worship that is full of the Holy Spirit's presence and activity can be no less than an experience which also makes much of Jesus Christ, in all His saving death and life.[16] Jesus said, "When the Advocate comes, whom I will send to you from the Father—the Spirit of truth who goes out from the Father—he will testify about me" (John 15:26). In short, the Spirit's agenda in manifesting His presence to us in worship is to show us our need for Jesus and then give Him to us.

Confessions of an Evolutionary Worship Snob

At this point, I need to confess something about my personal journey with all of this presence stuff. I began my Christian walk as a kind of "default charismatic," thinking and believing that God's presence was located solely in the surprising, unexpected, unplanned, goose-bump moments of worship. As a know-it-all teenager, I vilified the rigidity of tradition and branded it dead religion.

Then I went to college and studied the Bible "for real." In my worship thinking, I began swapping one snobbery for another. I turned on my own past and started directing my eye-rolling toward "those charismatics," as I experienced the presence and power of God in the Scriptures and the preaching of the Word, forever (I thought) leaving behind all that sappy, emotional stuff.

But then . . . *then* . . . I went to seminary and really started understanding things. I fell in love with all things liturgical and historical, locating God's presence primarily in the sacraments. I distanced my heart from those puritanical Bible-thumpers that insisted on "sermon-centric" worship, joining the crowd of haters who insisted that only we knew where the real action was in worship.

But later, as God lifted my head and opened my ears to listen to His Spirit's work in the broader church, among *all* the traditions, He brought friends into my life who cared about and invited me to experience afresh their expressions. I realized that we all might just be holding a piece of the presence puzzle.

---

16. As a side note, far too many thinkers and practitioners take an either-or approach to the debate about whether the Spirit is active in ordered structures of the liturgy or in all the surprising, unplanned, spontaneous "other places." I appreciate how Simon Chan, a Pentecostal theologian and an advocate for liturgical worship, argues for holding these two together: "The Spirit's personal indwelling could be characterized in two ways. First, in coming to indwell the church, the Spirit is the hidden person. In this way we could speak of the core practices of the church such as word and sacrament, and especially the liturgy, as the works of the Spirit. But the Spirit, second, also comes from *beyond* history to transform historical truth into a Pentecostal-charismatic event. This coming from beyond should give the church an expectation of a new Pentecost—indeed, a 'perpetual Pentecost'—in the liturgical celebration" (Chan, "The Holy Spirit as the Fulfillment of the Liturgy," 37).

Presence Across Traditions

I want to highlight three broad traditions of worship and show why each tradition is a gift to God's church, helping us to better understand, feel, know, hear, taste, and see God's presence in our worship services.[17]

God's Presence in Song: The Pentecostal/Charismatic Voice

Our Pentecostal and charismatic brothers and sisters testify that when we sing, God comes in palpable power. The Scriptures unashamedly declare that the Word of Christ dwells among us richly when we sing in worship (Col. 3:16).[18] In the Old Testament, the same scriptural language used to describe the sacrifices,[19] where God is mystically present and spiritually active, is used not only to depict the sacrifice's accompanying music but to characterize the musical experience *itself.*[20] Music as "sacrifice" is therefore loaded with all the rights and privileges of these Old Testament sacramental practices where God's presence was thickly available to His people.[21] Scripture also gives us several instances of divine theophany where God reveals Himself as music is played or alongside the people's singing (Ex. 19:16; 2 Chron. 5–7). Understanding music as a means of God's presence goes even further, though, when we think about the fact that the church, as the body of Christ (1 Cor. 12:27; Eph. 4:12), expresses a profound and unparalleled unity when she sings. If the church's unity is one of the ways Christ reveals Himself to the world, singing must be a pinnacle expression of that revelation.[22] No wonder Paul insists that singing is one of the ways that we are filled with the Spirit (Eph. 5:18–19).[23] As Pete Ward has pointed out, it has been our Pentecostal and

---

17. The following three sections signify *emphases* that are most dominant in those traditions, but it should be noted that voices may be found in nearly every tradition articulating God's presence in song, sermon, and sacrament. For instance, a remarkable Roman Catholic work, after an in-depth survey of Catholic liturgiology, argues strongly for the presence of Christ in the singing of the church. See Miriam Therese Winter, *Why Sing? Toward a Theology of Catholic Church Music* (Washington, D.C.: Pastoral Press, 1984), e.g., 231.

18. Much of what follows is indebted to the exegetical insights of Dr. Michael Farley, in group email correspondence on October 8, 2014.

19. Such language includes the mystically loaded biblical terms for *remembrance*: Heb. *zkr*, Gk. *anamnesis.*

20. On the accompanying music, cf. 1 Chron. 16:37–42; 23:30–32; 2 Chron. 5–7; 29:20–25; Pss. 27:6; 107:21–22; on the musical experience, cf. 1 Chron. 16:4 and the inscriptions of Psalms 38 and 70.

21. Michael Farley: "Sacrifices were tangible means of grace that God used to draw people near to him experientially and relationally, and thus they were a kind of sacrament. If worship music falls within the category of sacrifice, then it accomplishes the same broadly sacramental function, namely, to be a tangible means through which God reveals himself and enables us to experience his special presence with us" (email correspondence).

22. Cf. John 17:20–23. These ideas are fleshed out in Steven R. Guthrie, "The Wisdom of Song," in *Resonant Witness: Conversations between Music and Theology*, ed. Jeremy S. Begbie and Steven R. Guthrie (Grand Rapids, Mich.: Eerdmans, 2011), 382–85.

23. Though some translations obscure this by dividing this passage into discreet sentences or ideas,

charismatic brothers and sisters who have helped us recover an awareness of God's presence among us while we sing. They have reminded us that our songs aren't merely the accompaniment to the encounter but a real context of the encounter.[24]

God's Presence in Preaching: The Reformational Voice

The Protestant Reformation ushered in a mass revival of the church, and not a small part of that was an unleashing of the Holy Spirit's presence in the church through the preached Word. The Scriptures associate people's ability to hear God's Word with the power and presence of the Holy Spirit (Ezek. 2:2).[25] God's presence is *required* for preaching to be truly heard (Acts 16:14). God's transforming, life-changing, heart-turning presence is manifested in a special way when the Word of God is preached (Rom. 10:8–14).

Reformers like John Calvin rediscovered for us this unique vehicle of God's presence: "Is the Word of God being faithfully preached? Then we have Jesus Christ in our midst, as it were, as if he were presented before us hanging on the cross."[26] Just as God fills song with His presence, He fills preaching. As Martin Luther said, in preaching, "the Word which you hear [is the] Word of him who holds the whole world in his hand and who inhabits it from beginning to end."[27] Just as we can't speak without breath, so the Word cannot go forth without the Holy Spirit, the Breath of God. Preaching, then, is much more than instruction or teaching. The Reformers remind us that it is divine encounter, a deeply *real* spiritual experience.[28]

God's Presence in Baptism and the Lord's Supper: The Sacramental Voice

A third voice is what we might call the "sacramental traditions," which include many from the Reformation (Lutherans, Anglicans, Presbyterians) but extend into the voices of Roman Catholicism and Eastern Orthodoxy. These traditions

---

the original syntax of Paul's statement—an imperative verb, followed by a string of modifying participles—makes this clear: "be filled with the Spirit [by/as you are] . . . *speaking* . . . *singing* . . . *making melody* . . . *giving thanks* . . ." (Eph. 5:18–20 KJV, emphasis mine). See Guthrie, "The Wisdom of Song," 387–88, esp. n.20 on p. 388.

24. Ward, *Selling Worship*, 197–204.

25. John Calvin, *Commentaries on the Prophet Ezekiel*, vol. 1 (Grand Rapids, Mich.: Baker, 2003), 108: "This work of the Spirit, then, is joined with the word of God. But a distinction is made, that we may know that the external word is of no avail by itself, unless animated by the power of the Spirit."

26. John Calvin, *Sermons on Galatians*, trans. Kathy Childress (Carlisle, Pa.: Banner of Truth, 1996), 227.

27. Martin Luther, "The Adoration of the Sacrament (1523)," *Luther's Works*, vol. 36, ed. Abdel Ross Wentz (Philadelphia: Muhlenberg Press, 1958), 298.

28. "Proclamation is more like a sacrament than other oral communication such as teaching or informing" (Gerhard O. Forde, *Theology Is for Proclamation* [Minneapolis: Fortress, 1990], 147).

remind us that God comes down and meets us in baptism and the Lord's Supper.[29] The Bible describes baptism as being united with Christ in language too strong to be understood in merely symbolic and ritualistic terms. We are buried with Him and raised with Him (Col. 2:12; Rom. 6:4). Scripture describes baptism as being administered "by Christ" (Col. 2:11–12). Likewise, Jesus by His Spirit manifests Himself—He opens our eyes to see Him—when the bread is broken and given at the table (Luke 24:30–31). Both the bread and the wine are described by Paul as a "participation" in Jesus (1 Cor. 10:16). The sacramental traditions remind us that we can feel His presence in a powerful and multisensory way as we touch, taste, see, and smell Jesus, through the Spirit, in baptism and Communion.

Each tradition represented may understandably want to argue the finer points of their perspective by giving primacy to one of these three over the others. But the exciting picture painted by these three perspectives can be a kind of win-win where, as Christians, we're freed up to experience God's special, unique, and tangible presence among us in all kinds of ways in the worship service.[30] The bigger takeaways for us here are that, first, worship is no ordinary event; it is filled with God's very presence. And second, the way God reveals His presence in worship is unique and irreplaceable by any other means. We can't find this kind of experience praying alone in our quiet times, hiking on a hillside, or tuning in on a live streamed service. What happens in worship can't be replicated or refabricated in any other way because God reserves special gifts of His presence for the physical and corporate worship gatherings of the church.[31]

Worship Pastors as Pointers

Let's be clear about one thing. Worship leaders do not, as it's sometimes said, "usher people into the presence of God." Statements like these are why some are understandably hesitant to call us "worship leaders." We don't want to give people

---

29. Of course, Roman Catholicism and Eastern Orthodoxy include other sacraments besides these two.

30. I find this unifying vision of song, sermon, and sacrament similar to the spirit behind Gerhard Forde's lamentation of the "unfortunate competition" between Word and sacrament: "Churches are split between emphasizing one or the other, and within individual churches themselves what is said in the sermon may be quite at odds with what is done in the sacraments . . . People are then cut adrift between Word and sacrament; their allegiance to one or the other is reduced to a matter of preference. One or the other of them is then bound to lose. Churches divide into sacramental and nonsacramental communions and people develop tastes for one type of service or the other. As such, both Word and sacrament will lose out, because the vitality of both depends upon their complementarity and reinforcement of one another in the deed of proclamation." See Forde, *Theology Is for Proclamation*, 148–49.

31. Two books that have done more for my own reenchantment than any others, and which have served as underlying foundations for this chapter, are Jean-Jacques von Allmen, *Worship: Its Theology and Practice* (New York: Oxford, 1965), and John Jefferson Davis, *Worship and the Reality of God: An Evangelical Theology of Real Presence* (Downers Grove, Ill.: InterVarsity, 2010).

the false idea that we're somehow mediators of God's presence or that we are necessary for people to relate to God. The Bible is clear about this. There is one mediator between God and humanity: Jesus Christ (1 Tim. 2:5). *Jesus alone* ushers us into God's presence. *Jesus alone* can "present you before his glorious presence without fault" (Jude 1:24). *Jesus alone* opens up a way and gives us "confidence to enter the Most Holy Place" (Heb. 10:19). Jesus Christ is the one and only true Worship Leader.[32]

This truth means that we're free from the burden of trying to manufacture God's presence and cajole God's people to see it. Our job is simple. Though we don't usher people into God's presence, we stubbornly, insistently point to the One who does.

Waking Up the Church to the Presence

As we point to Jesus, there are at least three pastoral moves we can make to help God's people more clearly see how He is present by the power of His Spirit. And though God's presence can't be contained or manufactured, as worship pastors we're called to lead our people in building expectation of and sensitivity to the movements of God among us as we gather.

1. We should continually cultivate a sensitive awareness in ourselves. This awareness has to begin with us. If we don't believe in God's presence, pray for it, and long for it, our disenchantment has the potential to spread like a contagion to our flocks. But the opposite is true as well. A fervent anticipation and expectation of God's presence in worship is equally contagious. We need to regularly pray for God to infect us and our congregations with that precious, mystical hope. Additionally, our emotions must be dialed in, not checked out.[33] Experiencing God's presence is inseparable from our emotions, and we shouldn't be scared of engaging them. To know God's presence is to delight in Him (Ps. 21:6). As the psalmist did, we need to cultivate a longing for God's courts—a hunger to sing, hear, and taste the gospel in worship (Ps. 84:1–2).

2. We should build the language of presence and encounter into worship. God's presence is seen through the eyes of faith. Developing these eyes of faith requires faithful coaching. I will sometimes begin a worship service by saying to our congregation, "I know it seems like what we're doing is just routine church. I know it seems like this is an ordinary place. But make no mistake. God is really here!" Other times, I'll begin with a provocative question, such as, "When you came

---

32. Hebrews 8:1–2 is quite explicit about this. There, Jesus is literally called "the Liturgist" ("the *one who serves* [Gk. *leitourgos*] in the sanctuary").

33. See more on emotions in chapter 13, "The Worship Pastor as Emotional Shepherd."

today, did you arrive with the expectation that God would actually be here?" Yet other times, a strong passage about the evocative nature of God's presence is helpful as a Call to Worship: "In your presence there is fullness of joy; at your right hand are pleasures forevermore" (Ps. 16:11 ESV).

Many liturgical traditions use Prayers of Invocation or Collects to invite the Spirit's presence and work at the beginning of worship. Some traditions have made use of songs of invocation that entreat the Spirit to "come and fill this place."[34] As shepherds, we need to faithfully and routinely pastor the thought of God's presence into people's heads, until the encounter is so rich that even people who *don't* know Jesus are forced to cry, "God is really among you!" (1 Cor. 14:25).[35]

3. We should make room for both effects of killing and making alive in our services. If God's presence truly "cuts both ways," then the best thing we can do is to provide spaces in our worship—however free form or scripted our services might be—for the Holy Spirit to do His work of death and resurrection in us. This can mean adding a confession of sin—whether through song, prayer, or a Scripture reading. In worship, we need an opportunity to feel the "holy heat" of the sun of righteousness before we can find healing in His wings (Mal. 4:2).

When we take our pastoral call seriously, we become as wide-eyed as Peter Pan, seeing all the enchanted wonder of the Neverland of worship, where God is truly present. Do you *really* believe it?

O Holy Spirit, open our eyes and fill us with wonder.

---

34. This might be a good place to point out some theological confusion we can experience related to God's omnipresence and His unique presence in a worship service. The Scriptures affirm God's presence everywhere (e.g., Ps. 139:7; Jer. 23:24; Col. 1:17). How is it then that God can "fill" a place He is already in? We need here to understand the "filling" language as related to our *perception* of God's presence as well as God-given *special dispensations* of that awareness. Though God is omnipresent, part of our language of invocation ("come, Holy Spirit") is to ask for a greater awareness of His work and power among us as we engage in specific rituals He has uniquely chosen to be present in—i.e., singing, preaching, and sacraments, as we have outlined above. In short, asking the omnipresent God to "fill" a place is to ask Him to *manifest* that presence in greater power and perceptibility.

35. Notice, too, the context of this passage. This is one of those instances where God's presence is felt much more as judgment than comfort. His nearness really does cut both ways.

3

THE WORSHIP PASTOR AS DOXOLOGICAL PHILOSOPHER

He who has a "why" to live can bear almost any "how."
—Friedrich Nietzsche, 1889[1]

A frustrated man storms up to you before the start of the service, his finger pointing at your drummer. "I heard he was playing in a bar a few weeks ago! You can't have him playing in our worship services!" How do you respond?

You're hanging out with a teenager in your congregation one Tuesday, and he says to you, "Man, I just can't get into most of the music you guys play on Sunday morning. House music is my thing. Can you guys do some EDM worship songs?" What do you say to him?

You're getting coffee with a college student who is home on summer break. She says that she's struggled to find a church at school, so she's been listening to worship music and podcasting sermons in her dorm room. How do you advise her?

You're sitting in a team meeting with other leaders in your church. The person who helps lead your Christian education and discipleship programs says, "Worship is going really well, but we need to beef up our education so that we can make disciples who are really in the Word. I recommend that we shorten our worship services by fifteen minutes so that we have more time to do what Jesus called us to do—make disciples." What is your response in that moment?

A congregant comes up to you after a stirring sermon about social justice, and with passion in her eyes she says, "I have an idea. Once a month, why don't we cancel our worship services and instead mobilize everyone to do a communitywide service project during the worship hour?" What do you think? Is this a good idea?

Your leadership team is debriefing worship, and once again the problem of

---

1. A popular translation of Friedrich Nietzsche's, "Hat man sein *warum*? des Lebens, so verträgt man sich fast mit jedem *wie*?" quoted in *Friedrich Nietzsche Sämtliche Werke*, 2nd ed., vol. 10, ed. Mazzino Montinari and Giorgio Colli (Berlin: de Gruyter, 1999), 480.

noisy kids in worship comes up. Someone suggests the idea of having a separate children's service. Is this something positive? How do you evaluate this suggestion?

An older woman in your congregation comes to you in the middle of the week and hands you a piece of paper, saying, "God gave me this song, and He wants us to sing it as a church. You need to lead it next Sunday." You look at the song, and while the words aren't half bad, the melody is awkward and hard to follow. But God "gave her" the song. What do you do now?

You get an email from a couple—good friends—in your congregation who tell you that they're thinking of heading up to the mountains this coming Sunday and worshiping God as they take in His grandeur on a hike instead of coming to the service. They ask you if you think that's okay. Do you? What do you say to them?

You're approached by a middle-aged woman who says that God has given her a gift and she wants to serve the church by playing piano with the worship band. You audition her, and she fumbles notes, struggles to keep up, and can't seem to hold a consistent rhythm. She knows she did badly but insists, "I've been given a gift, and I want to serve my church in this way." What factors play into your response to her?

The Worship Pastor as a Philosopher

If you've been leading worship for any considerable amount of time, no doubt you've been faced with many questions, perhaps some similar to the ones I just asked. And as different as each question is, there is a question *beneath* all the questions, something they all have in common. It's this: "What's your philosophy of worship on [x]?" Given what you understand about worship—what the Bible teaches and you believe—how does that knowledge apply to these circumstances? These are all philosophical questions, and even if you don't consider yourself a philosopher, you will find yourself answering these types of questions on a regular basis. Whether you know it or not, everyone is operating out of some kind of philosophy.

The woman who suggests replacing worship with a community service project is asking the philosophical question, Is corporate worship interchangeable with the worship of acts of service? The couple headed to the mountains is asking the philosophical question, Can I experience God in the same way in the mountains alone as I can with the gathered church on Sunday morning? The Christian education leader is asking the philosophical question, Does worship do anything to contribute to our formation (and education) as disciples of Jesus?

"Philosophy" might sound like something for intellectuals and professional theologians. But philosophers are just people who ask, why? And worship leaders who take their pastoral role seriously must start asking why about everything they do in worship. Worship pastors are not content to do things just because "we've always done it that way" (which is itself a philosophy—traditionalism), nor should we mindlessly follow the latest fad or idea simply because it works (another philosophy—pragmatism). We may be practical thinkers, but we cannot let pragmatics drive our decision-making. We need to think, reflect, and prayerfully apply what we believe. Being a pastor means that our doxology (our worship) should be informed by our philosophy. A worship pastor is a doxological philosopher.

The Holy Spirit's Work in Scripture and Community[2]

Every worship leader has a philosophy of worship. The worship leader who leads only Christian radio hits from the last five years has a philosophy: new is better than old. The worship planner who allows a Q&A session/dialogue to substitute for the sermon has a philosophy: preaching is not an essential part of corporate worship. What makes a worship leader a worship pastor is not *having* a philosophy of worship. It's *owning* it, taking the time to think it through.

Thinking through a philosophy of worship isn't easy. It's an ongoing task. This is because the Scripture from which our philosophy emerges is always speaking *to* and *in* a local church and its context. A philosophy of worship is best created on the ground in the context of your community rather than in a closed-door theological laboratory with your Bible and some books. Certainly there is a place for reading and study, and we always want Scripture's unchanging truth to be the bedrock of our philosophy of worship, but we never ask these questions in a timeless, cultureless vacuum. The same Holy Spirit who breathed the Bible (2 Tim. 3:16) is alive *in the church*.[3] Philosophical questions are best asked and revisited *in community*. Developing a philosophy of worship is a lifetime endeavor where convictions are refined as questions are asked of the Scriptures and applied back into the community.

I emphasize the Holy Spirit's work in community because some might be

---

2. This section is indebted to the many conversations I have had with Chuck Fromm, head of Worship Leader Media, and to the several resources he has pointed me to, including the insights of Robert J. Schreiter, *Constructing Local Theologies* (Maryknoll, N.Y.: Orbis, 1994).

3. Simon Chan points out how the historic creeds of the church (particularly the Apostles' and Nicene) place the Spirit and the church in surprisingly close proximity. In fact, Chan argues that pneumatology might be just as an appropriate umbrella for ecclesiology as Christology. I'm not completely with Chan on all points, but he's given me pause to think more critically about the Spirit's intimate connection to the church. See Simon Chan, "The Liturgy as the Work of the Spirit: A Theological Perspective," in *The Spirit in Worship—Worship in the Spirit*, ed. Teresa Berger and Bryan D. Spinks (Collegeville, Mo.: Liturgical Press, 2009), 41–57.

tempted to develop a philosophy and then try imposing it on the church. This can end up putting God in a box and stifling the Spirit's freedom in worship. Instead, I'm advocating an interactive development of a philosophy of worship, a dynamic experience where the Holy Spirit—breathing in both church and Scripture, with the latter as the ultimate and final rule—allows the application of timeless truth to take place in an organic, contextualized way. If something surprising happens in the community that challenges our philosophy of worship, we don't need to be afraid that Scripture's authority is being questioned. We can be more open and humbly ask, "Is our understanding of Scripture on this point accurate?" A doxological philosopher who has a pastoral heart develops convictions and operates out of them but is always sensitive to how the application of that philosophy is interacting with the church. Before we dive into the questions we should ask in developing a philosophy of worship, let me give you one not-so-commendable example of how a philosophy has worked in my leadership.

Creating Pharisees with My Philosophy

Several years ago, I was a part of a church plant whose worship was more or less a blank canvas. At that point in my journey, I had developed a severe distaste for all things connected with the contemporary Christian music scene. More than that, I had constructed a philosophy around that conviction, one that I believed was scripturally sound. We would be a church who sang only hymns and psalms. No radio tunes. No Top-40 material. And that philosophy became the badge I wore. I found that as our church plant grew, the people I pastored in worship were being shaped around these convictions. Some began wearing them as a badge themselves.

Then I started to notice that in my conversations about worship with my fellow church members, we were proudly identifying as "not one of *those* kinds of churches." And I felt the conviction of the Holy Spirit telling me, "You see what you're doing? You're creating little Pharisees." As new people were being enfolded in our church life who didn't share our convictions, I saw their confusion and alienation when they asked why certain songs were absent from our worship. My philosophy was bearing some odd-looking fruit. I had to pause and ask some hard questions.

As I went back to the Scriptures and took a more honest look at the broader worship music world, I began to see that my philosophical grid was pretty tight. I was throwing out a whole lot of baby with the bathwater. Scripture's rule of love (1 Corinthians 13) pressed me to be a wider listener, and it took my philosophy's interaction with the people in our church to help me to figure that out.

How to Develop Your Own Philosophy of Worship

I'm a firm believer that while Scripture presents a timeless and unchanging message, developing a philosophy of worship is ultimately a *local* enterprise. So the rest of this chapter won't be me telling you what your philosophy should be. Instead, I'm going to propose a guided method for determining your philosophy of worship—the basic questions you need to ask.[4] In several places, I've added further questions in the footnotes, which will help you flesh out the implications of the more basic questions. Your own context will likely bring up even more questions than the ones listed here, but these should get you started and help you become a more intentional, pastorally equipped doxological philosopher.

1. Defining Worship

Developing a philosophy of worship begins with defining it. But defining worship can be difficult because the term includes several layers of meaning. Understanding these layers is vital. (See fig. 1.) The first and broadest layer is worship conceived as an activity in which all human beings—religious or not—are engaged. The second layer narrows when we begin to ask, "What makes worship uniquely *Christian*?" The third layer exists as an even narrower sphere of weekly gathered worship, where God's worshiping people join together to enact certain rituals and receive unique gifts of God's presence and grace.

Each inner layer specifies and narrows the previous while remaining included in it. Layer 1, "Worship," could be thought of as every single human being's responsive, whole-life giving to someone or something. This is an affirmation that worship is a fundamental orientation of humanity. Everyone worships. Layer 2 aims this holistic worship more specifically as responsive, whole-life giving to God, through Christ, by the Spirit. This is uniquely *Christian* worship.[5] Layer 3 focuses the Christian's all-of-life worship into a concentrated and repeated event we call gathered Christian worship: responsive, whole-life giving to God, through Christ, by the Spirit, enacted with the people of God through certain practices.

These three layers are helpful in categorizing our usage of the term *worship*, because some philosophies of worship unknowingly articulate one layer as the total package, which can lead to problems. For instance, if we speak of worship as layer 3, we downplay if not leave out how the Christian life outside of Sunday, through mission and vocation, is very much an act of worship, as understood in layer 2. The reverse is true as well. Some mission-minded thinkers want to

---

4. Inevitably, you will discover *my* answers to many of these questions as you read this book.

5. On this Trinitarian shape of worship's practice and trajectory, see especially James B. Torrance, *Worship, Community, and the Triune God of Grace* (Downers Grove, Ill.: InterVarsity, 1997).

emphasize layer 2 as the sum of worship. In doing so, they have downplayed the role of weekly, corporate worship in the life of the believer.[6]

Figure 1

LAYERS OF MEANING IN WORSHIP

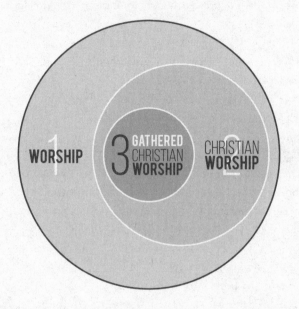

So with these categorical thoughts in mind, I would encourage you to strive, with your Bible in hand and the church (both locally and universally) before you, to answer these questions:

- How do you define worship as a transcultural human reality, and how does this definition play into your understanding of how human beings live and make decisions?
- How do you define Christian worship, and how does this definition inform the Christian's life and decisions?
- How do you define gathered Christian worship?
- How do these three definitions relate to one another, and how does that relationship inform the worship pastor's role?[7]

---

6. For more on the inseparable relationship between worship and mission, see chapter 9, "The Worship Pastor as Missionary."

7. Expanding questions: Is gathered worship able to be replaced or substituted? Can a church

With these definitions in place, you can begin answering important philosophical questions that expand outward:

- Who is worship for? God? Us? The world? All three?[8]
- What role does gathered worship play in the Christian life?
  - Is it merely beneficial? Or is it necessary?
  - Does God do anything unique in the context of gathered, corporate worship that He ordinarily reserves for only that time and place? If so, what does He do?
- What is happening in gathered worship?
  - Is worship merely helpful, formative ritual?
  - Does supernatural activity take place?
  - If so, what is happening? Address issues of God's presence/encounter with God.

2. Form and Content of (Gathered) Worship

At this point, a good philosophy of worship will narrow its focus to the questions surrounding gathered worship, particularly its form and content. This quest begins by determining what guiding voices are allowed at the table in determining the form and content:

- What role does Scripture play?
  - How does the Bible inform worship?
  - Do we do *only* those things that Scripture tells us explicitly to do? Or are we free to do something in worship so long as Scripture doesn't forbid it?[9]
- What roles do Christian tradition and history play?
  - What obligation, if any, does Christian worship now have to engage elements, structure, and content of Christian worship of the past?
- What role does cultural context play?

engage in worship by a corporate deed of mercy? (For example, does a community service day substitute for what corporate worship is and does?) Can individuals just as easily and rightly worship God on their own—on an individual retreat, in the wilderness, in nature, in a solitary place, in their own private devotional life—instead of attending and participating in gathered worship?

8. Expanding questions: How should we think of worship in relation to the non-Christian? Are non-Christians capable of worshiping God? In what way(s) is gathered worship "for" non-Christians? Does corporate worship evangelize? Is corporate worship an evangelistic rally? How should we think of worship with regards to accessibility and intelligibility?

9. This is known in liturgical/historical theology as the debate between the "regulative principle," articulated in the former question, and the "normative principle," articulated in the latter question. This debate rose to the fore during and after the Protestant Reformation as varying traditions dialogued about worship and scriptural authority.

- How should biblical Christian worship be contextualized to given times, places, and cultures?
- What role do cultural forms and expressions play in worship?
- Should worship reflect the culture, be distinct from culture, or be a balance of the former and the latter?
- What role does the Holy Spirit play?
  - Does the Holy Spirit (a) work through and alongside the guiding voices, (b) subvert and surprise those guiding voices, or (c) engage in some combination of (a) and (b)?

Once we understand the role of these guiding voices, we can allow them to speak into the form of worship—its structure—and the content of worship—its elements.

- Should worship take on a specific structure or shape?
  - How does the gospel (i.e., how we are made right and enter into relationship with God) inform worship's structure?
  - Do the structures of Old Testament worship (i.e., the sacrificial system, the feasts and festivals, and other rituals) have any carryover and bearing on New Testament worshiping communities? If so, what?
- What elements of worship are nonnegotiable?
  - Are there universals for Christian worship that transcend context? If so, what are they?
  - Is preaching a nonnegotiable element? If so, what form(s) can it take and not take?[10]
  - Are the ordinances/sacraments of baptism and the Lord's Supper to be included in this list of nonnegotiable elements?[11]

3. Expression of Worship

How worship is expressed is an important question in our day and age. Because of technology and a host of other factors, you and I are more exposed than ever to just how diverse the church is. Polish Christians can watch YouTube videos of vibrant African worship gatherings. Rural Methodists can trek a few hundred miles to attend a worship night led by a charismatic worship team in a big city. A small-town Guatemalan seminarian can study the praise gatherings of a

---

10. Expanding questions: What *is* preaching? Can a sermon be replaced by an artistic presentation such as a dramatic play? Can a sermon be replaced by a dialogue or conversation between pastor and congregation? Can a sermon be replaced by an extended testimony?

11. Expanding question: Should the Lord's Supper be celebrated with a specific regularity (i.e., quarterly, monthly, weekly)?

megachurch in Seoul, South Korea. In our globalized postmodernity, we are all collectively aware of many of the different worship expressions that exist in the world, and this awareness presses us more urgently to ask these kinds of questions:

- What human faculties—mind, body, will, emotions—should be expressed in worship, and how are they best employed?[12]
- What is the acceptable scope, range, and balance of human expression in worship?
  - Should worship be loud, energetic, and upbeat?
  - Should it be soft, quiet, and reverential?
- What roles do music and particularly singing play in corporate worship?
  - Is singing necessary? If so, why is it valuable and what does it accomplish?
  - Is music unique among the different art forms when it comes to use and implementation in corporate worship?[13]
  - What factors go into determining appropriate musical styles in worship (historical, situational, ethnic, theological, architectural, etc.)?
  - Is musical style an amoral category, purely based on preference?
  - Is special music (a moment when the congregation is not singing but music is being presented) appropriate and/or beneficial?
  - What factors play into determining appropriate dynamic/volume levels for music accompanying congregational song?
- How is worship's expression relative to one's cultural context?[14]
- How does the fact that the universal church transcends cultures, times, and nations inform worship in any one local church?
  - Does a local church bear the responsibility of reflecting its multicultural nature in the actual expression of worship?[15]

---

12. Expanding questions: Are there certain bodily actions more suitable for gathered, *corporate* worship? Should everyone be utterly free to express worship in their own way in the service?

13. Expanding questions: Is singing through music a more suited artistic expression for corporate worship than, for example, setting up canvases for individuals to paint or stations for people to journal or write poetry?

14. Expanding questions: Is there any sense in which issues of "propriety" (i.e., what is appropriate) in worship expression are relative based on cultural context? What might be some of those expressions that would work in some contexts but not yours? Are there liabilities inherent in certain cultural contexts and expressions that need to be challenged, pastored, shepherded, or abandoned?

15. Expanding questions: Should the worship of a given community engage elements of cultural expression from *outside* the community for the sake of connecting with more of its multicultural, universal identity? For example, should a Dutch Reformed community in northwest Washington consider singing a Brazilian praise song in Portuguese? Or should a Pentecostal church in Sydney, Australia, consider incorporating a prayer or reading from the Christian community in Nepal? Or, closer to home, should a predominantly white church in Southern California consider incorporating instrumental styles borne out of a Latino context in a neighboring suburb?

○ How does the church's transcultural identity address issues of nationalism and patriotism in the worship service (i.e., national flags, patriotic songs, etc.)?

If you're feeling overwhelmed right now, you're in good company. (I feel overwhelmed just having typed all this out!) You may even be in a bit of a panic, worried that you don't have answers to all these questions. That's okay. Remember, your philosophy can and does develop over time. Sometimes the best moment to answer a question is when it hits you. My encouragement would be for you to comb through the list and ask, "Which of these questions is most urgent for us right now?"

At the same time, don't ignore the questions that aren't as pressing. If you simply react to circumstances you will get behind the eight ball on some very important issues, and figuring out the answer when the question arises may be too late. The question may arise precisely because your philosophy is nebulous or fails to address that topic.

Moving Up and Down the Abstraction Ladder

Your philosophy should be useful. While it sits on the upper shelf and is filled with meta-concepts and abstract principles, it needs to be a tool you can take down from the shelf and actually use. It's one thing to have a philosophy about whether or not a non-Christian instrumentalist can be a part of your worship's musical team (an abstract determination); it's quite another to apply this philosophy on the ground when you meet Avery, an accomplished guitar player who doesn't know Jesus but seems to be in a tender and teachable place. Don't just create an abstract philosophy. Think about how you will put it into action when situations arise in your church.

We can fail our philosophy in two ways. First, we can develop a philosophy of worship and never use it. There it sits, on the upper shelf, useless and unapplied. But we also fail when we use it carelessly, swinging it around like an anvil without carefully and prayerfully applying and translating it to real people and real situations. These problems can be avoided if we're committed to developing habits that allow us to move "up and down the abstraction ladder."[16]

In any ministry we are faced with thousands of little, seemingly insignificant questions. Amid the barrage of decisions we face each day, we are often tempted

---

16. I was introduced to this phrase by my preaching professor at Denver Seminary, Dr. Scott Wenig.

to shoot from the hip—"Sure, go ahead and dial up the mains 5 dBs"; "Yeah, let's add that announcement into the middle of our service"; "No problem, we can bump Communion to next month because we don't have time in our service this Sunday." Being a worship pastor who is a doxological philosopher means that you develop habits and instincts as you make decisions. You learn to pause long enough to take a quick jaunt up the abstraction ladder and ask what your philosophy has to say to the situation. If you're not used to doing this, it can be quite exhausting at first. It may feel like you are overthinking everything. It may disrupt the flow for a while. Yet the more you put your philosophy in constant dialogue with your reality, the more your philosophy becomes the "culture" of your leadership and decision-making. Philosophizing begins to happen more naturally, and it feels less like a chore. Your philosophy "becomes" you.

This dialogue between our philosophy and our reality keeps us humbly openhanded because the Holy Spirit of Scripture, which is the center point of all philosophical questions asked, is the same Spirit working in real time in our church. We can say freely that while God's truth is unchanging, our apprehension of it is ever marred by sin. Thank God that His Spirit is active and speaking at both ends of the abstraction ladder—correcting, refining, and honing our philosophies until the day when faith will be made sight.

O Christ, You are the Way, the Truth, and the Life.
Lead us to worship You in Spirit and Truth.

4

THE WORSHIP PASTOR
AS DISCIPLE MAKER

Father, I want those you have given me to be with me where I am, and
to see my glory, the glory you have given me because you loved me before
the creation of the world.

—*Jesus (John 17:24)*

In darker moments during my early days as a worship leader, I struggled to believe that I was contributing anything of value to the spiritual growth of my fellow church members. Sure, I was a part of the big event where everyone came together and got excited about Jesus, but I had been taught to believe that the real formation, the real Christian life, real discipleship, happened "out there." Whenever I read or heard anyone talk about Jesus' Great Commission (Matt. 28:18–20) and how we should all be making disciples, I felt guilty. I wasn't leading any Bible studies. I wasn't organizing a small group. I wasn't evangelizing the lost or mentoring people over coffee. I was just planning and arranging songs, rehearsing musicians, and belting out tunes in desperate hope that someone in the congregation would sing along with me.

From time to time I would receive those blessed words of encouragement that are so life-giving for people in our position. One woman who was battling cancer told me, "That song we sang on Sunday ministered to me while I was getting my chemo treatment. It gave me words to cry out to God." A man mentioned, "That prayer you prayed gave me a new perspective on heaven, and I'm filled with hope." A young woman shared, "The benediction you speak at the end of every service gives me peace for the entire week."

I began to see these words of encouragement as way-markers on the maps of people's faith journeys. It was as though they were coming up to me and pointing to their faith maps and saying, "Look at this moment in my life. That's what God did through you." I had two immediate reactions. First, goose bumps: Praise God that He'd use a clueless sinner like me. Second, lightbulb: I was making disciples.

The Heart of the Great Commission

I now understand that I misunderstood what disciple making looks like. I thought that discipleship was about all those things outside the worship service, usually accompanied by a curriculum or twelve-week study. I may have even heard this dichotomy a time or two: "There's worship, and then there's discipleship." Or this trichotomy: "The church is called to three things: worship, evangelism, and discipleship." None of this was very helpful. It drove deep wedges between things that God never intended for us to separate. Take another look at the Great Commission: "Therefore go and make disciples of all nations, baptizing them in the name of the Father and of the Son and of the Holy Spirit, and teaching them to obey everything I have commanded you" (Matt. 28:19–20).

Have you ever thought about the two ways Jesus calls us to make disciples? We make them by *baptizing* and *teaching*, actions that find their principal expression *in worship*.[1] The early church understood this. One of the first records of Christian worship outside the New Testament is the *Didache*,[2] a how-to manual for some of the church's worship practices.[3] This document links Jesus' teaching here in Matthew with the worship of the church. Though the actions of teaching and baptizing can and do happen outside the weekly gathering of the people of God, Christianity has always seen the worship service as the nucleus of disciple making. In the language of my tradition, Word and sacrament (teaching/preaching and baptism/communion) find their pinnacle expression as acts of worship. Worship stands at the center of what it means to make disciples.

Worship leaders, make no mistake. Your leading of others in worship serves to fulfill the Great Commission.

Build the Body, Not Your Ego

Paul told the Ephesian Christians that God appointed church leaders "so that the body of Christ may be built up" (Eph. 4:12; cf. 1 Cor. 14:26). As we think of our worship leading as a disciple-making enterprise, we must first leave behind any notion of celebrity or rock stardom. Harold Best once said, "When a Christian musician goes about making music, the concept of the community/body should

---

1. See John Frame, *Contemporary Worship Music: A Biblical Defense* (Phillipsburg, N.J.: Presbyterian and Reformed, 1997), 20–21.

2. The dating of the *Didache* ranges widely. It has been proposed that it was written before AD 50 all the way through the third century. See *The Apostolic Fathers: Greek Texts and English Translations*, ed. and rev. Michael W. Holmes (Grand Rapids, Mich.: Baker, 1992), 247.

3. Robbie F. Castleman, *Story Shaped Worship: Following Patterns from the Bible and History* (Downers Grove, Ill.: InterVarsity, 2013), 155.

drive every note and every moment in which every note is heard. And the only object for every Christian musician is to build the body up into the stature and fullness of its head, Jesus Christ."[4] So what would it look like if a worship leader began filtering every decision they made and every action they took through the grid, "Does this build up the body?" The rock star status of many worship leaders is poisonous to churches because it turns the focus in worship from building up the body to making much of the leader. If you and I are fixated on making a name for ourselves, expanding our platform, building our reputation, increasing our fan base, garnering more adulation, and showing off our chops, there is no room left for the building up of the church. When our ego has inflated our head to such an ungodly size that there is no room for anyone else in the sanctuary, we've become worship leaders *of* ourselves, *for* ourselves, *by* ourselves.

The guiding question for a worship pastor as a disciple maker is: "Does this build up the body?" And that question serves as the umbrella for everything that we do in worship. The rest of this book is really just an expansion of this idea—how worship pastors make disciples through the ministry of worship in the church. Put another way, this book is one long answer to the question of how we build up the body as we lead people in worship.

Making Disciples through the Worship Service

In recent years there has been a resurgence of interest in the idea of spiritual formation. Leaders like Richard Foster and Dallas Willard have reintroduced the idea that being formed into the image and likeness of Christ is a central feature of being made disciples.[5] And though some in this contemporary movement have gone in an individualistic direction, worship is often described among the "corporate disciplines" which contribute to our formation.[6]

James K. A. Smith's recent work, *Desiring the Kingdom,* expands on this concept of worship as formation.[7] In it, Smith argues for a retooling of our understanding of the wiring of human beings. His contention, following Augustine, is that we are essentially desiring creatures driven more by what our hearts truly love (our "affections"), rather than fundamentally thinking creatures driven by information, ideas, and arguments. Formation, in this scheme, centers far more on rightly

---

4. Harold Best, *Music through the Eyes of Faith* (San Francisco: HarperSanFrancisco, 1993), 36.

5. Cf. Richard Foster, *Celebration of Discipline: The Path to Spiritual Growth* (San Francisco: HarperSanFrancisco, 1978); Dallas Willard, *The Spirit of the Disciplines: Understanding How God Changes Lives* (San Francisco: HarperSanFrancisco, 1988).

6. Foster, *Celebration of Discipline,* 158–74.

7. James K. A. Smith, *Desiring the Kingdom: Worship, Worldview, and Cultural Formation* (Grand Rapids, Mich.: Baker, 2009).

ordered love, not because belief is unimportant but because our desires sit much more at the core of who we are and how we are persuaded and changed. Smith's argument is that if our loves are formed and ordered rightly, the rest (behavior, thinking, etc.) is likely to follow: "Being a disciple is not primarily a matter of getting the right ideas and doctrines and beliefs into your head in order to guarantee proper behavior; rather, it's a matter of being the kind of person who *loves* rightly."[8]

Smith goes on to argue that worship functions as a habit-forming "pedagogy of desire" whose practices help aim our hearts toward the right end—Christ and His kingdom. The best worship is filled with "rituals of ultimate concern," which, through the repetitive aiming of our desires toward Christ and His kingdom, form us as disciples. Smith makes the case that worship has all the trappings of a thick and robustly formative experience. Corporate worship's elements, practices, structures, and expression all have a shaping effect on us.

Worship as Equipping the Saints

Central to any disciple-making paradigm is the idea that the church's leaders are called and responsible for equipping the saints for the work of ministry (Eph. 4:12). The worship services you lead are putting tools into the hands of Christians, tools which help them to both love God and love others better (Matt. 22:37–39). As you plan and lead worship services, it's as if you are handing out spiritual shovels, pickaxes, and rakes, empowering Christians for a week of labor in the fields of discipleship. Worship leaders who understand their disciple-making role know that they are there to equip others in this work.

First, we equip people for ministry to God. It might make us uncomfortable to think that *we* minister to *God*, but this is exactly how the Bible describes worship leaders: "At that time the LORD set apart the tribe of Levi to carry the ark of the covenant of the LORD to stand before the LORD *to minister to him* and to bless in his name, to this day" (Deut. 10:8 ESV, emphasis mine).[9] The Bible describes worship as a ministry of response in which we offer ourselves as living sacrifices unto God (Rom. 12:1). When the people gather and are led in worship through singing, praying, hearing, offering, and receiving the Word (in preaching and in Communion and baptism), we are equipping the saints with the tools they need

---

8. Smith, *Desiring the Kingdom*, 32. The Protestant Reformation strove to recover this lost anthropology. Leaders like Luther, Calvin, Cranmer, and Melanchthon were thoroughly Augustinian in this regard. They sought to overturn the Aristotelian schema that humanity could be changed through education because the mind, as the anthropological center, could turn the will and ultimately control the desires. One could summarize this reversal, perhaps articulated best by Melanchthon, as, "What the heart loves, the will chooses, and the mind justifies." See esp. the discussion in Ashley Null, *Thomas Cranmer's Doctrine of Repentance: Renewing the Power to Love* (Oxford: Oxford University Press, 2000), 98–103.

9. See also Deut. 21:5; 1 Chron. 15:2; 2 Chron. 13:10; Ezek. 43:19.

to minister to God in a way that pleases Him. As we explored earlier, our ministry to God also has a formative effect on us. You can think of a disciple as an idolater who has been "factory recalled" by God. Discipleship is God's reclamation of that misdirected worship—loving other things in place of God. When we lead the flock in worship, we are equipping them as disciples by helping them realign their love toward God.[10]

Second, we equip people for ministry to one another. In addition to the vertical ministry to God, worship has a horizontal ministry to our brothers and sisters.[11] Our singing, for instance, is described in the Bible in both vertical and horizontal terms: "Let the message of Christ dwell among you richly as you teach and admonish one another with all wisdom through psalms, hymns, and songs from the Spirit, singing to God with gratitude in your hearts" (Col. 3:16).[12] The traditional doxology is a great example of a horizontally oriented worship song. In its verses we summon one another, along with the whole created order, to praise God:

> Praise God, from whom all blessings flow
> Praise Him, all creatures here below
> Praise Him above, ye heavenly hosts
> Praise Father, Son, and Holy Ghost

Our singing is a true ministry of the Word to one another. The African American worship tradition is a great example of this. I've noticed, both in my own church and in others, that when my African American brothers and sisters are singing they often look at each other, grabbing each other's shoulders and nearly preaching the songs to one another with nods, smiles, and gestures of affirmation. On one occasion, during a song about suffering and death, I witnessed an elderly woman in our congregation lean onto her aging husband's shoulder, as

---

10. These themes are developed well by Matt Papa, *Look and Live* (Bloomington, Minn.: Bethany House, 2014), 63–80.

11. Many worship commentators have noted the "vertical" and "horizontal" dynamics of worship, but for brief discussions, see John Frame, *Worship in Spirit and Truth: A Refreshing Study of the Principles and Practice of Biblical Worship* (Phillipsburg, N.J.: Presbyterian and Reformed, 1996), 7–8, and Bob Kauflin, *Worship Matters: Leading Others to Encounter the Greatness of God* (Wheaton, Ill.: Crossway, 2008), 175–79.

12. It is unfortunate that some English translations obscure the literal flow of the Greek text in the rendering of this pivotal verse on worship. In fact, the original NIV translation (not the updated 2011 NIV quoted above) did what many others do in unnecessarily inserting a conjunction "and" separating the idea of "teaching and admonishing" from "singing": "Let the word of Christ dwell in you richly as you teach and admonish one another with all wisdom, and as you sing psalms, hymns and spiritual songs with gratitude in your hearts to God" (NIV 1984). "Psalms," "hymns," and "spiritual songs" are all set in (most likely instrumental) dative construction in relation to the preceding participles, indicating that the teaching and admonishing happens *by means of* psalms, hymns, and spiritual songs.

if to admonish, "This is for us! Listen to what God has to say here." Prayer, too, is a horizontal ministry when we are worshiping as we cry out for each other's needs and for the needs of the world. Preaching, likewise, is a horizontal ministry from the preacher to the receiving congregation. Giving tithes and offerings is yet another horizontal act where we financially support each other and the worship and work of the church.

In all these ways and more, worship leaders pastor the congregation by facilitating and equipping the saints for this twofold ministry of loving God and loving others. From time to time we must remind our flocks about this active ministry while in the moment of worship. When we do so, we are helping describe for them their own formation as disciples who are being made into the image of Christ.

Forming People in the Gospel by Equipping Them with the Gospel

In discussions of formation and equipping we must never forget where the formative power of worship ultimately comes from. We could go on and on about rituals, practices, and habits, but they will have zero power to shape us as disciples without being anchored in the gospel of God's grace in Christ to sinners. For too long, we have believed that the gospel is our ticket in to be left at the door as we begin the long road of discipleship. We have unhelpfully held on to the idea that the gospel is for people who don't know Jesus, but once we have received Him, it's time to roll up our sleeves and get started on the hard work of becoming a disciple.

But the Bible tells us that the gospel is our perpetual fuel for the journey of discipleship. Great habit-forming worship can aim our heart all day long toward Christ and His kingdom, but the gospel is the only means to actually get us there. The gospel "is the *power* of God for salvation to everyone who believes" (Rom. 1:16 ESV, emphasis mine). Paul was concerned that believers who first receive the gospel do not abandon it but continue to walk in it: "Therefore, as you received Christ Jesus the Lord, so walk in him" (Col. 2:6 ESV). Thinking that the gospel is only a starting point to be left behind for the road of discipleship is to fall back into what Paul described as the "works of the law": "For by works of the law no human being will be justified in his sight, since through the law comes knowledge of sin. But now the righteousness of God has been manifested apart from the law, although the Law and the Prophets bear witness to it—the righteousness of God through faith in Jesus Christ for all who believe" (Rom. 3:20–22 ESV).

This fundamental insight is in danger of being lost on us if we fail to remember that it is the good news of God's justification of the ungodly that *alone* has the power to actually turn a human heart. If formation is truly based in the heart, in our desires, the gospel *alone* has the power to initially and perpetually reorient those desires. In this respect, formational practices can only be as formational as they point us to and orient us around Jesus' work in His life, death, and resurrection. Beholding Jesus' saving glory is the means of transformation (2 Cor. 3:18). God's love for us is the perpetual driving force for our love for Him and others (1 John 4:19). Worship practices may be inspiring and habit forming toward many ends, shaping us in all kinds of ways, but those practices will not form us into disciples of Jesus Christ unless they form us *in* the gospel and equip us *with* the gospel.[13]

Making Disciples beyond the Worship Service

When worship leaders begin to think pastorally, we develop a heart and concern for how Christ's precious disciples are following Him beyond the weekly gathering into the other six days of the week. We begin to ask, "How is the formative nature of worship evidenced in the way the people of God are following Christ throughout their daily lives?" We are interested in how gathered worship affects and forms people's worship in their day-to-day living.[14]

I started to notice the relationship of Sunday worship to my daily experience after spending time worshiping in a more liturgically oriented church during my college years. Part of this church's weekly service structure was a rehearsal of repentance, a Confession of Sin and an Assurance of Pardon. Week in and week out, we would have a time in our service where we publicly spoke out a congregational confession, followed by a time of silent confession for each individual. These confessions were followed by the pastor declaring a scriptural assurance of our pardon, telling us our sins were forgiven because of the work of Jesus. Over time, these weekly routines wore ruts into my soul, and I'd find them graciously haunting me the other six days of the week. I noticed that when I would stumble into sin, I had new instincts and a new inclination to confess my sin to God and preach to myself—really, to hear the Spirit preach to me—one of the verses the pastor would

---

13. For more on this, see chapter 6, "The Worship Pastor as Theological Dietician," and chapter 14, "The Worship Pastor as Liturgical Architect."

14. This dualism of worship is given several different names by different authors: "gathered" and "scattered" (Mike Cosper, *Rhythms of Grace: How the Church's Worship Tells the Story of the Gospel* [Wheaton, Ill.: Crossway, 2013], 76–82); "liturgical" and "private" (Simon Chan, *Liturgical Theology: The Church as Worshiping Community* [Downers Grove, Ill.: InterVarsity, 2006], 160–64); "gathered" and "extra-Sunday practices" (Smith, *Desiring the Kingdom*, 211–14); "event" and "everyday" (Bob Kauflin, *Worship Matters: Leading Others to Encounter the Greatness of God* [Wheaton, Ill.: Crossway, 2008], 205–10). An overlapping sphere of thought, though more nuanced, is "adoration" and "action" (Miroslav Volf, "Worship as Adoration and Action: Reflections on a Christian Way of Being-in-the-World," in *Worship: Adoration and Action*, ed. D. A. Carson [Grand Rapids, Mich.: Baker, 1993], 203–11).

recite. I'd hear in my head and heart the words from our Sunday service: "There is therefore now no condemnation for those who are in Christ Jesus" (Rom. 8:1 ESV). Our weekly worship gatherings were teaching me how to repent and apply the gospel in my daily life any and every time the waves of guilt would hit.

There is an inseparable relationship between one's daily worship and our weekly gathered worship. Some have described this relationship as symbiotic—an interdependent connection. This idea cuts against the grain of what many of us have grown up with, having been taught that our personal relationship with God is either most important or, worse, solely important. But this privatized vision of discipleship underestimates the formative nature of corporate worship. Our private spirituality is formed and fueled by the public spirituality of weekly worship.[15] This is what Simon Chan is getting at when he says:

> Unfortunately, there is a tendency to treat daily prayers as "private devotions," divorced from the corporate prayer of the church, although this was not the case in the past. Daily prayers need to be theologically informed if they are to be spiritually sustaining. They were originally part and parcel of the church's liturgical life. We are spiritually nourished by being in the church—a branch of the vine, a member of the body. To divorce private prayer from liturgical prayer is to cut the branch from the vine. We need to see our own quiet times as joined with the corporate prayer of the church. They are not just "my private prayers" but belong to the whole church.[16]

A worship pastor must develop a keen sensitivity to what is going on in the lives of his or her flock Monday through Saturday. A worship pastor's role is more than oversight of the music and content of the Sunday morning service. He or she must also take into account the daily worship of the people of God. We have a vested interest, therefore, in making disciples both *through the service* and *beyond the service*. We'll look more at this in the following chapters.

> *Gracious Father, we ask that You would continue to call*
> *and make disciples through us as we plan and lead only*
> *through Christ and by the power of the Holy Spirit.*

---

15. Smith describes the symbiosis between private and public spirituality this way: "The sacramental intensity of liturgical practices (recalling that the sacraments are also *more* than practices) provides a center of gravity that then orients and nourishes other Christian practices, which are extensions of latent possibilities for practice in Christian worship" (*Desiring the Kingdom*, 213).

16. Chan, *Liturgical Theology*, 161. Chan goes on to beautifully describe how the joining of the private and corporate prayers of the church functions on a mystical and spiritual level *as the prayers of Christ Himself.*

5

THE WORSHIP PASTOR
AS PRAYER LEADER

Whoever sings, prays twice.

—attr. to Augustine of Hippo, fourth cent.

"Now close your eyes, fold your hands, and bow your heads." I can't tell you how many times I heard those words when I was young. From the portraits of Jesus in Gethsemane to the icons of saints in cathedrals, we've all been taught that the posture of prayer is *that* posture—eyes closed, head down. But did you know that when the early Christians gathered to pray, they didn't look anything like that? The posture they adopted for prayer in worship looked more like a charismatic revival than a Catholic mass. And while I may be overstating things a bit, there is evidence that when the early church prayed in worship, they weren't sitting around quietly with their eyes closed.

An early Christian fresco, painted in the latter half of the third century, depicts a worshiper in prayer.[1] The believer is standing, both hands raised, with eyes wide open, looking straight up to heaven. The prayer posture of the ancient church looked strangely similar to the worshiping postures of much of the modern church. And there is a good reason for that.

"We Need More Praying in Worship!"

An eager man approached me and several other church leaders with a concerned look on his face. Lovingly, if a bit accusingly, he asked us why we weren't devoting more time in our service to prayer. The music was fine; the preaching was wonderful. "But when are we going to get a chance to really *pray*?" he insisted. I have to admit I felt pretty bad hearing his words. What kind of deadbeat worship

---

1. *Lunette with Orante.* Catacomb of Priscilla, Rome, Italy. I first saw this fresco on the cover of the excellent book by Lester Ruth, Carrie Steenwyk, and John D. Witvliet, *Walking Where Jesus Walked: Worship in Fourth-Century Jerusalem* (Grand Rapids, Mich.: Eerdmans, 2010).

leader doesn't leave room for prayer in worship? What kind of worship leader doesn't even think about leaving room? How could I have missed that?

As I processed his complaint with a few good friends and mentors, I began to realize that the problem wasn't that we didn't make room for prayer in worship. It was that this man's vision of prayer (and my own) was far too narrow. He and I had thought that praying could only look certain ways—perhaps huddled groups of intercessors or down-in-front healing prayer by the elders. As good as those forms of prayer are, both the Bible and the church across time give us a more comprehensive picture of prayer.

Worship *Is* Prayer

When I was young, I thought prayer was talking *to* God. Then, as I grew older, I realized that prayer was talking *with* God. Prayer is a dialogue, a back-and-forth. In prayer we speak, but we also listen. In one sense, a worship service is just one long prayer—God speaks, we respond, repeat, repeat, repeat. Think back on the most recent worship gathering you were a part of. What actions were rehearsed? What language was used? Our worship is full of the actions and language of prayer. And many worshipers preceding our contemporary generation understood this intuitively. In the nineteenth century, Presbyterian pastor Matthew Henry wrote *A Method for Prayer*, a book that was just as much about public worship as it was about private devotion. Several centuries earlier, the reformer Thomas Cranmer sketched new worship services for the English people. He called this book the *Book of Common Prayer*. Thinking of worship as prayer has its roots in the Jewish origins of the Christian faith. Consider that when Jesus denounced the moneychangers' desecration of Israel's worship space, he quoted Isaiah in calling the temple a "house of prayer" (Matt. 21:13; Isa. 56:7). For most Jews and Christians down through the history of the church, the concepts of worship and prayer were fairly synonymous. The concerns of the man who had approached me wanting more prayer in worship would have struck them as odd because worship *is* prayer, from beginning to end!

What are the implications of this idea as we pastor others in worship? First, it means that worship leaders are the main facilitators of the church's corporate prayer encounter with God. The liturgies we employ, the song sets we put together, and the gaps that we fill everywhere else become the very words that the bride of Christ will utter to her Bridegroom. And when we think about the fact that the vast majority of worshipers in our churches won't seek or receive training and education in prayer elsewhere, this means that the worship service is *the* central training ground and vocabulary builder for a Christian's prayers throughout the week. We're not only facilitating prayer on Sundays, we're training Christians to pray Monday through Saturday. Whether or not you think of yourself as a pastor, if you're planning and leading worship, you're pastoring your flock's prayer life. So make no mistake. At the end of the day, Worship Pastor, if nothing else, you're a prayer leader.

The Church's Speechwriter

One way of better understanding your role as a prayer leader is to think of yourself as a speechwriter.[2] A speechwriter is someone who is tasked with giving an important person (like the president of the United States) words that both need to be said and sound like them. When the speech is handed over and delivered from the mouth and personality of the orator, it ceases to be the speechwriter's work and becomes the words of the speaker.

Worship leaders are charged by God to put the words of prayer on the lips of the people. The liturgies and song sets we lead become the church's "speech" to God that week, and that speech shapes the prayer life (or lack thereof) of the people the other six days of the week.

Speechwriters will agonize over every last word of the speeches they write— paying careful attention to inflection, sentence length, flow, argumentation, emotion, and even the nonverbal communication beyond the words themselves. As the church's speechwriters, we need to exercise a similar level of care and attention with the words we place into the mouths of God's people. Do we model thoughtful, intentional, passionate, and faithful speech to God? Do we mirror the breadth of prayer we find in the Bible (especially the Psalms)—from shouts of joy, to tears of shame, to moans of lamentation?[3]

Those who lead in highly liturgical contexts (where the "script" is largely packaged) aren't off the hook here. Just as speechwriters care about the delivery as much as the words themselves, liturgists have a responsibility to model and mirror the affective hues of the words they give to the people of God. The dispassionate liturgical leader, whose liturgy may be filled to the brim with perfect words, is just as irresponsible a prayer leader as the modern worship leader whose passionate song set is loaded with shallow words.[4] Poor prayer leading is an equal opportunity offense.

---

2. I owe this helpful metaphor to pastor Graham Gladstone from email correspondence on November 18, 2014.

3. For those looking to expand their church's prayer vocabulary in worship, I heartily recommend Debra Rienstra and Ron Rienstra, *Worship Words: Discipling Language for Faithful Ministry* (Grand Rapids, Mich.: Baker, 2009).

4. See more on this in chapter 13, "The Worship Pastor as Emotional Shepherd."

Cultivating Concern for the Prayerful
Heart of the Congregation

As prayer leaders, our job is to champion prayer's fervor and sincerity in the worship service. In all the rituals of our worship, we want our prayer practices to be filled with meaning and heart. Here we move beyond scriptwriting and facilitating. We are concerned for more than the outward actions of prayer. We long for our people's hearts to be inwardly aligned with those actions.

Of course, once we start talking about the heart, we are stepping into God territory. It is God and His gospel alone that ultimately turns hearts and kindles true Christian fervor. Nevertheless, God uses the means of prayers communicated through fallible human vessels to accomplish this work. A real prayer leader doesn't shirk this responsibility by saying, "That's God's thing. I'll do my part; He'll do His." The pastoral instinct of the worship leader kicks in and says, "It's part of my call to be concerned about this." So while God alone moves hearts in sincere prayer, a worship pastor continually cultivates a longing to see it happen. We want our worship services to be filled with real prayer. We ache for it to happen. And we plead with God to make it so.[5]

(Re)Filling Our Prayer
with Meaning

We could say that our worship services are nothing other than a collection of prayer rituals—various practices like singing, reading, hearing, praying, preaching, eating, drinking, and baptizing, where we as a community are in constant dialogue with God . . . sometimes listening, sometimes responding. And, just in case we are scared by the word *ritual*, as though it makes something rote or drains it of meaning, we should recognize with sociologists that we human beings "ritualize our activities *to express their significance*."[6] We make something a ritual because we believe it's important. Certain streams of modern worship "ritualize" spontaneous sung prayer by providing regular space in their worship service for people to, as is said, "sing your own song to the Lord." They do so because those moments have become meaningful contexts for God's power to move in prayer.

---

5. Let me point out, though, that the idea of "empty ritual" and "going through the motions" being *intrinsically bad* should be challenged. Of course, we want full engagement in worship. But James K. A. Smith reminds us that "the motions" aren't without formative consequence, and we can take heart. *Desiring the Kingdom: Worship, Worldview, and Cultural Formation* (Grand Rapids, Mich.: Baker, 2009), 166–67; see especially 167 n.29.

6. Lawrence A. Hoffman, *The Art of Public Prayer: Not for Clergy Only*, 2nd ed. (Woodstock, Vt.: Skylight Paths, 1999), 36 (emphasis mine).

Anglicans have ritualized the Communion liturgy because they understand the Lord's Supper as a unique and intimate place of prayer where Jesus reveals Himself to His people in the power of the Spirit. We should not automatically assume that rituals are bad or evil. Just the opposite. They exist because they provide something important for worship. We just never want them to downgrade into *mere* ritual—heartless practice. So whatever your tradition's prayer rituals are, from scripted liturgy to unscripted spontaneity, your task is to determine how to continually reinspire these practices with meaning. How do we shape contexts for God to kindle the flames of sincerity and integrity (wholeness)? Let's look quickly at four ways we can do this.

First, ask God for it. Don't skip over this, even if you know it's the first thing you should do. How often we forget that God is a loving Father who delights in giving good gifts to His kids (Matt. 7:11)! If you're finding your worship services lack a fervent and prayerful atmosphere, start by asking God for it. Ask God to fill you and your people with the Spirit of earnest prayer.

Second, cultivate a prayer-filled life. Fill your weekly rhythms with moments to get away and pray, and make your day-to-day regular activities a consistent time to converse with God. I often leave conversations with people only to pick up a dialogue with God about it then and there. This is the spirit behind praying without ceasing (1 Thess. 5:17).

Third, investigate the meaning—the why—behind your worship service's various prayer practices, and then tell your people about the meaning of those practices in worship.[7] I sometimes begin a worship service, after welcoming people, by tackling one topic in one minute. I'll ask a question like, "Why do we hear a Call to Worship every week?" Then I answer, "Because worship is our conversation with God, and the Call is God's invitation into that dialogue." When I lead our church in a time of confession, instead of the bland instruction, "You may be seated," I'll say, "Let's bow our bodies as we're seated and confess our sins to God." Little, unobtrusive interjections like these go a long way in filling our prayer times with meaning.

Fourth, fill your prayer practices with the appropriate emotion. We will talk about this more in the chapter on emotional shepherding. But emotion is always one of the key components to a meaningful, holistic experience, and our emotional leadership (body language, countenance, rhetoric, expression) can either help or hinder people's meaningful engagement in worship's prayer practices.

---

7. Hoffman suggests two helpful questions to dig into the *meaning* of our practices: (1) "How did the practice begin?"; (2) "What did the practice mean to the original practitioners?" These two questions, time and again, have inspired worship with meaning for myself and the people I lead. Hoffman, *The Art of Public Prayer*, 34–35.

Song: The Unique Power of Musical Prayer

For many of us, singing is one of the primary prayer practices of our worship. And it should be. It's high on God's radar. When talking about worship, Paul made a close association between singing and praying: "I will *pray* with my spirit, but I will also *pray* with my understanding; I will *sing* with my spirit, but I will also *sing* with my understanding" (1 Cor. 14:15, emphasis mine). It's also important to remember that though the Bible contains many prayers (e.g., 1 Kings 18:36–37; John 17), the greatest concentration is in a collection of prayers intended to be sung—the Psalms. Singing is God's gift to us to make our corporate prayer easy, meaningful, and holistic. Augustine is credited with saying, "Whoever sings, prays twice." Song amplifies the experience of prayer. Why is this?

The Science of Song: Music and Movement

Musicologists have pointed out that music's expressive power lies in its ability to mimic human gesture and physicality.[8] Sad music often sounds like human sighing and groaning. Think of Samuel Barber's famous *Adagio for Strings*. Frantic music sounds like the jitters of a fast heart rate. Think of Beethoven's Fifth Symphony. Sinister, sneaky music can sound like a person's careful, crouched movement. Think of Mancini's *Pink Panther* theme. Dance music sounds like the stomping and clapping of a group of people bouncing in rhythm. Think of disco and EDM. Robert Jourdain and Brian Wren take these ideas a step farther by saying that when we hear music, our brains receive the stimuli of these musical gestures similarly to how they process the stimuli of our nervous system in physical movement.[9] Our aural perception of music and physical perception of movement are closely related.

How does this insight relate to the connection between singing and prayer in worship? It indicates that something profound and rich, something moving (literally), happens to us in sung prayer that does not happen in mere spoken prayer. Music may not add to the propositional content of our prayers, but as music moves us, it amplifies and extends the reach of our apprehension, understanding, and experience of those prayers.[10] Music adds to prayer and indeed helps us "pray twice."

8. See the explanation of this in Jeremy S. Begbie, "Faithful Feelings: Music and Emotion in Worship," in *Resonant Witness: Conversations Between Music and Theology*, ed. Jeremy S. Begbie and Steven R. Guthrie (Grand Rapids, Mich.: Eerdmans, 2011), 340–49.

9. See Brian Wren, *Praying Twice: The Music and Words of Congregational Song* (Louisville, Ky.: Westminster John Knox, 2000), 61, citing Robert Jourdain, *Music, the Brain, and Ecstasy: How Music Captures Our Imagination* (New York: William Morrow Paperbacks, 2008), 303.

10. Similarly, Begbie says of our emotions, "They are capable of advancing and assisting our 'grasping of the truth.'" "Faithful Feelings," 333.

The Power of Song: What Music Does to Our Prayer in Worship

In an uplifting blog post, worship pastor Matthew Westerholm encourages us that, because of congregational song, our prayer lives are better than we think.[11] Riffing on reformer John Calvin's very edifying treatment of prayer,[12] Westerholm says that our song leadership as worship leaders performs at least four pastoral functions for our people. Let these be an encouragement to you that you may already be performing several pastoral functions in your ministry.

First, singing our prayers unites the gathered church. When someone is speaking a prayer "up front," it's understandably hard for everyone's hearts to be unified around that person's prayer. But song is a powerfully unifying medium. When we sing, we have many different voices with many different timbres coming together in harmony, all singing one thing. Singing is one of the activities that enables us to see and hear the church's union in Christ (Eph. 4:3–6).[13] Singing embodies and actualizes our identity as the church;[14] we pray "with one mind and one voice" (Rom. 15:6). In this way, the church learns who she is in the doing.[15]

Second, singing our prayers focuses our wandering thoughts. I don't know about you, but I find that when I am led in prayer by someone else's voice, I have a hard time staying focused. But when I am singing that same prayer, I am more engaged and less likely to drift. Song focuses our attention on the prayer we are praying.

Third, singing our prayers enflames our withering affections. If you're like me, you sometimes struggle to feel like you believe what you pray. Both individual and corporate prayer can feel less like easy love and more like heavy labor. Song has a way of kindling the inner affections, stirring up passion and love within us.

---

11. Matthew Westerholm, "Your Prayer Life Is Better Than You Think," *Desiring God*, January 25, 2015, accessed May 16, 2015, http://www.desiringgod.org/articles/your-prayer-life-is-better-than-you-think. Permission was granted by the author to reprint his ideas here.

12. John Calvin, *Institutes of the Christian Religion* III.20.31–32.

13. This is why, with some, I'm comfortable giving song lowercase *s* "sacramental" status, as I tried to articulate in chapter 2, "The Worship Pastor as Corporate Mystic." While singing doesn't mediate the presence of God in the same way that the sacraments of baptism and the Lord's Supper do, music is still sacramen*tal*.

14. This is what Oswald Bayer was getting at in speaking of the whole of worship when he said, "The restoration of the church from its corruption, as an order of creation, which God accomplished through Christ, is given and distributed to us as a gift in the Christian divine service" (*Theology the Lutheran Way*, ed. and trans. Jeffrey G. Silcock and Mark C. Mattes [Grand Rapids, Mich.: Eerdmans, 2007], 88).

15. Taking his cues from Michael Polanyi on "tacit knowledge" and Susan Wood on "participatory knowledge," Steven Guthrie beautifully said, "In song, we share in the life and activity of the church. We learn—we come to *know*—its ways, not by having these articulated for us verbally and conceptually, but by participating in them. We come to a lived and (we might say) a kinesthetic understanding of what the church *is*, by taking part in what the church *does*" (Steven R. Guthrie, "The Wisdom of Song," in *Resonant Witness: Conversations between Music and Theology*, ed. Jeremy S. Begbie and Steven R. Guthrie [Grand Rapids, Mich.: Eerdmans, 2011], 396, emphasis in original).

Music props up our emotions, preventing them from falling to the left or the right so that the source of our prayer comes not just from our lips but from our hearts.

Fourth, singing our prayers engages our entire bodies. Praying can often devolve into a mere "heady" exercise. Singing forces rapid, successive rushes of air in and out of our lungs. The muscles in our abdomen, chest, neck, throat, and shoulders cooperate to support the very physical exercise of holding notes and articulating phrases. No wonder John Wesley, in his Rules for Congregational Singing, said, "Sing lustily—and with good courage. Beware of singing as if you were half-dead or half-asleep; but lift up your voice with strength. Be no more afraid of your voice now, no more ashamed of its being heard, than when you sang the songs of Satan." How many times have you looked upon a congregation and felt like God's worshipers in prayer looked more like the walking dead than the praying living? If you want your people to *really pray*, encourage them to *really sing*. When you do this, you are pastoring them toward a stronger, more lively prayer life.

Missional Prayer

When we sing our prayers together, we help our church fulfill God's mission of revealing Himself to the world. Sung prayer is missional, even when it happens right in the middle of the worship service. Theologian Jürgen Moltmann emphasizes that part of the image of God in humanity (Gen. 1:26–27) can only be seen as we are unified in community. Because God is Trinity—a unity of three Persons—so we, as image bearers of God's communal oneness, become a kind of revelation of God to the world when we sing our prayers.[16] When the world hears our harmony, they witness the manifestation of this particular aspect of the image of God. Singing our prayers, in this sense, makes it easier for the world to see God so that they can say, "God is really among you!" (1 Cor. 14:25).

Hopefully you are beginning to see just how incredible your role is as a worship pastor. And as a prayer leader, you pastor people's prayer lives by facilitating a corporate dialogue between the church and her Father, through the Son, by the Spirit. What we're doing, week after week, has a formative impact on how the believers in our care speak to God in worship and throughout the week. And when we fill worship with meaning, intention, and faithful leadership, we ultimately are able to point believers to the only perfect Worshiper and our true

---

16. Jürgen Moltmann, *God in Creation: A New Theology of Creation and the Spirit of God* (San Francisco: Harper and Row, 1985), 220–22. See discussion in Guthrie, "The Wisdom of Song," 391–94.

Prayer Leader—Jesus Christ—who both teaches us to pray (Matt. 6:9–13) and perfects our prayers as they rise to God as a sweet aroma (Rev. 8:3–4).

O great Prayer Leader, Jesus Christ, as we gather each week to worship You, teach us to pray to our Father, by Your Spirit, until we can't tell where praying ends and life begins. Amen.

6

THE WORSHIP PASTOR AS THEOLOGICAL DIETICIAN

We will begin with worship, or as we prefer to call it, the divine service.
This means starting at the beginning, for whatever passes for theology
grows out of the divine service.

—Oswald Bayer, 1994[1]

James' Falling Out

James attends an evangelical church near you. The worship is vibrant, joyful, and uplifting. The messages are positive and encouraging. Church is filled with a lot of smiling faces and sincere happiness. The music is made up of the latest, greatest Christian radio hits. James learns from all of this that a relationship with God is light and easy. Christianity feels like freedom and success—all day, every day.

But then tragedy strikes. James' wife is diagnosed with terminal cancer. The next ten months are a living hell as James watches his precious love wither before his eyes, then die. Throughout the journey, James seeks God for answers. But he feels a growing disparity between his life's circumstances and what worship told him faith should feel like. "It doesn't seem like Christians are supposed to suffer," he thought, "so maybe there's something wrong with me." After his wife's death, he starts to question everything, not all at once, but in little moments here and there. Worship starts to wear on him. He isn't feeling others' joy and excitement, and all the shiny happiness is actually making his heart grow more bitter. Fast-forward to a year after his wife's death: James is now a professed atheist.

---

1. Oswald Bayer, *Theology the Lutheran Way*, ed. and trans. Jeffrey G. Silcock and Mark C. Mattes (Grand Rapids, Mich.: Eerdmans, 2007), 85.

Worship taught James a lot, both in what it did say and what it didn't say. James learned that faith equals joy and happiness—that faith and suffering are incompatible—because worship never addressed the dark things. God was a God of blessing. Suffering didn't fit into the equation of faith, so when it happened, James had no categories for relating to God through suffering. He was given no language to cry out, no voice for lamentation. Left with these realities, people usually do one of two things: they question *their* faith ("I must not be a real Christian"), or they question *the* faith ("God must not be real; Christianity must be a sham"). James, quite understandably, chose the latter.

As worship leaders, we have a pressing question before us: If all that the people of God had were the worship services we plan and lead, what would they know about Him, and how would they relate to Him?[2] Can you see from this story how serious this question is? For people like James, faith very much teeters on the precipice of worship's answers to the heavy questions of life—like those of the compatibility of God and suffering. Still, some might think the question unfair. Why should the burden for a biblical theology of suffering be placed solely on worship? Obviously, worship leaders alone cannot address the questions that people have, but we must also recognize that the people in our churches, by and large, aren't studying their Bibles much on their own, nor do the majority of them avail themselves of the educational and spiritual resources offered by the church. For many, corporate worship is where they learn about God. That's it.[3]

So while it's unfair to place the weight of catechesis squarely on the shoulders of the weekly service, at the same time we need to recognize that gathered worship (not the classroom) is often ground zero—where the Word of God forms every believer's theology. Learning theology is not just a heady exercise of fact memorization. It is an integrated way of knowing and being known by God. And worship is the context where primary theology takes place, where we are *theologized*.[4]

---

2. I'm grateful to Bob Kauflin, who has now trained several generations of worship leaders to ask this kind of question. See for example his article, "What Happens When We Sing in Worship?" *Christianity.com*, accessed May 21, 2015, http://www.christianity.com/newsletters/features/what-happens-when-we-sing-in-worship-11627945.html.

3. For this reason and more, we are beginning to observe the shocking similarities of theology, worship, and outlook between medieval Roman Christianity and twenty-first-century North American evangelicalism: a theologically uninformed laity; an active, mediated worship up front performed by the leaders; a passive, observant congregation in the pews; worship leaders as the "conjurers" of the divine presence through certain rituals.

4. I highly recommend two discussions worth digesting: (1) On worship as primary theology: Simon Chan, *Liturgical Theology: The Church as Worshiping Community* (Downers Grove, Ill.: InterVarsity, 2006), 48–52; and (2) On theology beginning and ending with worship: Oswald Bayer, *Theology the Lutheran Way* (Grand Rapids, Mich.: Eerdmans, 2007), 88–96.

The Dietician

The metaphor of dietician is a perfect way to think about how a worship leader engages in "theological pastoring" as they plan and lead worship.[5] A dietician's job is to lead their client toward optimized health through regimented meal planning with nutritious foods in a balanced variety. They take into account the complexity of the human body's needs while helping avoid the dangers of allergens, toxins, and other foods that could be harmful. So, too, part of pastoring a congregation through worship leading is thinking of yourself as a "theological dietician."

There is an obvious first step here: training and study in the art of knowing God. If we are to be theological dieticians for our flocks, we must first be committed and passionate theologians ourselves. We must seek God in His Word and learn of Him as that Word speaks and births faith in worship. We must allow the Word to "theologize" us and commit ourselves to studying God the way a man in love studies a woman—learning to understand God's habits, behaviors, thoughts, loves, and hates.

How Worship Theologizes

As we kindle the flames of being lifelong theologians ourselves, we also need to consider how worship feeds theology to people. If studying theology is like a dietician learning about food, then studying how worship theologizes is like a dietician learning how to administer meal plans. With this analogy in mind, let's look at some ways of breaking worship down into food groups. We'll look at roughly four "food groups": sermon, sacrament, structure, and song. We'll deal with the first two together.

Food Groups 1 and 2: Sermon and Sacrament

In talking about worship as a theological diet, we easily slip into a default way of thinking about worship as instruction. If we think of theology as another set of facts to be cognitively appropriated, we end up reducing worship to knowing *about* God rather than knowing *Him*.[6] Nowhere does this weakened view of theology rear its ugly head more than in our understanding of sermon and sacrament.[7] A sermon should be an amazing encounter with the living Christ as He is given to His people by His Spirit through creaturely preaching. Instead, sermons are

---

5. As best I can trace, this idea originated with John Witvliet, "Soul Food for the People of God," *Liturgical Ministry* 10 (Spring 2001): 101–10.

6. This classic distinction is made by J. I. Packer, *Knowing God* (Downers Grove, Ill.: InterVarsity, 1973), esp. chapter 1.

7. Some traditions call the sacraments "ordinances."

often reduced to teaching, knowledge transfer, or good advice. Likewise, the sacraments, which should also be experiences of the presence and power of Christ by the Spirit, are reduced to mere ritualistic "illustrations" of the gospel. Against the idea that our theological formation is merely our appropriation of information, we must see that we are theologized by knowing God through encounters, borne of His Word in preaching, baptism, and the Lord's Supper. We learn things about God and how to relate to Him as we experience these supernatural events.[8]

Food Group 3: Structure

If people are talking about theology in worship, most of those discussions center around content—what we are learning about God in the prayers, the words of our songs, the propositions of our sermons. But theologizing happens through the structure of our worship as well, in the ordering of our song sets and liturgical readings and prayers.

We can get started thinking about this by asking the question we posed in the introduction: How do I approach God rightly? Worship boils down to God's coming to us and our responsive approach, and how we answer this question of approach in our structure defines the difference between worship which is truly Christian and worship which is not. We will cover this in detail in chapter 14, "The Worship Pastor as Liturgical Architect," but here we can simply say that our structure says a great deal about our theology of worship, and it shapes the way people know and encounter God. In short, we can answer this crucial question of how we approach God in one of two ways: either we come into God's presence directly and on our own (pagan worship), or we come through the Mediator (Christian worship). The structure of our worship services must be Christ centered—even Christ mediated. If it is not, we pour poison on every theological meal we prepare, and our people cannot be nourished.[9]

Food Group 4: Song

As the worship leader, you may not have much control over the content of the sermon and the sacrament. Sometimes even the structure is not something you set. But for most worship leaders today, the songs are something you can choose and arrange. So for the remainder of this chapter I will focus on the songs we

---

8. See more on this in chapter 2, "The Worship Pastor as Corporate Mystic."

9. One of the richest insights of Bryan Chapell's outstanding work, *Christ-Centered Worship: Letting the Gospel Shape Our Practice* (Grand Rapids, Mich.: Baker, 2009), is that in every major stream of the history of Christian worship, amid many divergent themes, variations, and expressions, we can discern a similar Christ- and gospel-shaped *structure*. This structure, Chapell argues, constitutes the core of uniquely Christian worship. This is what I believe the 1996 Nairobi Statement on Worship and Culture points to when it talks about Christianity's "shared core liturgical structure" (2.3).

sing. Improvising on a theme of Martyn Lloyd-Jones,[10] my friend Kevin Twit is known for saying, "Hymns are theology on fire." By this he means that our songs are nothing more and nothing less than theology enflamed, engulfing our hearts. Sung worship is one of the most holistic ways we can experience (hear, "know") theology, because song summons our whole self—mind, body, soul, intellect, will, emotions. When we sing about God, His works, and our response to Him, we are being deeply, indelibly theologized.

At the end of Moses' ministry, in order to impart to his people the gravity of knowing God and remembering His mighty deeds (i.e., theology), he gave them a song (Deut. 32:1–43). And at the end of it, Moses was careful to point out that the song's lyrics "are not just idle words for you—they are your life" (Deut. 32:47). We need to see what Moses saw, the theologizing power of song. O worship pastor, the songs you choose each week bear the weight of *life*.

Many have pointed out that when people walk away from a worship service, they carry with them, more than anything else, the songs. A sermon rarely rattles around in your head on repeat. You don't find yourself humming a responsive reading a few days later. Of all the elements of worship, our songs probably have the most prolonged digestion rate. Their theology is "slow release." They stick, haunt, and preach. The question is, what are they preaching to our people? How do we take the diet of song seriously?

Planning the Diet

If we're thinking like a dietician, we develop meal plans with certain goals and objectives in mind, and we foster habits that help us to regularly see those goals through. I'd like to briefly outline four goals for leading worship.

1. We aim for a balanced diet. Just like the human body needs different types of foods, so the body of Christ needs theological variety. How do we get in tune with the breadth of theological nutrition? A great place to start is the book of Psalms. Martin Luther called the Psalms our "little Bible," and John Calvin described it as "an anatomy of all the parts of the soul."[11] Worship leaders immersed in the Psalms acquire a taste for its varied theological themes—joy, praise, lamentation, suffering, glory, fear, hope, guilt, history, love, hate, war, peace, community, family, and so on. And this developed palate helps us discern what is lacking in our church's sung theological diets. Our flock's dietary imbalances become

---

10. Martyn Lloyd-Jones, *Preaching and Preachers* (Grand Rapids, Mich.: Zondervan, 1972), 97: "What is preaching? Logic on fire! Eloquent reason!"

11. Martin Luther, "Preface to the Psalter (1528)," in *Luther's Works*, vol. 35, ed. E. Theodore Bachmann (Philadelphia: Fortress, 1960), 254; John Calvin, *Commentary on the Book of Psalms*, vol. 1, trans. James Anderson (Grand Rapids, Mich.: Baker, 2003), xxxvii.

exposed. Through the lens of the Psalms and the rest of the Bible, we discern certain dichotomies, paradoxes, and tensions that are the building blocks of a well-rounded theological diet. Here is a sampling:

- transcendence and immanence
- cognitive and emotional
- internal (heart) and external (body) expression
- vertical and horizontal
- planned and spontaneous
- structured and free
- traditional and innovative
- historic and contextualized
- for the church and for non-Christians[12]
- joy and reverence
- activity and stillness
- loud and quiet
- individual and corporate
- singing about ourselves and singing about God
- us to God (human address) and God to us (divine address)
- earthly and heavenly
- physical and spiritual
- verbose/content-heavy and sparse/meditative
- objective and subjective content[13]
- One God and Three Persons[14]
- Divinity and humanity of Christ

A worship pastor is attuned to dichotomies like these and is sensitive to how their own church or worship tradition naturally leans one way or another. A few

12. The list up to this point combines and edits lists from Bob Kauflin, *Worship Matters: Leading Others to Encounter the Greatness of God* (Wheaton, Ill.: Crossway, 2008), 153–210, and Chapell, *Christ-Centered Worship*, 137.

13. See the helpful treatment of this particular subject in Andrew W. Blackwood, *The Fine Art of Public Worship* (New York: Abingdon-Cokesbury, 1939), 17–20.

14. One very eye-opening study revealed to me how "under-Trinitized" our modern worship songs are. The Trinity, the foundational and formational doctrine of the Christian faith, can be quite vague to us if we're only singing about God generically or about Jesus and the Spirit in broad ways. We need worship music that helps us interact with God as Triune as well as the Persons specifically in their unique roles in our lives. We need to be engaging in God's threeness and oneness. See Lester Ruth, "How Great Is Our God: The Trinity in Contemporary Worship Music," in *The Message in the Music: Studying Contemporary Praise and Worship*, ed. Robert Woods and Brian Walrath (Nashville: Abingdon, 2007), 29–42. For more on worship and the Trinity, see Zac Hicks, "The Worship Leader and the Trinity," in *Doxology and Theology: How the Gospel Forms the Worship Leader*, ed. Matt Boswell (Nashville: Broadman and Holman, 2013), 59–74.

years ago, a new intern of mine offered a very wise perspective when she pointed out that our worship services were filled with songs and prayers that were content heavy—hymns with lofty language and few repeated ideas, phrases, or refrains. She said, "I never feel like there's any time to digest what is being said because a lot of heavy ideas are going by so quickly." This fresh perspective told me that there was a dietary imbalance in our worship. There was very little time for meditation and release from the barrage of terms and concepts, and this imbalance stifled the worshipful atmosphere of our services. In response we made a course correction and added moments of meditation and pause. We began to incorporate songs with more repetition and fewer words. Our services began to feel like they had more breathing room, and our people were becoming more holistically engaged in worship.

2. We develop criteria for food selection. When we select songs, it's important that we determine criteria ahead of time so that we don't go into the grocery store blind. We ask questions like, "What are the best foods for my flock?" and, "What kind of food does my flock need right now?" We can boil down our process of song selection to two types of listening. First, we continually listen to new and old worship music, and second, we carefully listen to the hurts, needs, dreams, and aspirations of our flock. For the former, here are the kinds of questions I ask:

- Is it singable?
- Does the music complement the lyrics?
- Is it theologically precise?
- Is it logically coherent?
- Is it aimed Godward?[15]
- Is it in line with the gospel?

Asking these questions may feel like analyzing a song in a laboratory. But we are not research scientists. We are pastors who serve local churches. We need our lab research to be in dialogue with our field testing. We need to be relationally invested in the people of our church, and we need to be dialed in to the big and small events that affect our communities. Only when this kind of double listening takes place are we properly equipped to offer selections to our people. For instance, you may have found a wonderful, upbeat, joyful song ready to introduce to your

---

15. I used to phrase this question, "Is it God-centered?" largely because of the observation that so many current worship songs were "me-centered." Unfortunately, this emphasis has yielded a knee-jerk reaction against any and all songs that utilize first person pronouns. The Psalms, yet again, are instructive here. They are filled with personal, individual references from the "me" perspective. Perhaps the difference, then, is the aim. One always gets the sense in reading the "me" Psalms that they are aimed Godward even when they are deeply personal.

congregation, but a recent national event spurred on by racial unrest has your congregation feeling the weight of suffering and injustice. Though the song passes your criteria with flying colors, your congregation is not in a place to receive it.

3. We carefully introduce new foods. A dietician knows that new foods can't be introduced quickly or in large quantities. So it is with songs. A congregation's confidence to sing is tied up in how familiar the songs are, and if you introduce too many new songs at once, you may find them losing their appetite to sing. Many worship leaders who lack this pastoral instinct have successfully silenced their congregation's voice here. I generally introduce no more than one song a month, and I will usually utilize it three out of the four weeks so that the congregation has plenty of time to get used to it. Even as there are so many wonderful new worship songs and arrangements out there that stir our hearts, a pastoral spirit keeps in check those urges to overload our congregations with too much.

4. We aim for long-term health. This is where (1) through (3) come together. There is a temptation in our jobs to operate solely within the week-to-week grind. Many pressures (some of them beyond us) make it hard for us to step out of this tyranny of the urgent. For the sake of pastoring people well, we must lift our heads above the weekly fray to develop habits of long-range planning and mapping our congregation's theological diet in worship, especially with songs. The balanced diet we've described is impossible to administer if we don't prayer-fully plan for it. Just as no one meal can contain the full gamut of nutrition, so it is impossible for every week's service to incorporate the entire theological spectrum mentioned above. Long-range planning allows a pastor to see how a congregation is being broadly theologized over the course of weeks and months. For me, in addition to my weekly use of Planning Center Online (PCO, one of the best universal worship planning platforms), I have a Google document where I collect my long-range ideas. This document serves as my planning mechanism for tentative service sketches (before I commit to them in PCO). The helpfulness here is that I can see several weeks' worth of services on my screen at once. I'm able to assess, at a bird's eye view, how well I am balancing some of the above tensions and dichotomies.

What They Want versus What They Need

Any dietician knows that the optimal diet isn't always something the client can stomach immediately. The meal planner must juggle the reality of giving their client what they want versus what they need. The same is true of a pastor. We live in the tension of where the people are, which means we have to make compromises now to get people where we want them to be in the future. Some people call this selling out. I call this pastoral ministry on the ground. Perhaps the song everyone in your congregation is dying to sing isn't the most theologically rich or musically lasting piece of work. Perhaps you have a list a mile long of better songs just waiting to be introduced. The reality is if you're going to lead in a way that people will follow, you need to at least occasionally give them what they want.

Of course, we're not talking about permitting singing outright heresy or incorporating polarizing, fringe musical styles. But a dietician is careful and strategic about offering people comfort foods along the way toward a healthy diet. Ultimately, this is just good pastoral work, which requires ongoing prayer and wisdom. And just in case some idealists out there think this is going too far, we only need to look at the pastoral leadership of our sovereign God, who offered His people an earthly king when it wasn't His best for them (1 Samuel 8) and a tabernacle and temple when He alone could be their true abiding place (John 1:1–14).

That said, there are some serious problems we need to avoid in our worship diets. I want to end this chapter by focusing on one in particular.

The Old Adam's Comfort Food and the New Adam's Feast

There is one kind of comfort food that we should be especially leery of weaving into our people's diets. Consider it the "high fructose corn syrup" of worship—it is toxic, cancer producing, and ultimately deadly. To expose it, we need to unpack the biblical idea of the Old Adam (and Eve), which Paul called the "old self" (Rom. 6:6; Eph. 4:22; Col. 3:9), the "sinful nature" (Rom. 7:18, 25), or sometimes the "flesh" (Rom. 7:5, 8:3–13). The Old Adam remains in Christians, even after salvation, as a vestige of the old world, which is passing away. This Adam's "primary and highest affection is love of self."[16] The Christian's lifelong battle against the flesh (Gal. 5:13–26) means that the Old Adam is vehemently opposed to the gospel, because its preceding word demands, "To be born anew, one must consequently first die."[17] This word of death to the Old Adam (i.e., the law, see especially 2 Corinthians 3) is shocking and untenable because it says, "You contribute nothing to your salvation." The Old Adam, being completely self-focused and self-absorbed, hungers for any word that will encourage him to love himself. The Old Adam is always looking for some edge, some foot in the door, some way

---

16. Philip Melanchthon, *Commonplaces: Loci Communes 1521*, trans. Christian Preus (St. Louis, Mo.: Concordia, 2014), 38.

17. Martin Luther, "Heidelberg Disputation (1518)," in *Luther's Works*, vol. 31, ed. Helmut T. Lehmann (Philadelphia: Fortress, 1957), 55. For a thorough treatment on the subject of the death of the Old Adam, see Oswald Bayer, *Living by Faith: Justification and Sanctification*, trans. Geoffrey W. Bromiley (Grand Rapids, Mich.: Eerdmans, 2003), 19–41.

to insist that he only needs a "little improvement," not death and resurrection.[18] Yet there is no room for self-love when you are told, "You have no righteousness (law: Isa. 64:6; Rom. 3:10–18; Phil. 3:9), but Christ is all your righteousness (gospel: 1 Cor. 1:30; Rom. 3:21–26; Phil. 3:9)." In short, the Old Adam hates the gospel because he loves himself.

Because the Old Adam is desperate for attention, he has extremely ticklish ears. He is looking for something, anything to grab onto which gives him credit for his hard work for God. And when he hears it—worse, when he sings it—an adrenaline rush surges through the flesh, and he rises up.

We need to ask hard and honest questions about the comfort foods which unknowingly feed the Old Adam's appetite in our songs. Old Adam loves to sing about what he is doing for God. And even when placed in response to the gospel, singing about what we are doing for God can very quickly cause Old Adam to rise up and stop the ears of faith from hearing and remembering those blessed words, "It is finished," drowning them out with his own shouts, "Look at what *I'm* doing!" When we sing too much about our surrender for God, our living for His name, our triumph, our zeal, our giving it all away, our passion, our fervor, and our commitment, we are making room for what Paul calls "confidence in the flesh" (Phil. 3:3–4).

Our worship song landscape today, in both traditional and modern circles, is overloaded with this kind of comfort food. For the sake of our churches and the gospel we treasure—which alone has the power to save and sanctify us (Rom. 1:16; 1 Cor. 1:30–31; 1 Thess. 5:23–24)—we need a lot more singing about Christ and His finished work of life and death and a lot less singing about our work.[19] If the Old Adam is to die, he must be starved.[20]

The beauty here is this: the table that is cleared of the Old Adam's comfort foods now has ample room for the New Adam's feast (Rom. 5:12–21). If we want our congregations to be healthy and vibrant, let us allow the Spirit to lavishly

---

18. Bayer, *Living by Faith*, 21: "The need that lies deeply within each of us to prove our right to exist—not simply to be there, but to gain recognition by what we can afford and accomplish—is put to death. This will to achieve and thus to secure recognition by being active and productive has become part of our nature, our second and evil nature. This nature 'is very unwilling to die and to suffer, and it is a bitter holy day for nature to cease from its own work and be dead'" (ending quote: Martin Luther).

19. I've written quite a bit about this over the years on my blog (www.zachicks.com) under the tag "triumphalism." Usually a Google search of my name along with that tag brings up the various posts that will tease this all out in more concrete detail (i.e., worship song analysis, album reviews, etc.).

20. Many will ask, "Where, then, is room for songs of consecration, dedication, and response?" The answer must be, "minimally and sparingly." The irony of such songs is that they often do not contain the Word within them that gives them the power to follow through on what they describe. If the gospel alone is the source of all righteousness and good works, and if we want our people to dedicate themselves to God in thought, word, and deed, we need far more emphasis in our worship services on the gospel and far less on our response to the gospel. Only the gospel can produce what the law demands.

serve up large portions of Jesus. Let's sing songs that revel in all His perfect, law-abiding work, His impeccable track record, His overabundance of merit, His righteous earning of the Father's full pleasure . . . *for us.* Let's sing songs that glory in His saving death, His blood-bought ransom, His complete payment of debt, His unflinching absorption of the Father's wrath, His heroic sacrifice, His full and final suffering, His finished work . . . *for us.*[21]

Being theologized, at the end of the day, is nothing more and nothing less than being given Jesus. And, thankfully, Jesus plus nothing equals everything.[22]

O Holy Spirit, serve us Jesus!

---

21. What we are talking about here are the classic theological categories of Christ's active (perfect, holy living) and passive (suffering for our sin) obedience, both of which we need to be singing about.

22. I'm forever grateful for and indebted to the preaching and teaching ministry of my friend Tullian Tchividjian, whose books, *Jesus + Nothing = Everything* (Wheaton, Ill.: Crossway, 2011), and *One Way Love: Inexhaustible Grace for an Exhausted World* (Colorado Springs: Cook, 2013), champion these thoughts like few others.

7

THE WORSHIP PASTOR
AS WAR GENERAL

This little babe, so few days old,
Is come to rifle Satan's fold;
All hell doth at his presence quake.
Though he himself for cold do shake,
For in this weak unarmèd wise
The gates of hell he will surprise.
—Robert Southwell, 1595[1]

It was Saturday night, and we were at each other's throats again. I'm not sure what we were fighting about—money, parenting, in-laws, schedules—but it was escalating quickly. My wife, Abby, is the classic conflict avoider. I, on the other hand, am the textbook confronter, and we were once again pushing all the right buttons like only a deeply committed, patient, tender, loving couple could. Yelling. Tears. Gestures. Silence. Blood pressure was high and tolerance low. Our Saturday night track record for these blowups was batting a thousand over the last month, and those conflicts, often unresolved as I stepped up to lead worship the next morning, loomed heavy over us, smothering our joy, tainting my leadership, and casting a cloud over the service.

Through some wise counsel and straight up divine intervention, Abby and I began sniffing the smelling salts. Our eyes were opened wide to the truth that we were caught up in an epic, cosmic narrative—good and evil, natural and supernatural. Only this story was no fiction. It was more real than the book or device you're holding right now. Abby and I saw that our recurrent Saturday night fights were spiritual disruptions intended to hijack the worship of God's people the next day.

---

1. Robert Southwell, "New Heaven, New War" (1595). Public Domain.

Worship Is War

The enemy hates the worship of God more than anything else. Recall, for instance, his temptation of Jesus in the wilderness. What was the final test? What was the pinnacle of his attack? After showing Jesus the kingdoms of the world, Satan said, "All this I will give you, if you will bow down and worship me" (Matt. 4:8–9). The top bullet point in the devil's exhaustingly long job description is, "Rob Jesus of as much worship as you possibly can."

Worship leaders who are pastorally alert and sober minded need to recognize that they have a big target on their backs. Our vocations put us dangerously out in front on the battle lines of a cosmic spiritual war. We fail to see the fight for what it is, much like fish fail to see water. It's all around us, but our cultural climate has largely made us blind to how real it is. Part of this is what John Jefferson Davis calls the "thinning and flattening of the doxological imagination,"[2] where our worship services have become nothing more than role play devoid of a sense of God's real presence. Perhaps it's modernism's fault that our world seems so dull and disenchanted,[3] but this is where we are, desensitized to the spiritual violence that is inescapable for every Christian. Wake up, sleeper. We've got a fight on our hands. Worship is war.

Even a casual survey of God's inspired songbook, the Psalms, reveals that gathered, corporate worship is full of conflict, struggle, warring, and wrestling enemies. "Praise be to the LORD my Rock, who trains my hands for war, my fingers for battle" is how one inspired worship song begins (Ps. 144:1). "The praise of children and infants" is described as intended, among other things, "to silence the foe and the avenger" (Ps. 8:2).

This war is multifaceted, and it's even more complex than the battle against the "rulers and principalities" that comprise the "spiritual forces of evil in the heavenly realms" (Eph. 6:12). Ancient Christians can help us here.

A Three-Front War

In earliest Christianity, when adult converts were brought forth for baptism, they took vows. Among the precious words spoken was a life-defining oath of renunciation. Church father Tertullian recorded one of the earliest renderings of this vow.[4] As this vow developed over time, it took a three-part form similar to

---

2. John Jefferson Davis, *Worship and the Reality of God: An Evangelical Theology of Real Presence* (Downers Grove, Ill.: InterVarsity, 2010), 78.

3. See chapter 2, "The Worship Pastor as Corporate Mystic."

4. Tertullian, *De Corona*, iii: "When we are going to enter the water, but a little before, in the

the rendering we find in the original prayer book of England, penned by Thomas Cranmer in 1549:

> Q: Dost thou forsake the devil and all his works?
> A: I forsake them.
> Q: Dost thou forsake the vain pomp and glory of the world, with all the covetous desires of the same?
> A: I forsake them.
> Q: Dost thou forsake all the carnal desires of the flesh, so that thou wilt not follow and be led by them?
> A: I forsake them.[5]

These three facets of renunciation are spoken in the context of warfare—against hell, the world, and the flesh—and they nicely summarize the three fronts on which worship's battle is fought.

1. The Assault on Hell

The most obvious front of the war is the spiritual battle fought against Satan and "all his hellish crew."[6] Worship is the front lines of humanity's struggle against the devil because worship is the front lines of the enemy's rebellion against God. Worship and spiritual/physical war share an ancient common ancestry.[7] Theologian Peter Leithart points out that the first battles of Joshua's conquest were fought on the same ground where Abraham had built altars centuries before, observing that Abraham's worship of the true God was the "preconquest" of Canaan.[8] Physical worship incites spiritual rioting. In any location where true worship takes place, the supernatural realm erupts in frenzied activity.

We should not be surprised to find that the two most inspiring biblical

---

presence of the congregation and under the hand of the president, we solemnly profess that we disown the devil, and his pomp, and his angels."

5.   Thomas Cranmer, *The First and Second Prayer Books of Edward VI* (London: J. M. Dent and Sons, 1910/1957), 244, English modernized.

6.   From the hymn, "How Sad Our State by Nature Is" (1707–1709), by Isaac Watts.

7.   Some modern scholars, unaware of how beholden they are to a naturalistic worldview, try to draw sharp lines between physical and spiritual warfare in the biblical accounts, forgetting that the vast majority of human and religious history knew no such hard-and-fast distinction. For the ancients, physical war was a very spiritual activity. Conquering was a sign of the favor and power of the god of the victors, and ancient conquest was often preceded and followed up by ritualistic worship practices. Warfare of all kinds was and continues to be a physical-spiritual reality.

8.   Peter Leithart, *A House for My Name: A Survey of the Old Testament* (Moscow: Canon Press, 2000), 111. I owe this citation to my dearly departed sister in Christ, Kim Anderson, "Worship and Conquest," *Mother Lode*, October 28, 2005, accessed November 26, 2014, http://mother-lode.blogspot.com/2005/10/worship-and-conquest.html.

models for prayer[9]—the Lord's Prayer and the High Priestly Prayer—include petitions for deliverance not just from abstract "evil," but the Evil *One* (Matt. 6:13; John 17:15).[10] Scripture also highlights music as playing an important role in spiritual struggle. In addition to psalms which highlight the war of God's people against their enemies,[11] we find music in the foreground of individuals' spiritual confrontations with demons (1 Sam. 16:23; 18:9–11). One of the Bible's most ancient worship songs appears to have been written on the heels of battle and is full of imagery of God as Warrior (Ex. 15:1–18).

Worship is an affront to everything hell stands for.

2. The Assault on the World

Theologian Jean-Jacques von Allmen defines worship as a fierce protest against the values of the present age: "Every time the Church assembles to [worship], to 'proclaim the death of Christ' (1 Cor. 11:26), it proclaims also the end of the world and the failure of the world. It contradicts the world's claim to provide men with a valid justification for their existence, it renounces the world: it affirms . . . that it is only on the other side of death to this world that life can assume its meaning: on the other side of death to this world, that is, in resurrection with Christ."[12]

Our world, including the world in us, is hell-bent on self-justification. It wants to stand on its own two feet and cry out, "*I* am all there is!" The spirit of this world is the evil spirit of rugged independence, playing itself out in ten thousand places, from academic philosophy to popular culture.[13]

Worship's very nature is deeply offensive to this spirit. And *offensive* is too soft a word. Worship is murderous. Worship prophesies to the world, "You will be made new, but you first must die." In this respect, as von Allmen says, worship is a "prelude to the Last Judgment,"[14] where the future echoes backward into the present, reminding all creation where it is headed—before the throne of God

---

9. We remember that worship at its core is nothing more and nothing less than the *prayers* of the people in response to God's revelation. See chapter 5, "The Worship Pastor as Prayer Leader."

10. Many New Testament scholars have pointed out that the Greek term in these passages (*tou ponerou*) is best translated as personal ("evil one") rather than generic and abstract ("evil"), despite many English translations to the contrary. See for example Sharon Beekmann and Peter G. Bolt, *Silencing Satan: A Handbook of Biblical Demonology* (Eugene, Ore.: Wipf and Stock, 2012), 118.

11. "Enemies" (Heb. *'ôyêb, tsâr*) are mentioned no less than fifty-five times across the 150 psalms.

12. Jean-Jacques von Allmen, *Worship: Its Theology and Practice* (New York: Oxford, 1965), 63.

13. This is why Gerhard Forde suggests that we might better think of Adam and Eve's fall as an upward one. The fall wasn't so much a "downward plunge to some lower level in the great chain of being" as it was an "upward rebellion, an invasion of the realm of things 'above'"—to become God, to be independent from His sovereignty. See Gerhard O. Forde, *Theology Is for Proclamation* (Minneapolis: Fortress, 1990), 48.

14. Von Allmen, *Worship*, 64.

Almighty.[15] Worship, centered on the earth-altering events of the death and resurrection of Christ, inherently points to the consummation of those events—the
return of Christ—when the world will see full justice and full salvation.

Worship assaults the world by proclaiming its death.

3. The Assault on the Flesh

But worship gets even more personal, pointing its finger directly at you and at me.
The independent spirit of the world mentioned above does not appear out of thin
air. It originates from our individual sinful impulses and rebellious urges to be
free from God and be gods unto ourselves. Worship pins our flesh to the floor and
calls it what it is—sinful, rebellious, idolatrous. The Call to Worship which says,
"Come and worship the Lord!" also ironically mutters under its breath, "because
you haven't been doing a very good job of that on your own, have you?"

All this is because the flesh doesn't just stumble into sin; it *worships* its way
into sin.[16] The lust of the flesh is the fruit of idolatrous adoration, and the call
of worship is a summons away from the fleshly addictions to idols. Mike Cosper
points out that the context of the Psalms of Ascents (Psalms 120–134) exposed
this reality to those who were singing them. As sojourners would heed worship's
call and ascend the hill to Jerusalem, they would have to pass by various temp-
tations and say no to their flesh: "The mountains on the road to Jerusalem were
littered with temples and idols, little gods who offer protection from bandits and
thieves on the journey. The threat of attack would tempt weary travelers to go to
the mountains, worship one of these lesser gods and trust in it to save."[17]

Worship pronounces the end of our attempts at self-justification and puts a
stop to our self-salvation projects by declaring Christ as the only One who can
justify us before God. It proclaims death to the Old Adam in us who desperately
wants to stand before God on his own two feet and present his own works as
worthy of God's pleasure.[18] Worship provides humanity an encounter with the
raw holiness of God, displaying God's demand for perfection as unattainably
high, where the flesh can never reach.

Worship assaults the flesh by forcing it to cower in fear.[19]

---

15. See chapter 12, "The Worship Pastor as Mortician."

16. See Timothy S. Lane, "Godly Intoxication: The Church Can Minister to Addicts," *The Journal
of Biblical Counseling* 26, no. 2 (2012): 11.

17. Mike Cosper, *Rhythms of Grace: How the Church's Worship Tells the Story of the Gospel* (Wheaton,
Ill.: Crossway, 2013), 102.

18. See the discussion of the Old Adam in chapter 6, "The Worship Pastor as Theological Dietician."

19. Here is one painful and lamentable irony in the now historic "worship wars" over musical style
and personal preference. In these "wars," we have actually declared a truce in the war on the flesh by
allowing the flesh to retain its selfish desires for "my way." Worse yet, such wars have often allowed the

One Weapon: The Gospel

The lines between hell, the world, and the flesh aren't as clean as we're drawing them here. They're all wrapped up together in a common, cosmic struggle of a fallen created order and fallen human beings against a holy God. For this reason, God has offered one weapon that fights on all three fronts—the gospel of Jesus Christ.

One of the most frequently referenced passages in discussions about spiritual warfare is Ephesians 6:10–17 on the armor of God, but it is most often interpreted in terms of what *we* do: put on the belt of truth by being truthful; put on the breastplate of righteousness by being righteous, and so on. But as New Testament scholar Jonathan Linebaugh pointed out, the armor of God is actually not our armor but God's. Linebaugh said, "The armor talked about here is not *our* armor. It's called the armor *of God*. It's *His* armor . . . [it] has nothing to do with what we have; it has nothing to do with what we can perform—our attributes or our achievements. The armor of God is what God gives in the gospel . . . in the giving of His Son, Jesus Christ."[20]

Jesus Himself declares that He is the belt of truth (John 14:6). Jesus is the breastplate of righteousness (2 Cor. 5:21). Jesus is the peace that comes from the shoes of readiness (Rom. 5:1). Jesus is the helmet of salvation (Eph. 2:8–9). The sword of the Spirit is the Spirit's proclamation of Jesus, the Word of God, to us (John 15:26). The shield of faith is received by hearing the word of Christ (Rom. 10:17). In short, the command to put on the armor of God is a command to receive the work of God on us. God arms us by giving us Christ in the gospel.

This is the great, counterintuitive "mystery of the gospel" (Eph. 6:19), that the battle is fought through receiving a message of apparent weakness. As hymn writer Samuel Gandy said,

> By weakness and defeat,
> He won the glorious crown;
> Trod all His foes beneath His feet
> By being trodden down.[21]

This is what the apostle John meant when he recounted the words of the loud voice from heaven: "For the accuser of our brothers and sisters, who accuses them before our God day and night, has been hurled down. They triumphed over him

---

flesh to pseudo-sanctify its desires in seemingly biblical and godly argumentation. How far the flesh will go in aiding and abetting our heart's self-deception! Lord, have mercy.

20. Jonathan Linebaugh, "But God: Part 13 (Ephesians 6:10–17)," sermon, Coral Ridge Presbyterian Church, April 28, 2013.

21. Samuel Whitlock Gandy, "His Be the Victor's Name" (1838), alt. Public Domain.

by the blood of the Lamb" (Rev. 12:10–11). Jesus conquered His enemies in battle by bleeding out before them. What a Savior!

A General under the Warrior-King

So what does this all mean for the worship pastor? Well, if worship is warfare, then the worship leader functions as a kind of general, leading his or her troops in step behind the great Warrior-King, Jesus. But here's the catch. This battle is an odd one, at least from a worldly point of view. It is not waged by efforts of human action but by reception of divine action. To illustrate this, we have many Old Testament examples where God's victory over Israel's enemies happened through their passive worship. Under Jehoshaphat's leadership, the people of God worshiped God's enduring love while He routed the Edomites (2 Chron. 20:22). Speaking about this battle, the prophet Jahaziel declared, "The battle is not yours, but God's" (2 Chron. 20:15). And before the Israelites faced the Egyptians in battle, Moses declared to Israel, "The LORD will fight for you; you need only to be still" (Ex. 14:14).

A worship leader pastors a congregation to victory by highlighting the mystery of this unconventional war strategy. How? By cultivating a worship context that is saturated with the upside-down, countercultural message of the gospel. Instead of pacing before the troops, holding up a sword and chanting, "Kill them all!" the war general plans a worship service where the Spirit can stand before the congregation, holding up the cross and shouting, "Jesus paid it all!"

The gospel is an assault on hell because at the cross, Jesus made a public spectacle of Satan and his minions, disarming them in triumphant defeat (Col. 2:15). The gospel is an assault on the world because at the cross, Jesus showed that the world's conceptions of power and goodness were both misguided and woefully inadequate (Isa. 53:7–12). The gospel is an assault on our flesh because it declares that sin is dealt with and righteousness is provided fully, freely, as a gift (Eph. 2:8–9). In worship, the gospel is the only weapon we have, but it's all that we need. And until Jesus comes to claim final victory once and for all, worship pastors as war generals must be stubbornly committed to that declaration.

All of this tells us that our songs must be saturated with the proclamation of the person and work of Jesus Christ. As Matt Boswell wrote, "Choosing songs for Sunday is like choosing weapons for war."[22] We find songs that might be different in shape and size, but their cutting edge is always the same—the gospel. We are cautious about songs and expressions that glory too much in our own triumph, and we are liberal with songs and expressions that make much of Jesus. This also

---

22. Matt Boswell, Facebook post, January 16, 2014.

means that our prayers, comments, and in-between moments of worship are all aimed at directing our gaze on the Author and Perfecter of our faith (Heb. 12:2). We become less concerned with how we're experiencing God in worship (what some have called "worshiping worship") and more focused on Christ's experiences of death and resurrection on our behalf. This means that the very structure of our service, from beginning to end, serves to tell the story of the glory of God (gathering and praise), the gravity of sin (confession), and the grandeur of grace (assurance/absolution).[23] And finally, but perhaps chiefly, we plan services that prize preaching that savors Jesus and His saving grace and regularly emphasize the gospel-saturated and Spirit-filled historic worship practices of baptism and the Lord's Supper.

Ultimately, how do we lead the charge in the fight against hell, the world, and the flesh? By flooding all of worship's spotlights on Jesus so that every last one of us can fix our gaze upon worship's one true Warrior.

O great Lord of Hosts, lead us in worship as we witness
and receive Your mighty, victorious acts.

---

23. See chapter 14, "The Worship Pastor as Liturgical Architect." For more on absolution, see chapter 11, "The Worship Pastor as Caregiver," particularly the section titled, "Delivering the Cure."

8

THE WORSHIP PASTOR AS WATCHFUL PROPHET

If you are to do the work of a prophet, what you want is not a scepter,
but a hoe. The prophet does not rise to reign, but to root out the weeds.
                              —*Bernard of Clairvaux, twelfth century[1]*

Our engagement in works of justice arises out of worshipful life. It comes
not out of being activists but out of living in God's rest, every day.
                              —*Mark Labberton, 2007[2]*

The service had just ended, but I didn't expect to hear the words that came out of this man's mouth. Our band was finishing up our postlude when one of our congregants—a smelly, disheveled man just one socioeconomic notch above homelessness—burst onto the chancel. He was so overjoyed he couldn't contain himself. He gave me a wildly violent hug and proceeded to tell me with tears in his eyes how moved he was by the service's music that day. He fumbled out compliment after compliment, culminating with these sincere words, "Man, that was the best [bleep] ever!" There was no guile in him, no crassness about it. He was just a rough man with a tough past and a colorful tongue enjoying the glory of Jesus displayed in musical art.

Later that day, I was reflecting on the beauty of that moment and the victory of grace signified there. There are a lot of church contexts I know where a homeless man would feel judged and self-conscious about sitting in worship next to the pretty, well-dressed, and well-to-do. Our church context, thankfully, was different. The gospel was preached in such a way that it leveled some of the hierarchical aspects of social propriety. In a small way, that man's exclamation to

---

1. Bernard of Clairvaux, *On Consideration*, Book II, chapter VI, trans. George Lewis (Oxford: Clarendon, 1908), 4.6.
2. Mark Labberton, *The Dangerous Act of Worship: Living God's Call to Justice* (Downers Grove, Ill.: InterVarsity, 2007), 103.

me was a sign and foretaste of the kind of justice, peace, and reconciliation that marks the coming kingdom.

Our Prophetic Calling

No one championed justice more than the prophets. As lone voices in the wilderness, the prophets cried out as God's mouthpiece against unjust actions and structures. They were equal opportunity prosecutors, calling out God's people and godless pagans alike. When we listen to their collective voice, certain themes emerge which sound similar to the pastoral duties of leading worship. This wedding of prophecy and worship is explicitly found in places like 1 Chronicles 25:1, where David appointed certain priests to temple worship "for the ministry of prophesying, accompanied by harps, lyres, and cymbals." Or consider the multifaceted calling of the songwriter-prophet Habakkuk. Habakkuk heard from God of the coming judgment on His people for their sin and injustice. He wrestled with God, complaining to Him about the things that he heard (Hab. 1:1–17), and after exhausting his grievances, Habakkuk took his stand, stationing himself at a tower, watching and waiting for the Lord's answer (2:1). God answered (2:2–20), and Habakkuk was humbled. Then he wrote a worship song about it (3:1–19).

Worship leaders have a prophetic call similar to Habakkuk. Our job is to station ourselves as watchful prophets over the people of God. Before we flesh out exactly what that means, let's first look at what the Bible has to say about the relationship between worship and justice and how they meet in the prophetic call.

The Inseparable Link between Worship and Justice

Some two thousand years ago, right in the middle of a Jewish worship service, Jesus, the full and final Prophet, stood up and read aloud His gospel mission from the book of Isaiah:

> The Spirit of the Lord is on me,
>   because he has anointed me
>   to proclaim good news to the poor.
> He has sent me to proclaim freedom for the prisoners
>   and recovery of sight for the blind,
> to set the oppressed free,
>   to proclaim the year of the Lord's favor.
>   —*Luke 4:18–19*

In this moment, Jesus was teaching us that worship and justice are woven together in the gospel. In saying this, Jesus was following a well-trodden prophetic path. The prophet Amos had railed against Israel's severing of worship and justice, claiming that while the people fulfilled all the rituals for corporate worship, they ignored the very apparent needs of the poor and oppressed among them (Amos 2–4). Isaiah similarly chastised Israel's "pious" liturgical fasting while they ignored sharing bread with the hungry and housing the homeless (Isaiah 58). After a series of rhetorical questions about what kind of worship practices would most please the Lord, the prophet Micah declared that worship's highest call is "to do justice, and to love kindness, and to walk humbly with your God" (Mic. 6:8 ESV). Again and again, justice and worship are found in the prophets to be joined at the hip.[3]

God's inspired collection of worship songs, the Psalms, likewise bring worship and justice together. The entire Psalter is bookended by two Psalms (2 and 149) that herald and praise the Lord for executing justice. The middle of the Psalter extols the God who "will judge the world in righteousness and the peoples in his faithfulness" (Ps. 96:13; cf. 98:9). And in one of the supreme psalms of kingship, God discloses His royal agenda: He will pay attention to the poor and needy and turn the whole world right side up (Ps. 72:1–19).[4]

Many conversations about worship and justice rightly follow the path of the prophets. They discuss how the worship of justice making *outside* the gathered services of the church authenticates the worship *inside* those times.[5] As worship pastors, we need to be concerned about this dynamic. Being watchful prophets means that we don't leave justice and care to ministries and teams who do "outreach." We're concerned with how our Sunday worship practices are fleshed out in Monday through Saturday's application. We're involved with those conversations, we're getting our own hands dirty on the ground, and we're making sure that our flock is entering the blessed mess of caring for those in need.

We need to take our cues from Psalms and also see justice as something to be realized in gathered worship. We must not forget that even the justice-oriented psalms weren't just poems for individual meditation but corporate worship songs. So justice and worship are inseparably linked, and this link is experienced in gathered worship. This isn't just a matter of having justice-themed worship services.

---

3. See also Isa. 1:11–17 and Amos 5:14–24.

4. I owe these insights about the Psalms to N. T. Wright in his talk at the Justice Conference 2014, "A Discussion on Biblical Justice," online video, accessed June 23, 2015, https://vimeo.com/91642795.

5. See, for instance, Ken Wytsma, *Pursuing Justice: The Call to Live and Die for Bigger Things* (Nashville: Thomas Nelson, 2013), 221–32; Nicholas Wolterstorff, "Imitating God: Doing Justice as a Condition of Authentic Worship," *Reformed Worship* (June 2003), accessed June 22, 2015, http://www.reformedworship.org/article/june-2003/imitating-god-doing-justice-condition-authentic-worship.

Rather, it is understanding that a life of just actions and a concern for righteous living is a goal of worship. True worship inevitably produces justice the way true faith inevitably produces good works (James 2:14–26). Mark Labberton explains it this way: "If we don't lift our heads to see God in worship, we can't see what God wants to show us, which includes our neighbor. Then our neighbor becomes those we choose to see, not those God wants us to see."[6] Good worship creates a justice-seeking culture.

How does this play out, practically, in our worship services? Let's take a look at seven sketches of prophetic pastoring in worship: the worship leader as Word wielder, heresy fighter, future seer, idol expert, complacency disturber, alms giver, and protector of the sheep.

Seven Sketches of Prophetic Worship Pastoring

1. Word Wielder

A prophet is fiercely committed to the Word of God. A prophetic worship leader necessarily returns, again and again, to the starting point of our prophetic ministry as worship pastors—listening to God's Word. We work to establish "watchful" practices, like Habakkuk, stationing ourselves before the Scriptures to hear from God. The first move in taking prophetic action is always passive and receptive.[7] This posture of receptivity, of listening to God, is what equips us to be Word wielders. With the Word of God studied, memorized, and soaked into our bones, we're ready to let it flow out of us in worship. Being a Word wielder gets practical quickly, especially in contexts where we have opportunities to extemporaneously pray and speak over our flocks. There is a huge difference between the prayers and reflections of worship leaders soaked in the Word of God and those who have not spent time in the Word. Word wielders will quote and allude to Scripture rather than mindlessly summoning stock "Christian-ese" phraseology.

2. Heresy Fighter

In the early church, the rise of Arianism—the denial of the equality of the Son with the Father—threatened to undo the community of faith. The Council of Nicaea in 325 AD denounced Arius' teachings as heresy, but as Robbie Castleman observes, "the heresy of Arius had *already been defeated* in the worship of the

---

6. Labberton, *The Dangerous Act of Worship*, 102.
7. Martin Luther called this posture of the Christian the *vita passiva*, "the receptive life." See Oswald Bayer, *Theology the Lutheran Way*, ed. and trans. Jeffrey G. Silcock and Mark C. Mattes (Grand Rapids, Mich.: Eerdmans, 2007), 107–10.

church. The church for nearly three and a half centuries had remembered, regu-
lated and reenacted the patterns of worship set in the canon of Scripture through
hymn and early creedal summaries of the faith."[8] Worship rightly planned and
led carries with it the prophetic ability to root out and prevent the constant threat
of heresy. Watchful prophets are in tune with the heretical beliefs of their generation and culture, those ideas that are tickling the ears of their congregations
(2 Tim. 4:3), and they are careful to craft services that bring those beliefs face to
face with Christian orthodoxy.

For example, one common American "heresy" today is that we are self-made
people—that God helps those who help themselves. This is a modern Pelagianism
that ignores our desperate need for the grace of God. A watchful prophet addresses
this tendency with worship's weapons of confession—"God, we confess that we
don't have what it takes in us to earn your pleasure and favor"—and the gospel—
"Jesus came to do for us what we could never do for ourselves."

3. Future Seer

One of several scriptural words for prophet is *seer*,[9] because God's Word often
came to the prophets through visions (e.g., Isa. 6:1–3; Ezekiel 1). God revealed the
future to the prophets, whether calamity or blessing, and He tasked the prophets to declare this vision to His people. As worship leaders we have a prophetic,
future-seeing task as well, helping people to "see the end" in worship. The future-
seer's role is fleshed out in a worship song like Psalm 96. Notice how the end of
this psalm of praise seems to us to take a weird turn:

> Let all creation rejoice before the LORD, for he comes,
>   he comes to judge the earth.
> He will judge the world in righteousness
>   and the peoples in his faithfulness.
> *—Psalm 96:13*

Today we find the idea of rejoicing in God's judgment a bit uncomfortable.
But this language of judgment would have sounded very different to the ears of
the ancient Israelite. We need to retune our ears to hear "bring justice" as they did.
Israel could rejoice because God would bring justice—He would make all things
right—in the future.

We also fulfill our prophetic call as worship pastors by creating space in our

---

8. Robbie F. Castleman, *Story Shaped Worship: Following Patterns from the Bible and History*
(Downers Grove, Ill.: InterVarsity, 2013), 155, emphasis in original.

9. Heb. *rō'ěh* (1 Sam. 9:9) and *ḥōzěh* (e.g., 2 Chron. 19:2).

worship services to hold up a vision of the future before the people of God—to display before them that day when "everything sad will come untrue."[10] We sing eschatological songs. We make "Come, Lord Jesus" part of our prayers. In our confession and lamentation, we weave in the language of longing for God's full restoration of all things, including ourselves (2 Cor. 5:17–21).[11]

4. Idol Expert

Author and worship pastor Mike Cosper calls the prophetic battle against idolatry "the real worship wars." In the last chapter, we saw how the Psalms of Ascents (Psalms 120–134) depicted the people of God on pilgrimage up the hill to Jerusalem and how, along the way, they would have had to say no to many of the idols just off the path calling for their attention. Cosper says, "Like the ascending pilgrims of Psalm 121, we're surround[ed] by clamorous mountains advertising happiness, sex, and power, all available for consumption. Our entertainment in television, film, and literature paints the good life in this way, and it grips our heartstrings."[12]

Worship pastors must be watchful and skilled in identifying the idolatry that creeps into our worship. Sometimes this is the self-focus and self-absorbing nature of our worship songs. Or it can be the undiscerning way we employ cultural practices without doing necessary theological reflection and contextualization. Sometimes it is the way we allow consumerism to color how worship is led and received. Like the prophets of old, we must develop keen sensitivities to our culture's prized idols and the idols of our own hearts and then carefully guard our worship and worshipers from their unceasing allure.

5. Complacency Disturber

Musing on the politics of art, one writer clarified that art's purpose is "not to surrender to glamour and consumption but rather to embark on the act of *agitating consciences*."[13] This accurately describes the role of a prophet in the context of worship. Worship leaders—many of whom are prophetic creatives—are called to disrupt and disturb imaginations, "replacing hollow daydreams about status and fame with dreams of a kingdom that turns status on its head."[14] This is where the work of *identifying* idols moves further into *displacing* them. Just as the

---

10. J. R. R. Tolkien, *The Return of the King* (Boston: Houghton Mifflin, 1988), 230.

11. See chapter 12, "The Worship Pastor as Mortician."

12. Mike Cosper, *Rhythms of Grace: How the Church's Worship Tells the Story of the Gospel* (Wheaton, Ill.: Crossway, 2013), 103.

13. Joan Fontcuberta, quoted in Branca Lina Urta, "Joan Fontcuberta: What's Next: On Future of Photography," *It Is What It Is (blog)*, April 22, 2011, accessed June 23, 2015, https://brancolina.wordpress.com/2011/04/22/joan-fontcuberta-whats-next-on-future-of-photography/. Emphasis mine.

14. Cosper, *Rhythms of Grace*, 185.

law of God (the "ministry that brought death") was a required, deconstructive precursor to the gospel's resurrection (2 Cor. 3:7–9), so worship must at times "agitate the consciences" of the complacent.[15] I remember leading worship on a Super Bowl Sunday, calling out the idol in the room during my introductory remarks to worship by saying, "We're quick to jump up and down before screens displaying uniformed men on a patch of grass . . . Of how much more worth and value is the resurrected Christ who is with us now? Let's worship *that* God today." That prophetic moment unleashed a wave of the Holy Spirit among our people in that service.[16]

6. Alms Giver

God's special affection for the poor is all over the pages of the Bible. The law of God displays it (Ex. 23:6; Lev. 19:10; Deut. 15:7), the Psalms sing it (Pss. 12:5; 14:6; 22:26; 35:10), wisdom demands it (Prov. 14:31; 17:5), and the prophets declare it (Isa. 3:15; Ezek. 16:49; Zech. 7:10). Giving to the poor has been a part of Christian worship since the earliest times (Acts 2:45).[17] The prophetic side of our pastoral call as worship leaders should include a concern that giving to the poor, variously called almsgiving, benevolence, or love offerings, be a part of our churches' worship practices. Don't relegate this responsibility to the deacons, but speak out to communicate that we value ministry to the poor in our worship. Some churches will periodically take up an additional offering that goes exclusively to service of the poor and needy. Worship pastors must learn to care about these kinds of practices and incorporate them into worship services.

There is another kind of poverty, however, that often gets ignored in these conversations. Holly Ordway brings it to light: "Certainly, all the money used to build a church and make it beautiful could be given to the poor instead—but that would not be feeding the poor in their complete hunger."[18] We should have a watching care over our aesthetic poverty as well. From architecture to art to the quality of our music, we should be attentive to feed our people's aesthetic hunger,

---

15. This is something that worship has in common with modern art, and perhaps we as prophetic worship pastors can learn something through an engagement of modern art. Dan Siedell notes, "The tradition of modern art reminds us that all human creative work comes from the desire to be loved and the pain of not receiving that. . . . [Modern art] wrestles with our tendency to make our beliefs about ourselves and our world the center of the cosmos, to make ourselves the subject of our existential sentences, to be, as David Foster Wallace said, 'lords of our tiny skull-sized kingdoms.'" *Who's Afraid of Modern Art? Essays on Modern Art and Theology in Conversation* (Eugene, Ore.: Cascade, 2015), 9.

16. For a full account of this story, see my post: http://www.zachicks.com/blog/2012/2/6/when-the-holy-spirit-breaks-open-the-worship-service-or-the.html.

17. See Bryan Chapell's comments on the offertory and almsgiving in *Christ-Centered Worship: Letting the Gospel Shape Our Practice* (Grand Rapids, Mich.: Baker, 2009), 53.

18. Holly Ordway, "Worship and Identity: The Role of Beauty in the Church," *Transpositions*, April 2013, accessed June 23, 2015, http://www.transpositions.co.uk/ordway/.

especially in a day and age where stunningly beautiful art, from graphic design to movie scores, is simultaneously ubiquitous and disposable.[19]

7. Sheep Protector

Care for the poor even extends to an awareness of the many ways that people can feel marginalized in worship. The book of James points out the problem of "seat-ing arrangement" between rich and poor in the early church (James 2:2–4), but that's only the tip of the iceberg. What about children? How do they gain access and entry into our worship as vital participants? Or what about the people in our congregations who are ethnic minorities? Are we offering hospitality, seeking solidarity, and pursuing mutuality with those who are different from us?[20] When we think of the mentally and physically handicapped, are they merely a nuisance, or do we brainstorm how to disciple these brothers and sisters to grow in their understanding and expressions of worship? What about visitors? Are we sensitive to them, encouraging our congregations to both welcome them and give them space to comfortably "take a place at the edge of the assembly"?[21] Raising these questions in our contexts is of vital importance as we prophetically seek justice in worship and align ourselves with the heart of God. A sheep protector is concerned for those on the margins because these are the people most vulnerable to attack and susceptible to being forgotten.

Balancing Prophetic Ministry with Pastoral Sensitivity

Those who get excited about justice and other prophetic ministries can run the risk of leaving corpses in their wake if they fail to apply their prophetic call in a pastoral way. One of the preeminent prophets of the historic church was Martin Luther. He was a Word-wielding firebrand of ecclesiastical reformation, and he certainly was a worship pastor. He knew that reforming theology and reforming worship go hand in hand. Despite his burning passion for reformation, Luther was an advocate for patient liturgical renovation, sensitive to the fact that change is

---

19. Andrew W. Blackwood, *The Fine Art of Public Worship* (New York: Abingdon-Cokesbury, 1939), 81: "Anyone who has ministered in the back alleys of a city knows that the souls of the poor are being starved through lack of beauty, and that they wish the place where they worship to be different from the hovels where they dwell."

20. As Sandra Van Opstal explains, hospitality says, "We welcome you." Solidarity says, "We stand with you." Mutuality says, "We need you." These latter two take much more sacrifice and prophetic leadership. In fact, as Van Opstal points out, the third (mutuality) requires giving up leadership so that it may be shared. See Sandra Van Opstal, *The Next Worship: Glorifying God in a Diverse World* (Downers Grove, Ill.: InterVarsity, 2016), 62–75, 77–95.

21. Ruth A. Meyers, *Missional Worship, Worshipful Mission: Gathering as God's People, Going Out in God's Name* (Grand Rapids, Mich.: Eerdmans, 2014), 70.

slow and difficult for most people. While commenting on some proposed changes to the Roman Mass, he wrote: "For I have been hesitant and fearful, partly because of the weak in faith, who cannot suddenly exchange an old and accustomed order of worship for a new and unusual one, and more so because of the fickle and fastidious spirits who rush in like unclean swine without faith or reason, and who delight only in novelty and tire of it as quickly, when it has worn off."[22]

A prophetic ministry of worship should keep this "hesitant and fearful" approach in mind. We don't want to advocate what's right at the expense of our people rather than for them. It takes prayer, patience, wisdom, and relational checks and balances to execute our prophetic ministry with pastoral grace. From implementing changes to calling out idols, from rooting out heresy to guarding the marginalized, the prophetic blade we hold must be used for precision surgery, not mass slaughter. Lord, help us.

Our True Justice

Talking about worship and justice can feel weighty, not joyful. And the prophetic voice sounds decidedly conditional—"If you don't do justice, then your worship is an utter failure"—and in its conditionality, if we're honest, we all stand condemned. "There is no one who does justice, not even one" (Rom. 3:10, not so loosely paraphrased).[23] We need to remember, though, that there is One who met all the conditions the prophets demanded of the people—Jesus Christ, the Word of God. Sometimes we're so quick to rush to the *actions* of justice that we forget the *event* of justice that has set us free to engage in this work in the first place. All talk of justice should begin and end at the cross. One of Paul's choice phrases to talk about the work of the cross is "the justice of God" (Rom. 1:17; 3:5, 21–26; 9:30–10:6; Phil. 3:9; 2 Cor. 5:21).[24] At the cross, God's justice was executed fully and finally on our Substitute, and there is no condemnation left for us (Rom. 8:1).

David Ruis said it well: "The fragrance of worship is justice. Where there is no justice, there is no fragrance."[25] And because Jesus is justice, the fragrance of

---

22. Martin Luther, "An Order of Mass and Communion for the Church at Wittenberg (1523)," *Luther's Works*, vol. 53, ed. Ulrich S. Leupold (Philadelphia: Fortress, 1965), 19.

23. A uniquely English problem emerges in the biblical expression of "justice." In English, "justice, justify, justification" and "right, righteous" are two separate word groups. In Greek, as well as many other languages, they are all one word group (Gk. *dikaio-*).

24. Gk. *dikaiosune Theou*. For a definitive treatment on the subject of *dikaiosune Theou*, see Jonathan A. Linebaugh, *God, Grace, and Righteousness in Wisdom of Solomon and Paul's Letter to the Romans: Texts in Conversation* (Leiden, The Netherlands: Brill, 2013), and his "Debating Diagonal Δικαιοσύνη: The Epistle of Enoch and Paul in Theological Conversation," *Early Christianity* 1, no. 1 (2010): 107–28.

25. David Ruis, *The Justice God Is Seeking* (Ventura, Calif.: Regal, 2006), 18.

worship is ultimately the One who is both our great Prophet and our perfect Law Keeper. He proclaimed, more boldly than any of the prophets, what is required of us (Matt. 5–7), and then He fulfilled it (Matt. 3:15). This means that where there is no Jesus in worship, there is no fragrance . . . and there is no true justice. If we want to see justice roll down like a river in worship (Amos 5:24), then we must make much of Jesus Christ, who is the true "justice of God" (2 Cor. 5:21). Justice and worship meet at the well of God's amazing grace.

O Justice Bearer, Jesus Christ, make Your righteousness
the theme of our song and the fragrance of our worship
until the day when You make all things new.

9

THE WORSHIP PASTOR
AS MISSIONARY

*It is by its worship that the Church lives, it is there that its heart
beats. . . . As the heart is for the animal body, so [worship] is for Church
life a pump which sends into circulation and draws in again, it claims
and it sanctifies. It is from the life of worship . . . that the Church
spreads itself abroad into the world to mingle with it like leaven in the
dough, to give it savour like salt, to irradiate it like light.*

—*Jean-Jacques von Allmen, 1965*[1]

Wine experts talk about the debated and semi-mysterious concept of *terroir*, a
French word that seems to defy easy translation. Terroir is, in my understanding,
the conceptual arena for all the local factors that give rise to the unique features
of wines. What makes one wine different from another? Terroir is the catch-all
answer. One wine geek offers four traits of terroir that help us wrap our minds
around it: climate (warm or cold), soil (mineral content), terrain (altitude, landscape, weather patterns), and tradition (harvesting, processing, and fermentation
methods).[2]

Great winemakers are experts in their own vineyard's terroir. Sometimes the
terroir is easily definable, and other times it is more intuited. But either way, the
winemaker's knowledge and leadership of the vineyard are uniquely authoritative
and insightful in ways that might not easily be transferred to another region or
location.

Worship leaders who think and lead pastorally must learn to become experts
of their church's doxological terroir.[3] This means refusing a one-size-fits-all men-
tality that blindly reproduces worship expressions and practices inherited from

---

1. Jean-Jacques von Allmen, *Worship: Its Theology and Practice* (New York: Oxford, 1965), 55.
2. Madeline Puckette, "Terroir Definition for Wine," *Wine Folly*, November 6, 2013, accessed
June 30, 2015, http://winefolly.com/tutorial/terroir-definition-for-wine/.
3. I'm grateful to my friend Bruce Benedict who led me to this very helpful metaphor.

the past or imported from the culture. They are cognizant of the climate, soil, terrain, and tradition of their assembly and are always asking questions about how these intersect in gathered worship. Of course, this is all just another way of saying that worship pastors are called to be missionaries. Great missionaries faithfully labor to communicate a transcultural, timeless gospel into a particular time and place, and God's missionary call extends to worship leaders too.

The Church as the World's Circulatory System

In chapter 4, we saw that worship is embedded in Christ's Great Commission (Matt. 28:19–20). It's fair to say that worship and mission exist in symbiotic relationship, mutually supporting each other with life and energy.[4] To tease this out further,[5] I want us to think of the church as the world's "circulatory system," whose two basic structural components—the heart and the veins/arteries—can be compared to worship and mission.[6] (See fig. 2.)

If we think of the world as a body, then the church is the vehicle within it through which God chooses to carry His life-giving gospel. In this circulatory system of "gospel transport," worship is the heart, the central propulsion chamber where the gospel is given to the people of God, fueling and pressurizing us to be sent out. Mission, then, is the network of veins and arteries that take the gospel out, reaching further into the body for the purposes of gathering more regions of the world back in and under the life-giving influence of its center and heart. Just as the blood in arteries and veins follows a circular pattern away from and back to the heart, so mission goes out and gathers in, to be "repumped" by worship. Together, worship and mission operate as one unified system. The church is both doxological and missional.[7] Just as a heart has no purpose without veins and arteries, and just as those veins and arteries are useless without a heart, so worship is inherently missional and mission is essentially doxological.

---

4. Steven Bevans and Roger Schroeder go a step further, arguing that worship is actually a *subset* of mission (*Constants in Context: A Theology of Mission for Today* [Maryknoll, N.Y.: Orbis, 2004], 350ff). There is value in engaging this paradigm, but my concern is that worship would be unnecessarily downplayed in the life and rhythms of the local church when seen as a subset, rather than the fuel, for mission. This is one of the reasons I am inclined toward the heart and circulatory metaphor.

5. See the brilliant, complementary, and highly illustrative metaphors of a Möbius strip and a spinning top in Ruth A. Meyers, *Missional Worship, Worshipful Mission: Gathering as God's People, Going Out in God's Name* (Grand Rapids, Mich.: Eerdmans, 2014), 12–45.

6. I'm building on the work of several thinkers as I extend this metaphor. Many have alluded to the idea of the worship as the "heart" and "pulse" of the church and her mission (e.g., the Nairobi Statement on Worship and Culture [Geneva, Switzerland: Lutheran World Federation, 1996], 1.1), and I'm especially leaning on Jean-Jacques von Allmen, who introduced the metaphor of the circulatory system in *Worship*, 55.

7. And as many have pointed out in various ways, doxology and missiology reflect two central realities of God's very essence. As Trinity, the Father, Son, and Spirit are mutually self-giving and self-glorifying (God is doxological), and the Father *sends* the Son and Spirit (God is missional).

Figure 2

THE CIRCULATORY SYSTEM OF THE WORLD

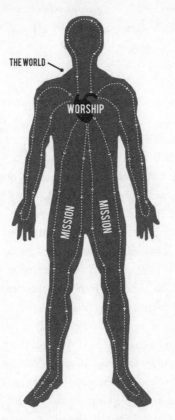

The reason we must view worship as the heart of mission is because it is where God initiates giving the gospel to the world. Several traditions call worship the place where God provides His "ordinary means" of grace—where the Father manifests Jesus to the world by the power of the Spirit through the preached Word, the sacraments, and prayer, both spoken and sung.[8] Though God can and does give Jesus to the world in a whole host of special, extraordinary ways, He ordinarily

---

8. The Reformed/Presbyterian tradition describes it this way through question and answer in the Westminster Shorter Catechism (1647), 88: "What are the outward and ordinary means whereby Christ communicates to us the benefits of redemption? The outward and ordinary means whereby Christ communicates to us the benefits of redemption are His ordinances, especially the Word, sacraments, and prayer."

and regularly (though no less miraculously) does so week in and week out as the people of God gather for worship.

But good worship, brimming with the gospel, cannot contain itself. When God out of the overflow of His love gives Jesus to His people in worship, the unavoidable spillover of this love is mission as the people go out and bear witness to Christ in the world in work (vocation), deeds of mercy (justice), and declaring the good news (evangelism). The result of the mission of "scattered worship" in the world is a harvest and ingathering of even more worshipers.[9] The process is cyclical and reproductive.

The interdependence of worship and mission helps us understand what certain Christian traditions mean when they say that what God gives in worship is "for the life of the world."[10] This interconnectedness also makes sense of one of the Greek words for worship, *leitourgia* (where we get the word *liturgy*), whose meaning evolved and deepened as the early church established patterns of worship in its first few centuries. *Leitourgia* gives a missional double meaning to the idea of worship as "public service": on the one hand, we worship before the watching public; on the other hand, worship serves the gospel *to* the public.[11]

The symbiotic relationship between worship and mission means, first of all, that it would be unthinkable to ever replace corporate, gathered worship with missional acts of evangelism and community service, just as it would be unthinkable to remove a heart and simply tie the remaining veins and arteries together. Missional momentum halts when the heart of worship is removed. Second, if your church is struggling to be a truly missional body, worship must be a very real place of examination. Is the gospel clear and present in worship, or is it crowded out by other things? Ironically, our quest for a more evangelistic worship service, friendly and easy to swallow for non-Christians, has often muted the gospel in worship, rendering the service impotent of missional, transformative power. While we should always strive for worship to be intelligible and understandable to non-Christians, nothing short of prizing the gospel and making much of Jesus will create the kind of awe-inspiring zeal in the church that causes the watching world to cry, "God is really among you!" (1 Cor. 14:25). If all this is true, then worship pastors truly are missionaries. But what is it, precisely, that missionaries do?

---

9. See Mike Cosper, *Rhythms of Grace: How the Church's Worship Tells the Story of the Gospel* (Wheaton, Ill.: Crossway, 2013), 81–82.

10. Cf. Evangelical Lutheran Church in America, *The Use of the Means of Grace*, Application 51B, 56 (quoted in Meyers, *Missional Worship*, 36); Alexander Schmemann, *For the Life of the World: Sacraments and Orthodoxy, 2nd ed.* (Crestwood, N.Y.: St. Vladimir's Seminary Press, 1973).

11. See the excellent summary of *leitourgia* in Meyers, *Missional Worship*, 25–29, 36.

The Primary Task of the Missionary

Every believer is called to bear witness to the gospel (Acts 1:8). What makes that witness bearing a missionary enterprise is how it is contextualized to a given culture, time, and place. Variously called "enculturation," "translation," "incarnational ministry," and more, contextualizing the timeless, universal gospel for the hearing of time-bound, localized people is the responsibility of the worship pastor who is called to be a missionary. Contextualization is ultimately rooted in Jesus' command to love one another (Mark 12:31; John 13:34), as Paul illustrates: "Though I am free and belong to no one, I have made myself a slave to everyone, to win as many as possible. . . . I do all this for the sake of the gospel, that I may share in its blessings" (1 Cor. 9:19–23).

It is worth noting how different worshiping traditions approach contextualization. For charismatic and free church traditions, contextualization might come a bit more easily, simply because their worship structures are more flexible. For those in more liturgical traditions, the creativity for contextualization might be a bit more constrained because of the liturgy's more fixed aspects. However, we should note that some of the most prominent Reformers—Luther, Calvin, and Cranmer—were all strong proponents of contextualized worship.[12] The traditions that claim the lineage of these thinkers would do well to think more critically about contextualization in their own denominations and parishes. With this in mind, let's explore in more detail the what and how of the contextualization process.

Contextualization: What Is Being Done?

Contextualization for the worship missionary is "localizing" the universal gospel. It is about establishing tradition. Some Protestants grow uncomfortable when the word *tradition* gets brought up. Something deep in our historical psyche reacts, "Isn't that a Catholic thing?" or, "Doesn't that undermine the authority of the Bible?" As we approach this topic of contextualization, I encourage you to keep two things in mind. First, the Bible itself speaks favorably, not suspiciously, of tradition. In the Pentateuch, God established worship traditions with the Israelites that became standard practices for centuries. Jesus Himself obediently observed them, even as He began to teach their fulfillment in Himself (e.g., John 7 and the

---

12. See Martin Luther, "An Order of Mass and Communion for the Church at Wittenberg (1523)," *Luther's Works*, vol. 53, ed. Ulrich S. Leupold (Philadelphia: Fortress, 1965), 37; John Calvin, *Institutes of the Christian Religion*, vol. 2, ed. John T. McNeill, trans. Ford Lewis Battles (Philadelphia: Westminster, 1960), 4.10.30, 1208; Thomas Cranmer, "Of Ceremonies, Why Some Be Abolished, and Some Retained," in *The Book of Common Prayer and Administration of the Sacraments, and Other Rites and Ceremonies in the Church of England* (1552).

Feast of Tabernacles).[13] The apostle Paul was also comfortable with the language of tradition when he encouraged the church at Thessalonica to, "Stand firm and hold to the traditions that you were taught by us" (2 Thess. 2:15 ESV).[14]

One helpful way of thinking about tradition is that it is simply one generation's attempt at contextualizing the gospel. As previous worshiping generations listened to the Scriptures, they sometimes knowingly, other times unknowingly, translated the gospel and its expression in worship to the hearers of their day. Now, we as Christians in the twenty-first century stand as receivers of past generations' attempts at contextualizing the gospel.[15] Some have referred to the enduring core—the common thread—of these practices of gospel contextualization as the "Great Tradition."[16] And while we don't receive the Great Tradition with the same authoritative weight as Scripture, we receive it as the testimonies and practices borne out of Scripture. We listen to the Great Tradition with humility and a teachable spirit, knowing that it is the collected and ancient wisdom of contextualization passed down to us.

The gospel is the summary message of Scripture, and the Great Tradition is a partner rather than an adversary in understanding that message. With this in mind, we're free to explore, learn from, and employ the traditional worship practices of the church as we think about our own contextualization. Nevertheless, we must always be discerning. You may want to periodically evaluate your traditions by asking these simple questions: Do these practices lead us toward or away from Christ? Do they contribute to His story, His glory, His salvation, His kingship? Writing about worship and tradition, reformer John Calvin noted, "Ceremonies, to be exercises of piety, ought to lead us straight to Christ."[17] Worship traditions that truly have the power to form us are those that point us Christward.[18] As mis-

---

13. Some will say that Jesus' confrontation of the Pharisees and teachers of the law shows that He opposed tradition (e.g., Luke 11:37–54). First, Jesus' opposition was focused on those things *added to* the traditions God had established. Second, Jesus was not concerned with the established traditions *themselves* as much as He was concerned with how they were used to abuse, foster self-righteousness, and lead people away from the heart of God.

14. Perhaps it is the suspicious Protestant impulse that led the NIV translators away from *traditions* and toward *teachings* in dealing with the Greek word *paradoseis* in this passage.

15. What I've just described is adapted from a line of thinking encountered in Robert J. Schreiter's concept of local theologies in *Constructing Local Theologies* (Maryknoll, N.Y.: Orbis, 1994).

16. See D. H. Williams, *Retrieving the Tradition and Renewing Evangelicalism: A Primer for Suspicious Protestants* (Grand Rapids, Mich.: Eerdmans, 1999); D. H. Williams, *Evangelicals and Tradition: The Formative Influence of the Early Church* (Grand Rapids, Mich.: Baker, 2005), 49; Jim Belcher, *Deep Church: A Third Way beyond Emerging and Traditional* (Downers Grove, Ill.: InterVarsity, 2009).

17. Calvin, *Institutes of the Christian Religion*, 4.10.29, 1207.

18. This idea was surely behind Thomas Cranmer's critique of so many of the unnecessary rituals of medieval worship when he said, "This over excessive multitude of Ceremonies was so great, and many of them so dark: that they did more confound and darken, than declare and set forth Christ's benefits to us" ("Of Ceremonies").

sionaries, we are committing ourselves to being lifelong students of three things: Scripture, the Great Tradition, and our context.

Contextualization: How Is It Done?

1. Studying the Scriptures

As we emphasized in chapters 3 and 6, worship pastors must be students of the Word of God, continually placing themselves under its authoritative voice, asking questions, and seeking answers. We need to humbly ask of the Word, "O God, how would You have us worship? What are the practices, structures, and expressions of worship which please You?" Answering these questions will lead to what academics call a biblical theology of worship. Thankfully, there are many resources to aid in this kind of study.[19]

2. Studying the Great Tradition

We will look more carefully at the worship practices of the Great Tradition when we discuss worship's structure in chapter 14. Just know that this study of historic Christian worship will be more or less familiar depending on your own tradition and experience. Typically, Christians in more liturgical traditions already have a tacit awareness of many Great Tradition practices simply because they are embedded in their liturgies. Yet Christians in free church and charismatic traditions may find historic Christian worship more unfamiliar. Regardless of your background, it is necessary for every worship leader to spend time exploring our Christian past and to humbly ask how previous worship pastors answered the same questions we are asking now. Two wonderful places to start are Robert Webber's *Worship Old and New* and Bryan Chapell's *Christ-Centered Worship*.[20]

---

19. See for example Daniel I. Block, *For the Glory of God: Recovering a Biblical Theology of Worship* (Grand Rapids, Mich.: Baker, 2014); Allen P. Ross, *Recalling the Hope of Glory: Biblical Worship from the Garden to the New Creation* (Grand Rapids, Mich.: Kregel, 2006); D. A. Carson, "Worship Under the Word," in *Worship by the Book*, ed. D. A. Carson (Grand Rapids, Mich.: Zondervan, 2002), 11–63; Robert Webber, *Worship Old and New*, rev. ed. (Grand Rapids, Mich.: Zondervan, 1994), 17–92; and David Peterson, *Engaging with God: A Biblical Theology of Worship* (Downers Grove, Ill.: InterVarsity, 1992). To set the stage on this subject, though, I highly recommend Michael Farley's very important article which safeguards against a narrow view of what biblical worship means. He brings up some issues of methodology that expose how often we can be talking past one another in such conversations: "What is 'Biblical' Worship? Biblical Hermeneutics and Evangelical Theologies of Worship," *Journal of the Evangelical Theological Society* 51, no. 3 (September 2008): 591–613.

20. Webber, *Worship Old and New*; Bryan Chapell, *Christ-Centered Worship: Letting the Gospel Shape Our Practice* (Grand Rapids, Mich.: Baker, 2009).

3. Studying Your Context

All the great missionaries of the past and those who are serving in ministry today must spend time and effort studying their mission field. The same is true for us as well. We can think of our context in two parts: our church with its habits and traditions, and our community—neighborhood, city, region, nation.

In the church, it's important to continually ask, "Who are we?" We need to ask this question, on the one hand, at the historical, institutional, and (where applicable) denominational level. We do this by exploring what the worship practices of our church and denomination have historically been, and we probe into why they were done that way.

While I want to encourage this type of engagement and study, I also want to zero in on a specific concern here. Regardless of whether our churches are more evangelical, mainline Protestant, or in some cases even Roman Catholic, many of us are involved in learning from the "tradition" of contemporary worship music and practices. The theology and history behind this modern, cross-denominational movement are very much worth studying, appreciating, and understanding because they are shaping the sensibilities of our people, and we need to discerningly place them in dialogue with Scripture and tradition. I encourage every worship pastor to take time to study the history and theology of contemporary worship.[21]

On the other hand, the question "Who are we?" also needs to be asked on the personal level:

- Who are the people God has gathered in our church?
- What are their worship backgrounds? What habits and practices are they used to? What habits and practices are foreign to them?
- What are their cultural backgrounds? How do those backgrounds shape the way they approach worship?
- How are people in our context moved? What are the rhetorical expressions and musical "languages" of our people's emotions?

---

21. Three helpful historical accounts of the rise of contemporary worship, especially among evangelicals, are worth noting: Larry Eskridge, *God's Forever Family: The Jesus People Movement in America* (New York: Oxford, 2013); Chuck Fromm, "Textual Communities and New Song in the Multimedia Age" (PhD diss., Fuller Theological Seminary, 2006); Cornelius Plantinga Jr. and Sue A. Rozeboom, *Discerning the Spirits: A Guide to Thinking About Christian Worship Today* (Grand Rapids, Mich.: Eerdmans, 2003), 13–46. I'm also very encouraged by the growing list of scholars across many disciplines (history, liturgics, sociology, anthropology, ethnomusicology) who are taking seriously the study of the contemporary worship movement—e.g., Joshua Busman, Monique Ingalls, Stephen Marini, Glenn Packiam, Deborah Smith Pollard, Wen Reagan, Lester Ruth, Martin Stringer, Mike Tapper.

Asking questions like these helps us guard against a naïve capitulation to the "cult of cool" that tends to steer us toward focusing on the young and hip of the next generation. Our cultural obsession with youth may have led us, as worship leaders, to neglect the needs of people from different generations and to ignore the biblical wisdom that admonishes us to listen to the Spirit's work among the older generations in our communities (Job 12:12; Prov. 7:6–8; 20:29; 1 Tim. 5:1–2). Proper contextualization—being a faithful missionary to your flock—involves listening to every voice, not just the young and attractive.

In addition to your church context, you will need to study your community as well, asking these types of questions:

- What makes my culture tick?
- What kinds of music, movies, and art do they listen to, enjoy, or find expression in?
- How do people in this context express various emotions—joy, fear, hope, longing, lamentation, wonder?
- What are my culture's values, and how are they represented in my city's life, layout, architecture, leisure activities?
- What moves people in my city and region? What drives decision-making for the people groups represented in my community?[22]

Bringing together considerations of your church and your community often means making some important decisions about worship expressions. Inevitably, some of your church's personal and institutional history and practices will stand in tension with what you might employ if you were thinking about the surrounding culture. For instance, one of the churches I have served claimed a strong traditional-classical heritage, complete with a large, expensive pipe organ. While this heritage was part of who we were, it stood in contrast to a city and region filled with a variety of cultures, many of which were disconnected from any Western classical heritage. We attempted to weave sensibilities together by combining modern musical styles and instrumentation with our organ. Every church is different, of course. Every worship leader will want to examine the local church's heritage and compare that with the culture of the community.

---

22. Figuring out what drives decision-making often exposes a culture's central values and priorities. Investigating these themes further, Tim Keller summarizes David Hesselgrave's categories of three basic ways to reason: (a) conceptual—making decisions through analysis and logic; (b) concrete relational—making decisions through relationships and practice; (c) intuitional—making decisions through insight and experience (*Center Church: Doing Balanced, Gospel-Centered Ministry in Your City* [Grand Rapids, Mich.: Zondervan, 2012], 122–23). Understanding and applying these concepts will greatly enhance one's ability to contextualize according to the "reasoning language" of a given culture.

Straddling this tension will be an ongoing matter of prayer and dialogue among your church leadership.

4. Listening to the Holy Spirit

One of the most important things to do when engaging in any kind of momentous decision-making is to listen to the Holy Spirit. This involves adopting a posture of prayer and Scripture meditation where we as individuals, leaders, and churches ask for the Holy Spirit's leadership, guidance, and movement. This listening posture seemed to be behind the decision-making of the New Testament church where we read that they made decisions because "it seemed good to the Holy Spirit and to us" (Acts 15:28). At the same time, I encourage you to think of studying the Scriptures, the Great Tradition, and our context as a way of listening to the Holy Spirit. In studying the Scriptures, we're committed to the Spirit's concrete, definitive, God-breathed revelation to the church and to the world. In studying the Great Tradition, we're open to how the Holy Spirit moved previous generations to form and express worship in the past. And in studying our context, we look at our church and world with eyes wide open to all the ways the Spirit is active in our communities and cities. Don't just look for God to speak in an audible voice to guide you. He can and will speak through His written Word, through tradition, and through the circumstances of your discernment process.

So how do we put this all together into our role as a worship pastor?

As we listen to the Scriptures and the Great Tradition and discern the Christward worship expressions in them, there will likely emerge a list of core, timeless worship practices. (See fig. 3.) These timeless worship practices must then be sifted and translated through the grid of our context to provide for us contextualized worship practices that make sense for our worshiping body. I start asking questions like, "How would a twenty-first-century South Floridian most naturally feel and express [x worship practice] (i.e., confession, praise, offering, etc.)?"

Be aware that this process is cyclical. It is not a static, once-for-all dynamic that we figure out and then move on from. It's ongoing. This means that we need to develop habits and rhythms that lead us to engage Scripture's authority, the Great Tradition, and our context while remaining in dialogue with the Holy Spirit.

This may seem fairly straightforward and tidy, but in reality it is far from clean and simple. Contextualization of local practices and the Great Tradition is hazardous work because "every translation is itself an interpretation," and therefore liable to the idolatries and blind spots of the culture out of which it emerged.[23] We are also doing all of this listening and discerning with broken ears and sinful hearts (Jer. 17:9). This is, again, why this study process must be ongoing, cyclical, and

---

23. Plantinga and Rozeboom, *Discerning the Spirits*, 50–51.

open-handedly dependent upon the dynamic work of the Holy Spirit. But it is also why it happens best in community rather than in our own personal laboratories.

Figure 3

CONTEXTUALIZING WORSHIP PRACTICES

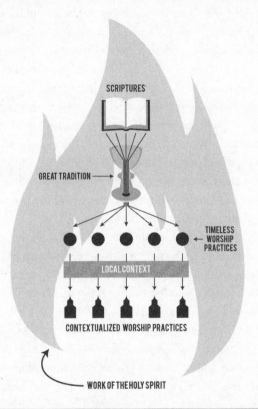

Learning to Be a Missionary in South Florida

When I first moved to take a new position in South Florida (a foreign mission field for me if there ever was one), I began asking questions about this new and strange culture. I wanted to better understand how to weave various music traditions in with some of the Great Tradition practices of our worship service. One of the most helpful moments for me was some time I spent recording an album with some of the local artists I was just getting to know—our church's drummer (who helped produce the record), our bassist, and a local engineer. As we spent time making music together, I listened and learned, paying attention to how they heard and felt the art. Through this I gained a greater understanding of the way music is integrated with emotion in the culture of South Florida. My time in the studio opened up several insights into how to better arrange our music in and around our worship practices, affixing the right kind of musical "affect," largely sculpted by the musical artists around me, to a given liturgical moment.

I discovered that South Floridians, in general, were intuitive in the way they experienced life, made decisions, and expressed themselves in worship. Most of the cultures represented in that region—from New Yorkers to Haitians to Brazilians—were highly emotive and expressive in the way they communicated. For our church, these insights led to our creating a highly musical liturgy, where we would journey primarily through worship songs, with the music helping to paint the emotions through expressions of praise, confession, absolution, offering, and communion. This also meant that I had to take musical arrangements from other contexts and "amp them up." Our songs of praise were generally sung louder than the originals, and I began setting them in higher keys than I had previously been used to. Our lamentations and confessions were intense and far less introspective than you might find in other contexts.

This missionary journey of understanding our tradition and our cultural context also brought me face to face with several challenges. I quickly learned that some biblical worship practices were harder for people in the South Florida culture to embrace and engage. For example, because South Florida was highly influenced by transplants from the cities of the northeast United States, we were not a terribly patient people. We drove fast and lived hard. This meant that having more reflective and meditative moments of worship would be challenging. South Florida also had a rich nightlife and a joyous, sometimes raucous, party culture. The more somber and sober aspects of worship from the Great Tradition were largely unfamiliar to our fast and sometimes chaotic pace of life. Contextualization of these aspects of worship was possible, but it would happen with care, patience, and by starting with small doses.

The missionary call of a worship pastor is ongoing. Mission and worship flow together as a single life-giving system. As missionaries, we must assume a posture of listening as the Holy Spirit speaks and works through Scripture, tradition, and our context. As we apply what we've heard to our worship practices, in a small way we mirror the life of God the Son, who took on flesh and gave Himself for us, "contextualizing" Divinity in humanity, full of grace and truth, that we might behold Him, glorify Him, and enjoy Him forever.

God the Father, our great Missionary God, Who sent Your only
Son, fill our worship with Your Spirit to make much of Jesus, until
every knee bows and every tongue confesses that He is Lord.

10

THE WORSHIP PASTOR AS ARTIST CHAPLAIN

The world does not need more (or any) "Christian artists." What the world does need, and needs desperately, are Christians who embrace our freedom in Christ to such a degree that we can listen to and participate in the art and culture that is at hand. What the world needs are more listeners, more receivers.

—Dan Siedell, 2015[1]

A few years ago at a hole-in-the-wall pizza joint, I learned a valuable lesson on what *not* to do as a pastor speaking to artists. A musician I was working with—we'll call him Ben—was relaying the story of his previous experience as a music director under pastoral supervision at another church. He loved his job, using his gifts to help build up a culture of great music making in the local church. What he didn't love was the weekly meeting in his pastor's office. Ben would arrive at the appointed time and hear the same opening question coming at him. Leaning in toward me, with intensely squinted eyes and an exaggerated southern accent, Ben gave his best impression: "How's your walk with Jesus?" Ben described these encounters as awkward and uncomfortable, and my reading between the lines told me that the pastor's well-meaning weekly interrogation actually served to push Ben away from Jesus rather than toward Him. The very means by which the pastor sought to encourage faith in this artist ultimately served to discourage.

"How's your walk?" isn't necessarily a bad question. It's a standard one many of us have learned to ask to get past the fluff of superficial chitchat and into the reality of the life of a disciple. But Ben's bristling at this question told me that our techniques for pastoring can't be one-size-fits-all. In talking with Ben and other artists like him, I've learned that some of our typical and standard approaches to

---

1. Daniel A. Siedell, *Who's Afraid of Modern Art? Essays on Modern Art and Theology in Conversation* (Eugene, Ore.: Cascade, 2015), 31.

"intentional" conversation need to be thrown away. If we do that, though, what goes in their place?

From One Artist to Another

In calling a worship pastor an "artist chaplain," I'm seeking to be deliberately ambiguous. This chapter will explore how we worship pastors are *artists' chaplains*—we're here to connect with and minister to the artists in our churches and communities. At the same time, we are *artist-chaplains*—artists ourselves, living in overlapping vocational spheres with other artists to whom we're called to minister.

I like the metaphor of chaplain because it calls to mind a more relational and itinerant ministry. Think of the old English friars who dragged their mule from village to village, meeting the people where they were, offering them the words and hope of Jesus. Or think of a hospital or military chaplain today. In these scenarios, people aren't coming to the church; the church is coming to them. I believe that many artists fall into this category. They need the ministry of a chaplain who will meet them where they are. I've witnessed through my own experience and observing the ministry of others how our calling as pastors can effectively turn us into a chaplain for and to other artists.

Why this focus on artists, though? What makes artists different from other vocations, and why should worship pastors focus their attention on them? Not long ago, I tweeted an off-the-cuff thought about my own church's ministry to several artists. Someone responded with a challenge: "Why should the church give special treatment to artists? What about engineers or teachers?" That's a fair question. As I reflected on it, my simple response was that as a worship pastor and an artist myself, those with artistic callings are the people whose life and work stand directly before me. I would agree that the church needs to minister to everyone. But I want to suggest that worship pastors—those involved in leading music and engaging people in the worship of God in creative ways—exist in unique proximity to artists and their communities. More than other pastors and staff and lay leaders, we have a unique calling to minister to individuals who find art making a key aspect of their vocational makeup.

"The Art of Arts"

I realize that some of you may not think of yourselves as artists. But I'll clear it up for you. Worship pastor, you are an artist. Part of your vocation involves tinkering in the realms of aesthetics, beauty, and expression. If you're like me, you may feel a sense of insecurity about calling yourself an artist, especially if you interact with other artists who, whether because of their concentrated investment, time, and study, or just because of their raw gifting, are likely better at their craft than you are at yours. I'll be the first to admit that I often feel like a second-class citizen in the artistic community.

And yet, as a worship leader and pastor I'm called to lead others, including those with strong artistic gifts. Here is a good place to begin if you struggle with insecurity as well. Recognize that pastoral ministry itself is an art form. I'm not the first to suggest this. It was the view of the early church as well. At the end of the sixth century, Gregory the Great encouraged pastors that "the care of souls is the art of arts."[2] This was more than just a metaphor or a fancy way of speaking. The church fathers recognized that there is an artistic dimension present in ministering to people. The same tools we employ to "hear" and receive an artist's work—time, contemplation, question asking, vulnerability—are the very tools we employ to truly hear and receive the artist herself.

Who Is an Artist, and How Do We Minister to Artists?

One of my favorite art thinkers, Dan Siedell, helpfully introduces us to the difficulty in defining who an artist is. Unlike other vocations whose boundaries are more clearly demarcated by degrees conferred (PhD for college professors), professional titles assumed (CPA for accountants), or places of employment (Cupertino for hardware engineers), artists "struggle with recognition and justification in an especially acute way."[3] In a cultural climate where we refer to a five-year-old's crayon drawing as art right alongside Rembrandt's *Self-Portrait as the Apostle Paul*, there is real confusion about who is and who is not an artist. Who defines what an artist is and does? As a chaplain to artists, you should be aware of this struggle, but answering this question is not essential to your ministry.

What is important is avoiding assumptions. We strive to receive a work of art for what it is rather than what we impose on it. And in the same way we should strive to receive artists for who they are rather than how we or our culture tend to stereotype them. Siedell explains it well: "The myth of the tortured artist—which has a long and distinguished history—who feels more deeply, struggles with depression, addiction, and alienation, is often used to put the artist 'over there,' away from 'us,' either on a pedestal or in the gutter."[4]

---

2. Quoted in *A Companion to Gregory the Great*, eds. Bronwen Neil and Matthew Dal Santo (Leiden, The Netherlands: Brill, 2013), 212.

3. Siedell, *Who's Afraid of Modern Art?* 58.

4. Ibid.

So don't begin with faulty assumptions. Our assumptions about people create stereotypes, and these create distance, a distance that weakens our pastoral ministry. It's not essential to define who is and is not an artist. Some people will draw their income and livelihood from their art making. Others will self-identify as artists, and we should receive them as such. Still others may not use that word to describe themselves but they clearly express creativity and artistry in formal and informal ways. I think of all of these people as artists and include them among the people I am called to minister to and with. Don't go out looking for the stereotypical artist. Simply ask, "Who are the artistic people doing creative work before me, in my life, in my relational spheres and networks?"

Thankfully, several helpful books have been written to provide you with practical and insightful tips on understanding and ministering to artists.[5] In what follows I won't repeat those insights. Instead, I want to offer a simple, twofold paradigm that can guide you to further reflection on your own calling and context.

What We (and the Church) Can Receive from Artists

Ministry as an artist to other artists always begins with receiving, then it moves on to giving. I realize this might sound odd at first, but I believe it is important to get the order right to avoid ministerial missteps. Remember Ben's weekly "walk with Jesus" interrogations? Ben was unable to receive that pastor's ministry because he had never been heard and understood by that pastor. To that pastor—even if he had good intentions—Ben was an object, not a subject. One of the most important ministries we offer to artists is to simply let them be heard. Here are just four of the many things we can seek to receive from the artists in our church.

1. Receiving Their Stories and Their Art

Each one of us desires to be known, understood, and accepted by others. Our ministry to artists begins here, by listening to their stories, asking them questions about themselves, and allowing them to share their background, training, hopes, fears, and dreams. In the act of listening, we need to be especially sensitive to the fact that in recent generations, the church has often adopted an adversarial and judgmental attitude toward culture, one where artistic endeavors are not valued and artists are the objects of moral condemnation by religious people. When people I've met for the first time ask me what I do and I say, "I work in a church,"

---

5. See especially W. David O. Taylor, ed., *For the Beauty of the Church: Casting a Vision for the Arts* (Grand Rapids, Mich.: Baker, 2010); Rory Noland, *The Heart of the Artist: A Character-Building Guide for You and Your Ministry Team* (Grand Rapids, Mich.: Zondervan, 1999).

I often see them wince slightly. Then their eyes glaze over as they rehearse whether they've cussed or said anything inappropriate in the conversation. The belief of many is that religious leaders stand on a moral platform, critiquing everyone else. Therefore, when we find ourselves in those precious, sacred moments of listening to artists (or anyone for that matter), it's especially important that we steer clear of offering advice or giving any hint that we're evaluating what is being said. We want to hear and receive, not judge and condemn.

One of the ways artists are heard is through the reception of their work. Whether we listen to their music with them or visit their home or studio, allowing their work to work on us is essential. It's important to know that we don't need to be experts in their field to receive their work. It might be that we are able to know them more deeply through the process of having them explain or guide us through their art. Listening, loving, and receiving with no strings attached and no hidden agendas can be our most effective ministry as artist chaplains.

2. Receiving Their Acquaintance with Inadequacy

As artists, we can all identify with Pope John Paul II's description of the artist's plight as the "suffering of insufficiency."[6] Artists, more than most, are acquainted with inadequacy. I've never known an artist who said they had produced a perfect work. Though the world may laud their masterpieces as sheer perfection, often-times an artist's own finished work exists for them as a thorny judgment on their artistry, a lasting testament to their imperfection: that one brush stroke that was too thick; that one note that was just a hair flat and needed some postproduction tuning; that one slight indentation at the base of the clay; that one hastily composed section because the deadline came too quickly. An artist's own work can be painful. As Siedell observes, this acquaintance with inadequacy is something common to us all, though we all experience it in different ways:

> The artist is *exactly* like us. Art, as Edvard Munch [*The Scream*] reminds us, comes from pain. And if we're honest with ourselves, we have to admit that most of our work comes from pain, the struggle for recognition, and the desire to close a wound that has remained open our entire lives. We struggle with the same existential problems and insecurities as Munch. We worry that our work, at the end of the day (or at the end of our lives), will mean nothing, will not matter. Yet our professions usually insulate us from confronting these questions as directly and powerfully as an artist does each time she goes into

6. Quoted in Barbara Nicolosi, "The Artist: What Exactly Is an Artist and How Do We Shepherd Them?" in *For the Beauty of the Church: Casting a Vision for the Arts*, ed. W. David O. Taylor (Grand Rapids, Mich.: Baker, 2010), 114.

her studio to work, and brings with her doubt, fear, and struggles—precisely the emotions that most of our professions have trained us to leave somewhere else, either at home or at the bar down the street.[7]

Artists are, for the church and the world, key harbingers of the gospel because they are (as painful as it is to say) experts in the knowledge of failure. The gospel is never good news for sinners unless it is preceded by the devastatingly bad news, "You are a failure" (Rom 3:10–18, 23). Failure and inadequacy are the elements that make the soil of our hearts fertile for the gospel to grow. Artists, in this respect, have a unique and powerful insight into the heart of Christianity, and they just might be—if known, understood, and *heard*—one of God's greatest gifts to the rest of the church.

3. Receiving Their Insight into Our Cities

In a day and age when churches are waking up to our own missionary callings to our neighborhoods and cities, one key aspect of effective ministry is properly "exegeting" the culture. All great missionaries understand what makes a culture tick. And local artists, in particular, often understand the makeup of their cities far better than people of other vocations. As I write this, an artist friend of mine is dealing with the politics of South Florida as he fulfills a commission to paint an enormous mural in one of the central parts of West Palm Beach. He's caught between the city officials, some citizens who are against the mural, and the supportive patron who funded the project. Weeks before that, he was interacting with the locals of Fort Lauderdale who were engaging with some of his drawings at an art walk. Artists are uniquely positioned within a community's life and rhythms, and their knowledge of what drives a city often carries better missionary insights than demographic studies, focus groups, or think tanks. As a part of their work, artists are listening to their cities and surroundings in a way that the rest of us aren't. The church needs those expert ears.

Sociologist Robert Schreiter includes artists among the four primary groups of "local theologians" who are expressing and shaping the beliefs of a given culture, "capturing the soul of a community." He provocatively asks, "The poets in the community, who can capture the rhythm and contour of the community's experience—cannot their work be considered a genuine local theology? Is not some of the more authentic theology, especially that which captures the imagination of the majority of people, to be found in their work rather than in theological monographs or church documents?"[8]

---

7. Siedell, *Who's Afraid of Modern Art?* 58.
8. Robert J. Schreiter, *Constructing Local Theologies* (Maryknoll, N.Y.: Orbis, 1994), 18–19.

I have found that the more involved I am in listening relationships with local poets—musicians, painters, dancers, filmmakers, writers—the more equipped I become to understand and minister to my immediate culture.

4. Receiving Their Aesthetic Wisdom

The church also has much to receive from artists, especially in the arena of aesthetic sensibility. Sadly, in some church settings a hyperbiblicism has deafened ears to the aesthetic input that artists can offer. This happens when all of the aesthetic decisions made in the church—the architecture, decorations, lighting, color, sound, and music—are made by pastors and leaders whose aesthetic sensibilities are underdeveloped or absent. In these settings, worship leaders can be advocates for new processes and models of decision-making where a diversity of views and appropriate voices come together and where the best of wisdom is brought to bear on aesthetic decisions. Can we make aesthetic choices together as artists, pastors, and other leaders working and wrestling together in deferential postures, taking God's gifts in one another seriously?

In one church I served, I tried to take the gifts of others seriously in my work with professional musicians. One musician in particular—Matt, our drummer—was one of the best musicians I had ever worked with. Matt was already present in his role as drummer when I arrived, and I quickly discerned that his gifts, training, and expertise far exceeded my own. I could have been threatened by Matt's skill as an artist and musician. I could have played a positional trump card and fostered a dynamic that made him merely my drummer. Instead I chose to let Matt's aesthetic voice and musical expertise be heard. Though it's a bit unorthodox, Matt and I served as co-leaders of our weekly rehearsals. More often than not, I ended up deferring to his advice and sensibilities. As a veteran musician who had played in almost every venue in our region, Matt's missionary understanding of the ins and outs of our culture had given him instincts worth listening to and heeding for the sake of our growth in worship.

In other chapters, we have noted the central role that our affections play in how we engage in worship. Artists of all stripes (alongside psychologists, counselors, and caregivers) are experts in the affections. Art resides largely in the affective realm, where feeling, perception, intuition, emotion, and ambiance are the communicative currency. Artists are instinctively and keenly sensitive to the ways our churches' aesthetic qualities are heard and felt by our people. Listening to their reflections offers them the opportunity to be heard, and it can strengthen your church's missionary effectiveness and enhance your worship experience.

What We (and the Church) Can Give to Artists

In response to the many things we can receive from artists in the church, there are also many things we can give to artists. I want to explore four of these gifts, and I want to begin by exposing a key theological insight that makes all the difference.

1. The Gift of Nonexploitative Love

Today we find ourselves at a point in Western Christianity where transformation is the predominant paradigm of our faith. What do I mean? To put it simply, we've so emphasized the fruit of salvation in Christ—a changed life—that the root of salvation—Jesus—has been knocked off center stage. Here is an example of how this shows up in our faith and practice. We ask the question: What does it mean to be a Christian? We answer: "A changed life." What's wrong with that? you might ask. Well, several things. While a changed life is our glorious testimony, it is not the heart of our faith. It is not the gospel. The Scriptures tell us that the heart of Christianity is substitution, not transformation: "God made him who had no sin to be sin for us, that *in him* we might become the righteousness of God" (2 Cor. 5:21, emphasis mine). At the root of my faith, it is not about me or my transformed life; it is about Christ and His life and death. Christianity does not begin with the good news of my life changed, but Christ's life *ex*changed.

Why point this out when talking about ministry to artists? Ultimately, if transformation is the prevailing paradigm of Christianity, we will approach ministry from a radically different (and ultimately harmful) angle. In a transformational scheme, we're always looking for the artist to produce evidence of their transformation—fruit, results, tangibles, measurables. When ministry takes this hue, artists become tools to be manipulated for our agendas. We instrumentalize, and therefore dehumanize, them. People become projects. Our driving question for them then always becomes, "How's your walk with Jesus?" We will be less desirous to truly know them and much more inclined to evaluate and use them as objects of our "transformative" ministry. Under a transformational scheme, ministry ultimately becomes exploitative.

However, if Christianity is primarily not about transformation but substitution, ministry is set free. Character development and improvement plans take a back seat to an unclanging kind of love. Our ministry to artists is freed up to bear all things, believe all things, hope all things, and endure all things (1 Cor. 13:1–7). We're free to listen open-endedly to an artist's hopes, dreams, fears, and frustrations (our job) without feeling the burden to fix them (God's job). We're unshackled to embody the kind of one-way love that the gospel alone ultimately provides.[9] That means we don't need to hang on to the compulsion to correct the questionable aspects of an artist's work or relationships. We can be the type of friend who looks at their sin as unflinchingly as the Father looks at ours through Christ. We can be the type of pastor who enters their world deeply and fully, just as Christ entered ours. If substitution is the hallmark of our faith, then we're free to simply declare and demonstrate the gospel. And, ironically, it is only this kind of no-strings-attached love that has the power to transform (2 Cor. 5:14–19).

2. The Gift of Shielding

I start with the love discussed in the previous paragraph because I know that many artists live in a heavy, burdensome reality. Dan Siedell highlights the raw brutality of life in the art world.[10] The "art-industrial complex," comprised of dealers, curators, critics, collectors, and artists, exists in a loose network of relationships which works most often like a pressurized cauldron of comparison, judgment, critique, conditional transactions, and one-upmanship. Siedell observes this world at work in the context of the auction: "It is the primary site in the art world in which men and women participate in . . . a life-or-death battle for mutual recognition. As such, it is one of the most profoundly theological locations in contemporary culture, where the ultimate value of life, a person's justification, is at stake with each lot and with each bid."[11] The auction might very well be the perfect microcosm to illustrate the world that the artist lives in on a day-to-day basis. As artist chaplains, Christ's love compels us to understand the artist's world for their sake.

Since artists often live with the constant pressure of being evaluated, judged, and criticized, part of our job is to provide an alternative to the "auction" where the critiquing happens. For artists (and hopefully for everyone), the church should feel like a haven where criticism ceases and grace abounds. A musician I once worked with on Sunday mornings shared with me one morning that a member of our congregation had told him—right before a worship service—that the hat he was wearing was offensive to God. The musician immediately felt bad and took off his hat, but throughout the service, he couldn't shake the feeling that he had been unfairly judged. When I heard this story, I knew that he needed the affirmation of the gospel. I apologized to him on behalf of the church and told him that I and the other leadership did not share the concerns of this member. I told him that what this member did was wrong and suggested (with a smirk) that he should wear a sombrero next week.

---

9. See Tullian Tchividjian, *One Way Love: Inexhaustible Grace for an Exhausted World* (Colorado Springs: Cook, 2013).

10. Siedell, *Who's Afraid of Modern Art?* 44–65.

11. Ibid., 50.

In moments like these, it's important that artists sense that church leaders stand with them. They need to understand that the church is not an arena of judgment. While we all, artists and nonartists, must live in a painfully graceless world, the church can and should offer something different. Our call as artist chaplains is to fend off the Pharisaical and legalistic spirit that can easily and quickly wound artists and obscure the ministry of the gospel to them. It also means that we stand as voices and advocates for artists to the broader church community that can sometimes misread (and subsequently judge) their behavior and work.

3. The Gift of Patronage—Meaningful Income, Work, and Advocacy

Most artists I know are in a perpetual state of hustling, running here and there to scrape together enough money to get by. One month's feast gives way to three months of famine. One of the more mission-oriented decisions I've seen churches make is to reserve a portion of their budget to pay musicians for their service to worship. Many churches, in the name of ministry, will justify shortchanging professional musicians by paying them next to nothing (or literally nothing). I believe that churches should be more generous than the world here, that we should pay adequate wages that at least match what musicians get paid elsewhere. If churches are seeking advice and input from artists (as I mentioned earlier), we should consider paying them for their consultation. I understand that not every church has the means to do this, but for those who do, this source of income values the work of the artist and can sometimes become a financial anchor in an artist's otherwise volatile budget. Sometimes we think of patronage purely in terms of commissioning an artist for a specific work. But a church's weekly employment of musicians can also be considered a form of patronage.

Patronage involves providing income, but it also involves giving artists meaningful work to do. In working with professional musicians, I've noted their appreciation and joy in being able to use their gifts to serve the church. These artists have noted to me the contrast between their work in the church and what they experience in other venues—the critical snobbery of concert halls, the disinterested inattentiveness in bars, the under appreciation at corporate events. Churches can become places where artists can make great music that serves an obviously edifying purpose—congregational singing, experiencing the presence of God. In doing this, we are offering them not only a "gig" but also meaningful work. Thoughtful artists pick up on this, and appreciative, supportive congregations become patrons in this way.

One artist chaplain who excelled here was a man whom many have thought of as an enemy to the arts—reformer John Calvin. History often forgets that Calvin encouraged Geneva to employ two of the best artists of his day, poet Clement Marot and composer Louis Bourgeois, for the ongoing work of developing a new Psalter. Calvin not only offered these artists patronage through income and meaningful work, he also became a patron in a third way by becoming a mediator and advocate for them before the city magistrates. When financial hard times hit Geneva, it is reported that the city had planned on cutting Bourgeois' salary in half. (Isn't it often the case that budget crises first put artists on the chopping block?) Additionally, some traditionalists voiced a strong dislike for the new music Bourgeois was composing. Calvin stood in the gap as a defender of and advocate for Bourgeois, offering the city several exhortations throughout the process.[12]

Sometimes our church leaders and congregants may see artists the way the Genevan council did. It's our job as artist chaplains to offer patronage to artists by being their advocate when they are becoming marginalized or misunderstood.

4. The Gift of the Gospel

Genesis records one of the first artifacts ever created—a garment of woven fig leaves (3:7). Adam and Eve used their creativity to reimagine earth's raw materials for the purpose of medicating the pain of guilt. Ever since we made those clothes, humanity has continued on this trajectory of using our gifts and talents to hide our shame and medicate our pain.[13] Many artists are, at some level, aware that their art making is an attempt to deal with the questions and problems that plague their soul—their guilt, shame, and need for justification. Art helps them answer the questions: Why do I exist? What purpose does my life have?

What does an artist chaplain bring to these questions? Artists, like all of us, crave understanding, acceptance, and validation. This thirst seeks to be quenched in many forms: validation by approval ("I'm acceptable when the art world tells me so"); validation through monetary success ("I am successful because I can sustain a living off my work"); validation by intellectual superiority ("My work is meaningful because most are too simpleminded to understand it"); validation by comparison ("At least I don't need a second job like most other artists I know"); and on and on it goes. The question every artist asks is the same one we're all asking: "How can I be justified?" This is what drives our passions, directs our pursuits, and dictates our plans. Justification sits at the core of all human endeavors, even art making.

More than anything, artists need the relieving word that their validation can

12. See Ross James Miller, "John Calvin and the Reformation of Church Music in the Sixteenth Century" (PhD diss., Claremont Graduate School, 1971), 120–21.

13. I'm grateful to Dr. Ashley Null for this profound insight into the Scriptures and the artist's heart in a lecture on "Cranmer's Advice to Contemporary Worship," given on January 6, 2015, at Trinity School for Ministry (Ambridge, Pa.).

be completely and irrevocably satisfied by the beautiful work of another. The news that Jesus' perfect life and substitutionary death comes to us as a free gift of once-for-all, full and final justification (Eph. 2:8–9) has the power to unshackle burdened artists. Freed from the need to be justified, their art can be even more what it should be—an act of worship for the glory of God and the blessing of their neighbor. No longer does the well of their creativity have to be tainted by the need to self-justify.

Dan Siedell movingly describes the experience of one such freed artist, Diego Velásquez (1599–1660), whose odd habit of wiping his brush on the corner of the very masterpieces he was painting exposed the depth of his own understanding of his freedom in Christ: "How could a human being so gifted care so little about his gift? Certainly, a human being whose identity is received as grace, whose relationship to God, the world, and himself was not defined by his work as an artist and the paintings he painted."[14] How many more artists out there are just waiting to receive what Velásquez embraced? As worship pastors, we have a glorious call to carry this message—a message that sets artists free to live, not for their art, but for the great Artist Himself. This means that our best and final ministry to artists is the preaching of the gospel of Jesus Christ, the Lamb of God who takes away the sins of the world.

O Creator God, Artist of artists, fill us up with Your grace to be messengers of Your gospel, until freedom abounds and art flourishes.

---

14. Siedell, *Who's Afraid of Modern Art?* 85.

11

THE WORSHIP PASTOR AS CAREGIVER

For centuries, the liturgy, actively celebrated, has been the most important form of pastoral care.

—*J. A. Jungmann, 1962*[1]

It is not only in worship that the community is edified and edifies itself. But it is here first that this continually takes place. And if it does not take place here, it does not take place anywhere.

—*Karl Barth, 1958*[2]

My wife, Abby, had just given birth to our first baby. We were enjoying a night out as new parents at a Denver Nuggets game when Abby noticed that something was wrong with her eyesight. She had mentioned concerns about her vision several months back, but we'd chalked it up to one of the many changes the body goes through during pregnancy. The blind spot she discovered at the basketball game, however, could not be ignored. A doctor examined her eyes and, after giving a concerned look, sent us to a specialist. The next day, another doctor gave us the news that Abby had a cancerous tumor growing inside her eye.

We needed to act immediately. Suddenly, our world had been turned upside down as we pondered the possibilities of imminent death and the thought of our newborn son growing up without a mom. Abby underwent radiation, which ultimately stopped the cancer, but the trauma of the ordeal left my precious wife mostly blind in one eye. During this painful time in the life of my young family, I was leading worship every week in our church.

On Abby's first Sunday back in church, as she was feeling an acute sense of grief over the loss of her eyesight, we sang the hymn, "Be Thou My Vision." For my wife, that song immediately took on a new meaning. It deeply comforted her.

---

1. J. A. Jungmann, *Pastoral Liturgy* (New York: Herder and Herder, 1962), 380.
2. Karl Barth, *Church Dogmatics*, trans. G. W. Bromiley, IV/2 (Edinburgh: T&T Clark, 1957), 638.

Abby shared her epiphany with me after the service. "I don't need my vision as long as God can be it for me," she said. As her husband, I can't not cry as I write this, and I can't not cry every time I sing that hymn now.

As the worship planner and leader that week, I will admit that I was oblivious to the potential ministry that the double meaning of that hymn would have for my wife. But Abby's comment that day helped me realize that worship wasn't a heavenly pause on her earthly grief. Nor was worship a means of helping her "get over" her grief. Worship was helping her to grieve. It was giving language to her tears. It gave her scattered prayers a script to follow. In the service, the Holy Spirit was applying pastoral care through the songs I led and the prayers I prayed. For the first time in my life, I understood in a very personal way that a worship leader has a pastoral ministry of giving care.

The Divorce of Worship and Pastoral Care

When we hear "pastoral care," we typically think of one-on-one, gut-wrenching meetings between a pastor and a hurting congregant. We think of counseling sessions, hospital calls, in-home visits, praying for individuals' needs, and presiding over funerals. These are all vital, indispensable care practices of any pastor. But the history of the church points us to a center, a starting place for pastoral care. The pastors of early Christianity saw the core of their ministry to sick, hurting, wounded sheep happening in the context of *leading worship*.[3] Worship is the ground zero of pastoral care. It is where all pastoral care rightly begins, and without it, all other forms of pastoral care lose their meaning and power. Before I show you why this is so, we need to address another question: How did we ever get to the place where we don't think of worship when we talk about pastoral care?

William Willimon has argued that modernity has overly individualized and psychologized the landscape of pastoral care.[4] He traces historically how, after the Reformation, pastoral care took an increasingly individualized shape: "A major

---

3. "For centuries, the liturgy, actively celebrated, has been the most important form of pastoral care. This was especially true of those centuries in which the liturgy was being created. Unfavourable conditions brought it about that in the late Middle Ages, in spite of the liturgy being celebrated and developed in numerous churches with great fervour and magnificence by collegiate clergy and monastic communities, a veil became drawn between the liturgy and the people, a veil through which the faithful could only dimly see what was happening at the altar. Even in all this we can still see how pastoral concern led to the development and adaptation of the liturgy." J. A. Jungmann, *Pastoral Liturgy*, 380.

4. William H. Willimon, *Worship as Pastoral Care* (Nashville: Abingdon, 1979), 31–40. He highlights the progression from Richard Baxter to Jonathan Edwards to William James on through the twentieth century with Andrew Boisen's pioneering of Clinical Pastoral Education (CPE), still a staple today in many seminary educations.

difference in the pastoral care of previous ages of the church and that of our modern era is the switch from care that utilized mostly corporate, priestly, liturgical actions to care that increasingly limited itself to individualistic, psychologically oriented techniques heavily influenced by prevailing secular therapies for healing, personal fulfillment, and self-help."[5]

The long-term impact of this shift is that pastoral care has been detheologized. Willimon points out that pastors have lost their ability to "hear the faith issues behind the psychological distress."[6] To put a finer point on it, our secular age has severed the biblical explanation for our pain and suffering, no longer speaking in categories of sin, the fall, justification, and forgiveness.[7] And worship, which addresses sin and salvation, appears to many to have no practical bearing on our psychological problems. The result has been the disassociation of pastoral care from corporate worship. I believe that we need a renewed vision for how worship functions as pastoral care.

Worship as the Ground Zero of Pastoral Care

"In worship, all the community's concerns meet and coalesce," Willimon says. Corporate worship is where we encounter God, ourselves, our judgment, and our grace.[8] It is where our most fundamental human problems and concerns are directly addressed by God and His Word. Worship is the nucleus of all pastoral care. Let's look at three ways in which worship addresses the pain of our human experience.

1. Worship acts as preventative treatment. The services we plan and lead can be thought of much like a regimen of vitamins for God's people, the body of Christ. Worship begins caring for us long before the crisis of sickness strikes by building up the immune system of our souls. Long before people are sitting in a pastor's office seeking counsel, they have likely been sitting in the pews for weeks, months, even years. The services we plan and lead have been offering them words and images of meaning and hope that can speak to their souls. Here's how one pastor put it: "The minister has a clear duty to counsel the ill and dying, but he should first have helped create a community with a religiocultural view of the meaning of illness and death. . . . The difficulty with much of pastoral counseling today is that more time is spent discussing the tools of counseling than in the

---

5. Ibid., 35–36.
6. Ibid., 43.
7. We spoke in chapter 2, "The Worship Pastor as Corporate Mystic," about how modernity is a "disenchanted" reality. The inability to see psychology's grounding in these fundamental human problems addressed by theology is yet more evidence of this disenchantment.
8. Willimon, *Worship as Pastoral Care*, 20–21.

more challenging process of developing the structure of meanings that should constitute the context for counseling."[9]

Worship sets our individual problems in a cosmic context where we consider ultimate things. Worship reminds us of the spiritual realm, of good and evil, of death and resurrection, and of the hope of future healing on the other side of present pain. I remember talking to a hurting woman in my congregation who, having gone through a series of miscarriages, was able to say through tears, "My only comfort in all of this . . . what I cling to . . . is that God is good, He is sovereign, He loves me, and He knows my pain." Where did she gain that cosmic structure of meaning? She learned it in her regular, habitual encounters with God's goodness, sovereignty, and grace in worship. And she learned this and embraced it well before her world caved in. Worship shaped her heart and soul, preparing her in advance for the inevitable suffering she would experience in this fallen world.

We see this time after time throughout the Psalms. The psalmist's present distress—whatever it may be—doesn't suddenly disappear. Instead, his pain is contextualized by the vast landscape of God's sovereign mercy. "How long, LORD? Will you forget me forever? . . . But I trust in your unfailing love" (Ps. 13:1, 5).[10] Recovery from grief begins with remembering God's greatness. Worship offers us this vision.

2. Worship contains some ingredients of care that you can't get anywhere else. Have you ever experienced a time when the medicine you'd been looking for could be found in only one pharmacy in town? Worship is that one pharmacy. It's the only place we can go to find a remedy for our spiritual terminal illness. In God's perfect wisdom, He has chosen to use specific human actions to be His ordinary vehicles for dispensing extraordinary grace. And He's chosen these actions to be put on display weekly when His people gather for worship. To the naked eye, these actions may look weak and ineffective. But by the power of the Holy Spirit, they are God's means of caring for His people.

I'm talking here about the preaching of the Word, baptism, and the Lord's Supper. These are God's supernatural care package, hand delivered to the world chiefly in worship.[11]

3. Worship gets to the heart of the matter. The various elements of worship just mentioned are powerful vehicles of pastoral ministry because they all address the heart of the human condition. As worship leaders, part of our caregiver's call is to recognize what makes Christianity unique among all other ideas of care and

---

9. Don S. Browning, *The Moral Context of Pastoral Care* (Philadelphia: Westminster Press, 1976), 109.
10. See also Psalms 4, 18, 31, 55, 57, and 102.
11. Read more on this in chapter 2, "The Worship Pastor as Corporate Mystic."

healing in the world. Christianity insists that sin and alienation from God are at the root of all of our social and psychological problems. The classic symptoms that cause people to seek care and counsel—guilt, shame, loneliness, depression, relational dysfunction, fear—find their ultimate answer at the cross.

The prophet Ezekiel chastised Israel's poor shepherding: "The weak you have not strengthened, the sick you have not healed, the injured you have not bound up, the strayed you have not brought back, the lost you have not sought, and with force and harshness you have ruled them. So they were scattered" (Ezek. 34:4–5 ESV). So God took back the reins: "I myself will be the shepherd of my sheep" (Ezek. 34:15 ESV). And what exactly was at the heart of God's strategy for strengthening weakness, healing diseases, binding injuries, and gathering the lost? Nothing less than atonement and resurrection by Christ in the Holy Spirit, through the vehicle of reclaimed worship: "I will sprinkle clean water on you . . . and from all your idols [i.e., your misdirected worship] I will cleanse you. And I will give you a new heart, and a new spirit I will put within you. And I will remove the heart of stone from your flesh and give you a heart of flesh. And I will put my Spirit within you, and cause you to walk in my statutes" (Ezek. 36:25–27 ESV).

Jesus would later describe His caregiving ministry in much the same way, claiming that the root of the sickness of our souls is our sin and unrighteousness (Mark 2:17), not the symptoms we are typically trying to directly treat.

The rest of the world at best offers bandaid therapy. They can give techniques for managing pain, fear, anger, and the like, but only the church through the Word can offer Jesus—the cure for every curse. If our worship is not offering Jesus to the world, we provide nothing more than the same bandaid solutions the rest of the world is offering, and we might as well close our doors because, to be honest, the world has bigger and better bandaids. While some "Christian" services can still feel quite therapeutic with very little mention of the person and work of Jesus, those feelings are always proven to be temporary and fruitless. True pastoral care in worship has something far better to offer than superficial wound care. In worship, God offers heart transplants (Ezek. 36:26) and resurrection from the dead (Eph. 2:1–5). And just as Moses lifted up the serpent in the wilderness for the people's healing, so our worship must display Christ high and lifted up (John 3:14).

The root of all pastoral care in worship is the ministry of the gospel because every last person's deepest need is not a motivational talk, a life adjustment, an inspiring song, a new outlook, or a soul makeover. We don't ultimately need New Year's resolutions. We need the New Adam's resurrection. Therefore, the most compassionate thing we can do as caregivers is to plan and lead services that offer the ministry of the gospel in lavish excess. How do we do this?

Diagnosing Sickness

First, we allow worship to diagnose people's true condition. Worship can't mess around. It needs to get to the bottom of things by offering the right diagnosis for the grief and pain of life. The world offers many dissatisfying diagnoses:

- You're just not thinking highly enough about yourself (self-esteem).
- You're just not trying hard enough to do the right thing (self-righteousness).
- You just need to apply yourself to solving your problems (self-help).
- You just need a vacation, better work-rest rhythms (self-regulation).
- You just need to discover the real you inside (self-actualization).
- You just haven't put your best foot forward (self-curation).

The irony of all these diagnoses is that they point us back to the problem—self. In the spirit of Augustine, Martin Luther described this plight of the human condition with the imaginative phrase, *incurvatus in se* ("curved in on itself").[12] Our problem in life and in worship is that we are hopeless navel-gazers. We are hunchbacked, curved down and in, just like Tolkien's Gollum—a once-healthy hobbit now permanently incurved because of his unrelenting self-absorption (his "precious").

A good caregiver sniffs out our fallen instinct in worship to curve in on ourselves—to look at our works, our victory, our effort. We hear this "triumphalism" in preaching that is nothing more than motivational talks filled with good advice about how to make our lives better through behavior modification. We hear it in well-meaning but self-focused song lyrics that make promises we know we can't keep ("Jesus, I'm going to give it all away for you!"; "God, I'm not turning back!"). We feel it rise in our souls as we sing of ourselves and how we're living for God, surrendering for God, sacrificing for God. And make no mistake. It feels really good . . . just like Gollum in his dark corner gazing at his precious. But a caregiver loves the Good Shepherd's sheep too much to allow for a triumphalism that keeps the flock's eyes fixed on themselves, where there is no hope.

Worship leaders, for the sake of Christ (our only hope), we must eradicate the plague of triumphalism from our worship.[13] Those songs, those lyrics, those

---

12. See Matt Jenson, *The Gravity of Sin: Augustine, Luther and Barth on homo incurvatus in se* (London: T&T Clark, 2006).

13. Some may say the critique is broad-brushed, but I find Paul Zahl's comment very poignant here: "The core problem with the charismatic renewal movement, from Van Nuys to Toronto, from Malmesbury to Antwerp, was its emphasis on victory rather than on the dereliction of the Cross, on sanctification rather than on redemption, on victorious living rather than on *simul justus et peccator* ("justified

statements, those prayers—they cannot do. Worship needs to offer the kind of diagnosis that so devastates our triumphal hope in self that we are forced to look outside ourselves for answers. We need worship to diagnose our terminal illness.

We must plan and lead worship services that put us face to face with the raw, white-hot glory of God. We need an encounter with God that first makes us feel like our flesh is being stripped off our bones, exposing everything. We need to sing, pray, read, and hear about God's perfections, attributes, law, and incomparable glory. We need psalms, hymns, and spiritual songs that pull the veil back from heaven until we see, with Isaiah and John, the Blazing One who is "Holy, holy, holy!" (Isa. 6:3; Rev. 4:8).

Make no mistake. This kind of diagnosis is uncomfortable. Have you ever thought about all the ways in worship that we consciously and unconsciously shield ourselves from the unsettling glory of God? Willimon points out some of the odd "worship behaviors" we employ to distance ourselves from the discomfort: "Even the incessant clearing of throats, whispering, coughing, rattling of gum wrappers, [the checking of phones,] and aimless activity that usually goes on in a congregation on Sunday morning may be a direct, if unconscious, attempt to avoid getting too close to the mystery."[14] All the distraction we witness in ourselves and others in worship may be part of the way that our flocks are dealing with the painful proximity of Holiness. How do we offer them relief?

Delivering the Cure

If worship diagnoses our problem accurately, it will settle for nothing less than the Divine Cure. "As long as sins are unknown," Martin Luther said, "there is no room for a cure, and no hope of one; for sins that think they betoken health and need no physician will not endure the healer's hand."[15] But imagine the catharsis, the relief, the hope, the splendor that the gospel can bring in worship when set against the backdrop of that diagnosis. This is why so many in liturgical traditions insist on the psychological and spiritual power of the moment of absolution,[16] when

---

and sinful at the same time"). The charismatic movement blew it because it wanted to pole-vault over Calvary on the way to Pentecost. (Who does not?) It flew right over the unevangelized dark continents of the Christian heart. It underestimated the awesome devastating force of inherited and continuing sin." Paul Zahl, "A Liturgical Worship Response," in *Exploring the Worship Spectrum*, ed. Paul A. Basden (Grand Rapids, Mich.: Zondervan, 2004), 154.

14. Willimon, *Worship as Pastoral Care*, 79.

15. Martin Luther, *The Bondage of the Will*, trans. J. I. Packer and O. R. Johnston (Grand Rapids, Mich.: Baker, 2012), 288.

16. For a brief but excellent defense of the use of absolution from a Reformed perspective, see James R. Thomson, "A Plea for the Absolution in the Reformed Churches," *Church Service Society Annual*, vol. 19 (1949): 33–40.

the people of God hear the simple, powerful, and direct words, "Your sins are forgiven!"[17] Our burdens find their ultimate relief only when we hear that Jesus' death on the cross paid for all our transgressions. Our sickness and sorrow find their ultimate hope only when we hear that Jesus' perfect life was enough to merit the Father's eternal, perpetual, irrevocable delight in us. Caregiver, where in your worship service will you provide the moment for weak and wounded sinners to look up to "behold the Lamb of God, who takes away the sins of the world" (John 1:29 ESV)? After the diagnosis has been made, give them the Cure! Read—no, declare—passages of Scripture that proclaim the gospel (e.g., John 3:16; Rom. 8:1; 1 John 2:1). Sing songs about Jesus' life and death, and (literally) for Christ's sake, tell them plainly and forcefully that their sins are forgiven! If these actions seem too bold, remember that Jesus, just before He departed, commissioned His disciples (and therefore us) with exactly that charge (John 20:23).

At this point you may be asking why, in a chapter on pastoral care and when the needs of people are plentiful and varied, I am emphasizing the role of the gospel instead of focusing on individual needs. It is because the forgiveness of sins is the great key that unlocks pastoral care's chest of tools. When people hear that their sins are forgiven, they have their greatest need—their guilt and alienation from God— dealt with. Our justification tells us now that the end is settled (Gal. 5:5). The gospel tells us that no matter what transpires in this life, God will say to us at its end, "Justified, righteous, holy, blameless, accepted, loved . . . *mine*." Our justification is a present declaration that seals our future security. Forgiveness changes everything.

Other Ways We Administer Care in Worship

When the gospel unlocks the ministry of care in our worship, we're freed as caregivers to shepherd God's love in a variety of ways.

1. The ministry of keeping things the same. Familiarity is a powerful, comforting balm for the instability we feel in the circumstances of life.[18] People enter worship disjointed and jostled. We show care and concern for our flocks when we seek to keep worship familiar. We don't throw too many curveballs at them. We don't make it difficult to engage. Worship's structure and songs should have a measure

---

17. Of the many things that the Reformers changed about medieval Roman Catholic worship, absolution remained untouched by many of them. One Anglican liturgiologist observes: "Our Reformers were guided by a sound psychological instinct when they refused to weaken the authoritative and emphatic form of Absolution provided in the Sarum Manual." W. K. Lowther Clarke, ed. *Liturgy and Worship: A Companion to the Prayer Books of the Anglican Communion* (London: SPCK, 1959), 529.

18. Willimon (*Worship as Pastoral Care*, 62): "Predictability of structure and liturgical sameness enable the worshiper to participate without having to think about it, without having to worry about what is going to happen next; and therefore the worshiper is free to wander into the untrodden paths of praise and prayer."

of predictability so that our people are not overly burdened by wondering what's next and they are freed to immerse themselves in God's presence. There is a time for introducing new things and changing old habits, but we should do this carefully and in small doses. Our goal is for people to experience worship as an easy yoke, a light burden.

2. The ministry of changing things. The flip side of this first point is that careful innovation and the injection of newness can become a ministry of care as well. As we are changing things, we avoid dead repetition and keep our flocks attentive and flexible to change. The inspiring spirit of worship in our services can often behave like the second law of thermodynamics—it's always eroding, fading, disintegrating. Newness and innovation fight against the natural tendency of our worship to become stale and lifeless. By introducing new songs, praying with fresh language, and offering variations in our liturgies (both in structure and content), we are caring for our people by stoking the flames of inspiration in them. Change is a wonderful deterrent against a Pharisaical, self-righteous spirit. It's painful how quickly "we always do it this way" degrades into "this is the only way God would have us do it." To some, the ministry of change may feel like a jolt, but most will eventually recognize it as a friendly repositioning of the logs to help get the fire going again.[19]

3. The ministry of hospitality. Worship pastors would do well to think about the roles of planning and leading worship in terms of hospitality. We do this by asking, "How do I create an environment where people feel included and brought in rather than excluded and shoved out?" At your church, for instance, think about how the dress and diversity of the people up front should mirror the congregation so that everyone can see someone "up there" with whom they can identify. You also might ask, "Do our songs and song arrangements make it easy for people to sing? Are the settings too high in the vocal range? Are the rhythms too difficult to follow?" These are context-specific questions (one size doesn't fit all), but a caregiver will ask them. I recall a few years ago when an African American couple came to me after worship and encouraged me to do more vocal ad-libbing between song phrases. I had always assumed that this "oversouling" was distracting (and it is to some people), but this couple told me that they felt encouraged and spurred on to sing by that practice, which was part of the dynamic in their worship tradition.[20] I'm always trying to learn more about what it means to be hospitable in my

19. This brings up a related issue. Sometimes the most caring thing we can do for people is *not* to give them what they want. Pope Gregory the Great (540–604) said long ago, "To put cushions under every elbow is to cherish with smooth flattery souls that are fallen away from rectitude in the pleasures of this world." *The Book of Pastoral Rule*, II.8; quoted in Andrew Purves, *Pastoral Theology in the Classical Tradition* (Louisville: Westminster John Knox, 2001), 72. There is a kind of care to be located in *denial* too.

20. Vocal improvisation in between and over congregational phrases certainly is a part of the call-and-response ethos of the historic African American worship tradition. This insight is an important

context. Mike Cosper points out that musical style is also an issue of hospitality. Our stylistic decisions will either help or hinder a sense of inclusion in worship.[21] This means that we need to be faithful listeners to our people and our immediate cultural context so that we can be hospitable, pastoral caregivers.

4. The ministry of pastoral prayer in worship. One of the blessings John Wimber and the Vineyard movement gave to the church was the practice of having hands-on, pastoral prayer during worship. This ministry time in the service, when people are prayed for by church leaders and other members, is a powerful pastoral moment. My friends in more charismatic churches remind me that this was the original purpose behind the practice of having "fire tunnels" in worship—a blitz of prayer for everyone in the room. Liturgical traditions likewise make room for their own version of the pastoral prayer, when the priest or pastor prays corporately for the specific care needs of the flock. Regardless of your tradition, consider how your worship service can make room for these kinds of practices.

5. The ministry of care outside of worship. One of the things that will most bless your ability to be a caregiver *in* worship is to be a caregiver the other six days of the week. Stay in tune with your church's care needs. Don't leave care for the deacons, care teams, or the other pastors. Make a hospital visit with a pastor. Check up over the phone or meet for coffee with the volunteers and leaders who assist with worship. Pray regularly with and for others' specific care needs. When you make the ministry of care part of your weekly rhythm, you will find yourself more in tune with the needs, hurts, joys, and triumphs of the body. You will plan worship with a new set of sensitivities that will prevent you from making unfortunate mistakes, like leading an energetic worship service on a week when a fresh wave of cancer diagnosis has hit your congregation. The worship pastor who cares for the flock *individually* will better care for them *corporately* in worship.

Be the Shepherd You Already Are

When we stand in front of people to lead them in worship, we are, quite literally, their "overseers." Peter has a word for us: "Be shepherds of God's flock that is under your care, *watching over them*—not because you must, but because you are willing, as God wants you to be; not pursuing dishonest gain, but eager to serve"

check to those who decry all forms of vocal ad-libs and freestyling by the worship leader. They fail to take into account that, for many years in the African American tradition, the leader's (and congregation's, for that matter) ad-libbed vocal flourishes were a part of the necessary "emotional content" of worship. This difference in cultural expression certainly creates a tension for multiethnic, multicultural worshiping communities, but even awareness of difficulties like this is half the battle for creating hospitable worship cultures.

21. Mike Cosper, *Rhythms of Grace: How the Church's Worship Tells the Story of the Gospel* (Wheaton, Ill.: Crossway, 2013), 181–82.

(1 Peter 5:2, emphasis mine). Before departing Ephesus, Paul gave a similar charge to the leaders there: "Keep watch over yourselves and all the flock of which the Holy Spirit has made you overseers. Be shepherds of the church of God, which he bought with his own blood" (Acts 20:28). The church is full of precious, blood-bought saints whose aches are real and needs are plentiful. Worship pastor, care for the flock of God.

*O Good Shepherd, be pleased to use the services we plan and
lead to care for the flock, ultimately leading them to You,
the Cure of souls, and Your finished work for us all.*

12

THE WORSHIP PASTOR
AS MORTICIAN

Beneath our feet and o'er our head,
Is equal warning given;
Beneath us lie the countless dead,
Above us, is the heaven.
Turn, Christian! turn; thy soul apply
To truths divinely given:
The bones, that underneath thee lie
Shall live for hell or heaven.

—Reginald Heber, 1812[1]

Christianity is nothing if not a way of thinking about death.
—John Witvliet, 2003[2]

I remember when I first got hold of Johnny Cash's later albums. Listening to them was an eerie experience. It was a true case of an artist embodying his subject matter. In his later years, Cash became laser focused on themes of ultimate significance—particularly pain, death, and the afterlife. His worn and warbled singing only intensified with his age, and as a result these albums chronicle the voice of an oracle on his deathbed, delivering prophecies with a divine kind of gravity. His 2002 album, *American IV*, is particularly ominous. Its opening track, "The Man Comes Around," begins with a haunting recitation of Revelation 6:1–2: "And I heard, as it were the noise of thunder, one of the four beasts saying, Come and see. And I saw, and behold a white horse" (KJV). Then a single acoustic chimes

---

1. Reginald Heber, "Beneath Our Feet and O'er Our Head," (1812). Public Domain.
2. John D. Witvliet, *Worship Seeking Understanding: Windows into Christian Practice* (Grand Rapids, Mich.: Baker, 2003), 291. Much of the language and spirit of this chapter is indebted to Witvliet's powerful explication here.

in with a surprisingly chipper C major groove, while Cash begins to narrate in an old-fashioned country cadence. The whole song is a perfect setup for the rest of the album's ongoing wresting with death and resurrection. But in the opening minutes, all you hear is the confident gallop of Death riding into town. He's here to bat cleanup, Cash announces.

These recordings are not casual listening material. They make me downright uncomfortable. Since the fall of Adam and Eve, death has been an unpleasant constant in the background of every human life. Cash makes us squirm because our age avoids looking death too squarely in the eye. Between plastic surgery, dieting techniques, modern medicine, our obsession with youth culture, and the strategic sequestering of the aged away from our homes and into "facilities," our mortality is hidden from us in ways that it has not been for previous generations.

Naming the Elephant in the Sanctuary

Though we've done all we can to distance ourselves from death, we can't hide from our fear of it. Death is the unspoken anxiety of North American culture. It prompts much of our odd, airbrushed, death-denying obsessions—from CrossFit to botox to gated communities to GMO-phobia. Our people bring all those fears right into the services we plan and lead. Each week, death is the biggest elephant in the sanctuary.

The Christian faith offers answers to the plague of death. Death, ushered into the world by our sin in the First Adam, is undone by the work of the Second: "For as in Adam all die, so in Christ all will be made alive" (1 Cor. 15:22). God tells us that our earthly death is not the end, that dying is not a wall but a doorway.[3] Because of this, Christians can look death in the face and rather pompously taunt with Paul, "Where, O death, is your victory? Where, O death, is your sting?" (1 Cor. 15:55). Jesus declawed death at the cross, and all death can do now is "paw" us into eternity.

A Christian view of death is part of a bigger picture of how everything will end—what theologians call "eschatology." Usually we think of eschatology, if we think of it at all, in the context of end-times scenarios where we're left behind or raptured away, but eschatology is far more than a schedule of events. A biblical view of the end is rooted in Christ's ultimate defeat of death and evil and His full and final redemption and re-creation of the world—a new heavens and a new earth. This eschatological vision is wonderfully summarized in the words of the Nicene Creed, "We look for the resurrection of the dead, and the life of the world to come."

---

3. Witvliet, *Worship Seeking Understanding*, 293.

As worship planners and leaders, we need to think about how we can present this vision of the future in a way that speaks to the very real and present fears we all bring into worship. The metaphor of a mortician, as odd as it sounds, is helpful here. Good morticians are skilled in the caring art of preparing bodies for burial.[4] I believe that a worship pastor is a mortician for the body of Christ, one who faithfully prepares the church for her encounter with death—not as a final experience of defeat—but as a transition into life everlasting.

Worship Is a Wormhole

It's time to get a little mystical. Sci-fi lovers, this is for you. As we think about how worship prepares us for death, let's ponder the wormhole. What's a wormhole? Wormholes are those legendary portals in space, speculated by some scientists and exploited in science fiction, through which unthinkably long galactic distances can be shortcut in an instant. If a ship travels through a wormhole, in the span of a few seconds it can cross distances that would normally take light-years to traverse. Worship is an eschatological wormhole. It shortcuts the gap between our present and God's future. Worship brings the end to us.[5] One of my favorite worship theologians, Jean-Jacques von Allmen, says it this way: "Worship is *par excellence* the sphere in which the future puts forth its buds in the present."[6] Using another metaphor, von Allmen says that worship is where the church gets to "try on its bridal garments."[7]

Heaven is a place of unceasing worship where the created order is gathered around the throne of God to marvel at His holiness (Revelation 4) and extol the worthiness of the Lamb (Revelation 5). It is where joy eradicates mourning (Rev. 7:17; 21:4) and where we all feast at "the great supper of God" (Rev. 19:17). It is the place of perpetual light and perfect healing (Rev. 22:2, 5). And worship is the portal where heaven leaks into our present existence in dribbles. It is the chink in time's armor, the hole in the dam between the now and the not yet. We struggle to see heaven, not because it's not there, but because seeing heaven requires God-given eyes of faith (Heb. 11:1). Our job as worship pastors is to create contexts in worship where eyes can be opened to the reality of heaven and the eschatological vision where God's purposes are realized.[8]

---

4. In many ways, this chapter is a subset of the previous, "The Worship Pastor as Caregiver."

5. Jeremy Begbie calls worship "an 'echo from the future,' a foretaste of something we'll see come to fruition when Christ returns and all things are made new, a not-yet life that we taste in part, but one day the exile will end" (qtd. in Mike Cosper, *Rhythms of Grace: How the Church's Worship Tells the Story of the Gospel* [Wheaton, Ill.: Crossway, 2013], 100).

6. Jean-Jacques von Allmen, *Worship: Its Theology and Practice* (New York: Oxford, 1965), 99.

7. Ibid.

8. There is something pertinent here in the biblical idea of remembrance (Heb. *zkr*; Gk. *anamnesis*)

Give 'em Heaven

If you've read the Bible from cover to cover, you've experienced the book of Revelation and how it hits you as the perfect ending to the story. And once you know the ending to the story, you likely find it there, in your thought, whenever you go back and read other passages. The entire Bible is written with an awareness of its ending. And worship is like that too. As morticians, our job is to prepare the body of Christ for the end, and we do that by planning worship services that are set against the backdrop of that ending.

When your church is gathering for worship, you can remind everyone that they're about to step into a moving stream. Heavenly worship is happening now. It is unceasing and perpetual: "Day and night they never stop saying: 'Holy, holy, holy is the Lord God Almighty,' who was, and is, and is to come" (Rev. 4:8). When we begin to worship as a gathered community each week, we aren't starting from scratch. We're jumping into heaven's praise on the third verse of the song.

So we need to remind people that our worship is connected to the ongoing, celestial worship of heaven. But that's only the tip of the iceberg. We also want to create space in our services for heaven to come down, for people to experience the reality of heaven in our gatherings. So how do we do that?

1. Singing, Praying, and Proclaiming Death

Heaven and earth are very different, yet in worship they are overlapping spheres. And death is one of the places where they clearly overlap. When we talk about heaven in our worship, we need to confront the truth about death. This might seem like a depressing question to think about, but it is necessary to ask: Is there room for death in our worship songs, prayers, readings, and transitional words? The answer we find in the Psalms, the worship and song book of the church, is unequivocally yes. Martin Luther was dissatisfied with the emotional impact

---

when thinking about the mysticism of time. Many ancient and modern commentators have noted that biblical remembrance is a loaded concept. See for instance Dom Gregory Dix, *The Shape of the Liturgy* (New York: Bloomsbury, 1945), 245; John Jefferson Davis, *Worship and the Reality of God: An Evangelical Theology of Real Presence* (Downers Grove, Ill.: InterVarsity, 2010), 137–55. Remembrance isn't a mere recalling of past events; it is a kind of time travel where those doing the remembering become mystically united with those who experienced the past event recalled. Biblical remembrance is why Moses could say to the Israelites who were getting ready to cross the Jordan, most of whom were *not* alive when God had made a covenant with Israel at Sinai, that they were *truly* present on that mountain and that God had made the covenant not merely with their ancestors but with *them* (Deut. 5:2–3). This is why when Jesus said of the Last Supper, "Do this in *remembrance* of me" (Luke 22:19; 1 Cor. 11:24–25), we have warrant to view this sacrament as much more than a mere symbolic memorial. At the Lord's Supper, we are time warped to the cross. Perhaps this is going too far, but I wonder if we can't say that in worship, the future "remembers" us. Heaven experiences an *anamnesis* where it crosses dimensions and becomes mystically yet truly present to us in the here and now.

of translating verses like Psalm 90:12 literally: "Teach us to number our days." While this translation is more faithful to the Hebrew and honoring to the poetic language, Luther wanted to be faithful to the psychology behind the passage when he translated it. So he changed the end to explicitly reference death: "Teach us to reflect on the fact that *we must die*."[9] Or how about this song lyric (Ps. 103:14–16):

> For he knows how we are formed,
>> he remembers that we are dust.
> The life of mortals is like grass,
>> they flourish like a flower of the field.
> The wind blows over it and it is gone,
>> and its place remembers it no more.

Is there room in our worship language for us to reflect on death? To come face to face with our mortality and acknowledge our dependence on God? Singing and praying about the reality of our death is formative. It develops godly sobriety in our people, grounding them in eternal truth in our hyped-up, ephemeral world.

Our understanding of the resurrection, the great and future promise given to us in Christ (Rom. 6:4–11; 1 Cor. 15:22), becomes more powerful as well, offering us relief and hope when it is preceded by a confrontation with the despair of earthly death. Resurrection Sunday was not possible without Good Friday. In the same way, worship's weekly celebration of resurrection needs us to have a firm grasp on the reality of death.

Worship's confrontation with death is not about being morose and morbid. It's being honest about our mortality, and it can be as simple as prayers that lament during confession, "God, we're mindful of the fact that our days are numbered, that not one of us is immune to the consequence of sin—death." It can be a hymn that sings, "Let all mortal flesh keep silence." It is beginning worship by reminding the congregation, "We've gathered today to remember that you and I, though headed for the grave, know that death isn't the last word. Jesus is. And in Him is life everlasting."

Songwriters, take heed. We have pastoral ground to plow here, and we can follow the lead of the church's most sacred, time-tested hymns. The unused, largely forgotten final verse of "O Sacred Head, Now Wounded" sings:

> Be Thou my Consolation, my shield when I must die;
> Remind me of Thy passion when my last hour draws nigh.

---

9. Quoted in James Limburg, *Psalms* (Louisville: Westminster John Knox, 2000), 309.

Mine eyes shall then behold Thee, upon Thy cross shall dwell,
My heart by faith enfolds Thee. Who dieth thus dies well.[10]

Previous generations of songwriters knew that Christianity's ground zero—the cross—is the place where we see not only Christ's death but also our own (Rom. 6:8; Gal. 2:20; Col. 2:20; 3:3). Worship pastors need to create space for us to sing, pray, and proclaim the reality of our own death in worship.

2. Multicultural Expression, Stylistic Diversity

Death is not the only reality we must introduce into our worship. Heaven will be a recreated place where all nations are gathered in worship (Rev. 5:9; 7:9). As worship pastors, we help prepare our flocks for what is beyond death as we explore those multicultural realities in our gatherings. Being a good mortician, then, can include a willingness to sensitively stretch our context's expressive and artistic boundaries through musical diversity. Some congregations and hymnals purposefully employ songs in other languages to remind the church that she is bigger than any one city, country, tribe, or culture, and that the church's end will be unified, multicultural worship.[11] Stylistic diversity of any kind, in this regard, helps our church fly into the wormhole, embodying and even experiencing the future in the present. Perhaps your church isn't ready to sing in another tongue. How about playing your existing songs with different arrangements and instrumentation, or even simply venturing out of a specific era of pop rock sound and into the blues, bluegrass, folk, gospel, Latin, or Dixie jazz?

Notice the shift we've just made there. A discussion about musical style got moved out of the sphere of personal preferences and into the realm of the pastoral, where matters of style are connected with theological and biblical truths. Our worship is not about consumers getting their products; it's a reflection of our eschatology. This is an example of what happens when a worship leader thinks more like a mortician and less like a maître d'. And over time our churches become more generous communities whose eyes are fixed heavenward.[12]

---

10. Attributed to Bernard of Clairvaux, 1153; translated by James Alexander, 1830. Public Domain. Francis of Assisi's classic hymn translated into English, "All Creatures of Our God and King," also has a verse dealing with mortality: "And thou most kind and gentle Death / Waiting to hush our latest breath / O praise Him! Alleluia! / Thou leadest home the child of God / And Christ our Lord the way hath trod."

11. Mainline Protestant denominations (Methodist, Lutheran, Episcopal, Presbyterian, Reformed, etc.), especially in recent decades, have been far more intentional about this than most more thoroughly evangelical traditions. See for example *Global Songs for Worship* (Grand Rapids, Mich.: Faith Alive, 2010); *Lift Up Your Hearts: Psalms, Hymns, and Spiritual Songs* (Grand Rapids, Mich.: Faith Alive, 2012); *Evangelical Lutheran Worship* (Minneapolis: Augsburg Fortress, 2006); *Glory to God: Psalms, Hymns, and Spiritual Songs* (Louisville: Westminster John Knox, 2013).

12. There is so much more to say on the topic of diversity and multicultural worship, and a great

3. Partying at the Table

Celebrating the Lord's Supper is one of the most eschatological events the church can experience in worship because it's the place where we "proclaim the Lord's death until he comes" (1 Cor. 11:26). When Jesus instituted the Supper, He pointed to the end: "I will not drink from this fruit of the vine from now on until that day when I drink it new with you in my Father's kingdom" (Matt. 26:29). Yes, Communion looks back to the cross, but it also looks forward to consummation. The table is a place where we rehearse for the great wedding supper of the Lamb (Rev. 19:6–9, 17–18), the party to end all parties, where everyone gets their fill and is drowned in joy.[13] If Communion points us forward on this trajectory, we as worship pastors need to make this celebration of the future feel less like a funeral and more like a wedding feast. And because music is a significant way that we experience this celebration, we have powerful affective tools at our disposal to set the joyful scene of the end in the present. Joyful experiences at the Lord's Table pastor our flocks to hunger and thirst for the day that is to come. We want our people to long for Christ's return so that their hearts naturally cry out, *Maranatha!* "Come, Lord Jesus" (Rev. 22:20).

Space for Suffering

Another way we prepare the body of Christ for the end is by making room in our worship for expressions of suffering. In our fallen world, suffering is unavoidable. Worship must train God's people to suffer well, and we do that by giving believers a vocabulary of suffering. The words we sing, pray, and speak arm them with ammunition so they're ready for the war of woe when it comes. Don't be afraid of singing songs that highlight suffering. You may find your congregation surprisingly ready (and needy) to come together and lament over what is happening in their lives. Again, we have a great resource in the Psalms, at least sixty-seven of which are regarded as lamentations, either in whole or in part. Knowing that suffering would be an inescapable part of the human experience, God ordained almost half of His inspired songbook to contain songs of suffering.

John Witvliet points out that the suffering psalms all contain three ingredients: honest lament, resilient hope, and stubborn solidarity.[14] We need all three of these ingredients. We need to be able to cry out honestly with words that help us express what suffering feels like:

---

starting place I heartily recommend is Sandra Maria Van Opstal, *The Next Worship: Glorifying God in a Diverse World* (Downers Grove, Ill.: InterVarsity, 2016).

13. See Peter J. Leithart, *Blessed Are the Hungry* (Moscow: Canon, 2000), 166–68.

14. Witvliet, *Worship Seeking Understanding*, 292–95.

- "My God, my God, why have you forsaken me?" (Ps. 22:1).
- "Why have you forgotten me?" (Ps. 42:9).
- "How long will you hide your face from me?" (Ps. 13:1).

This raw, honest language needs to be comingled with hope. So these same psalms continue:

- "You are my strength" (Ps. 22:19).
- "Put your hope in God, for I will yet praise him, my Savior and my God" (Ps. 42:11).
- "But I trust in your unfailing love" (Ps. 13:5).

And this hope-filled lament must be done in communal solidarity. Witvliet rightly insists: "Dying well is not possible alone. 'Dying well' is a verb that requires a plural subject. Dying is a social act. In the Christian community, one never dies alone (or at least the Christian community should not let this happen). The Christian community together faces death. Only the Christian *community*, with the strength and encouragement of God's Spirit, can ever be said to have faced death well."[15]

All three of these ingredients—honesty, hope, and solidarity—are necessary to suffer well, and this is why we need to be able to express our suffering in worship. Plan your worship sets and liturgies with these ingredients in mind.

Leading Worship for the Grieving

We mentioned earlier the need for songs which confront death and how many great hymns have included verses or expressions which deal with death. So why have those verses been edited out of so many hymnals today? There is a good pastoral reason for this. We need to be sensitive to how we wield the words of suffering and death before the people of God. Some people are in the throes of death's crises, and if we cavalierly brandish Death's name, we can inadvertently cut wide their bleeding heart. So our speech and song need to be pastorally sensitive, and we must go about our worship planning with prayer and wisdom, aware of the condition of our flock.

These thoughts lead us to a common pastoral ministry that doesn't often get discussed—funerals. Worship leaders are regularly called on to provide music and even service planning for memorial services. These times are precious and vital moments in the life of any worship pastor, and we should be ready to engage

---

15. Ibid., 294–95, emphasis in original.

them. Remember, funerals are church worship services. Here are three insights I've gained in planning and leading worship for families walking through the valley of the shadow of death.

1. Make service planning with families more like a counseling session and less like a business meeting. Meeting with a grieving family to go over the memorial service for a loved one is a sacred time and a key pastoral moment. Your normal weekly routines go out the window when someone dies and a funeral is being planned. Your job in that moment is to listen, listen, and listen some more. Expect the meeting to go longer than you think. Expect rabbit trails. Expect sobbing and silence. Expect numbness. Expect chaos. Expect indecision.

Grieving families often face a paralyzing amount of decisions. They are over-loaded with choices and details—casket, cremation, burial site, will, insurance, property. One of the best things we can do in this pastoral moment is to make service planning as easy as possible. Sometimes family members and friends come to you with a list of ideas. Make it easy for these ideas to be implemented. Other times, the family hasn't thought about what the service should look like at all. Come ready with a service template and ideas and options for songs and Scripture readings. If they're struggling to make a decision, make some for them. I often say, "A lot of people love this passage, and I think it would be perfect if one of your family members read it." Whatever you do, above all, "weep with those who weep" (Rom. 12:15). Funeral planning is less about getting the tasks done and more about ministering Christ's love and grace to weary mourners.

2. At the funeral, lean into pain and away from platitudes. I've seen how awk-wardness and a sense of the gravity of the memorial service can cause the best worship leaders to buckle under the pressure. In less liturgical settings, there may be an expectation that a worship leader should do some talking, and I've heard people say some really unfortunate things—even hurtful, wounding things— that can linger in the memories of friends and family members. My advice is to plan out what you're going to say, say it, and then (pardon me) shut up and play. Don't ad-lib. Our role in the service is to be a calm, stable, and sensitive presence, leaning into the pain of those around us. Avoid platitudes like, "She's in a better place," or, "We should all trust in God's sovereignty," and instead rely upon the Word of God and the hope of the gospel. A memorial service is a time, in Scripture and song, to make much of Jesus' death and the hope of resurrection. And it is a time to worship.

3. Be ready to break your normal rules. The ultimate goal of a funeral service, as with any time of worship, is the glory of God. That said, if there is one ser-vice when your planning and leadership should be aimed at a narrow group of people, it's this one. The memorial service is a vital way the Holy Spirit ministers particularly to the closest friends and family, and part of the purpose of your leadership in that time is to simply help the pain of death hurt a little bit less for them, if only for a brief moment. Because of this particular focus, unique to the funeral, I find myself breaking a lot of my normal "rules" in worship planning.

I'll be honest. I've sung some awful songs at funerals. I've sung cheesy country songs. I've sung old-school eye-roller worship songs with sappy sentimentality and spurious theology. I've sung and led hymns I can't stand. I've made a fool of myself and nearly violated my conscience. And would I do it again? Absolutely. Why? Because a pastor gets busy weeping with those who weep. And when the people are weeping, our job in that moment is to try to lessen the pain, not make sure we've got every single theological duck in a row. I'm not suggesting that you throw your theology out the window. But grief requires sensitivity to where people are in the moment. Was Jesus worried about compromise when a grieving, sinful woman was repenting as she washed His feet with her hair (Luke 7:36–50)? Was Jesus concerned about the religious establishment's raised eyebrows as He ministered to a broken, heathen adulteress at a well in Sychar (John 4)? Was He worried about all the "worship rules" associated with the Sabbath as He was healing the sick (Mark 3:1–5)? God help us if all our so-called convictions prevent us from running to the need right in front of us, from falling into the dirt with them, from being conduits of His grace, love, forgiveness, and comfort. Death demands the rule of love (1 Corinthians 13).

Moral compromise is not an option, of course. I am simply saying that some flexibility is required, more so in a funeral than in a regular worship service. We need to exercise pastoral instincts.

Only He Can Lead Us

In a day and age obsessed with now, the need for worship leaders to guide their people in honest preparation for death is more pressing than ever. And yet we must remember that there is truly only One who can lead us in worship, through death, and into life. So we look to Him who is able to keep us from stumbling and present us before His glorious presence without fault and with great joy (Jude 24).

Come, Lord Jesus, and lead us from death to life.

13

THE WORSHIP PASTOR AS EMOTIONAL SHEPHERD

The thing you have to do is make people feel their own emotions.
—Bob Dylan, 2012[1]

If Jesus is in your heart, someone should notify your face.
—1990s T-shirt

The story of martyr Dietrich Bonhoeffer is one of unflinching bravery in the face of torture, injustice, evil, and death. After an unsuccessful attempt to take the life of Adolf Hitler, Bonhoeffer and his crew were rounded up, placed in internment camps, and killed. Bonhoeffer spent some time in prison awaiting his death, and though that would be enough to make any man buckle, the accounts of his time there, drawn from the testimonies of others and his own letters, reveal a steady and spiritually strong Christian. What was the source of his faithful fortitude?

Jim Belcher shares a story of a secret training ground in the small German town of Finkenwalde where Bonhoeffer had spent time retreating from the world in a modern monastic community.[2] The two years Bonhoeffer spent as a leader at this underground seminary for the Confessing Church became what one biographer would call Bonhoeffer's "strength training for the moral crucible" to come.[3] Belcher concludes that it was the daily rituals, especially the rhythms of worship, which fortified Bonhoeffer's emotional muscles so he was prepared for the seismic ups and downs he would experience on the path to death in the internment camp.

The Nazis were masters of psychological and emotional warfare. This mastery commonly took the form of prescribed rituals and propaganda, and it is part of what enabled them to secure and subdue the German people's allegiance as the

---

1. Quoted in Bob Batchelor, *Bob Dylan: A Biography* (Santa Barbara, Calif.: Greenwood, 2014), 123.
2. Jim Belcher, "The Secret of Finkenwalde: Liturgical Treason," in *Bonhoeffer, Christ and Culture,* ed. Keith L. Johnson and Timothy Larsen (Downers Grove, Ill.: InterVarsity, 2013), 191–210.
3. Craig J. Slane, *Bonhoeffer as Martyr: Social Responsibility and Modern Christian Commitment* (Grand Rapids, Mich.: Brazos, 2004), 239; quoted in Belcher, "Secret," 199.

Third Reich rose to power. Bonhoeffer understood that to withstand the emotional onslaught that would break down the ordinary German, Christians needed a muscular "counter-liturgy."[4] His idea would be put to the test during his time in prison. Bonhoeffer embodied the reality that worship is where our emotions are trained and shepherded in the truth.

Why Should We Care About Emotional Formation?

For whatever reason, many people today believe that being emotional or expressing emotion is a sign of immaturity. As philosopher Robert Roberts bluntly puts it, "When we describe someone as an 'emotional type,' we do not intend to give a compliment."[5] Our suspicion of emotions leads us to believe that maturity means keeping them at bay or getting rid of them altogether.[6] We've all experienced what it is like when emotions run amuck. They turn people into relational hurricanes, where they leave nothing but the carnage of broken relationships in their path. But vilifying emotions is like throwing out the baby with the bathwater. Roberts and others argue that these "emotional problems" which plague humanity in general and worship in particular are not problems with emotions themselves but with poorly formed emotional responses.

Our emotions and affections are simply a part of our God-given makeup, our humanity. It's telling that we refer to emotionless people as "robots." We do this because we intuitively realize that when people lose the ability to feel and express emotion, we recognize their situation as less than human. When God summarized the central duty of humanity as loving Him with heart, soul, mind, and strength (Deut. 6:5; Matt. 22:37), He was saying that being human is a holistic endeavor. God wants *all* of us, including our emotions. If God's plan is to redeem and restore us as humans, then His best for us includes a good, healthy emotional life.

Getting to the Heart of the Matter[7]

As we saw in chapter 4, the Christian tradition in the line of Augustine argues that our affections—our faculties of desire and emotion—sit at the core of who we are. They influence how we operate even more than our other God-given

---

4. Belcher, "The Secret of Finkenwalde," 202.

5. Robert C. Roberts, *Spiritual Emotions: A Psychology of Christian Virtues* (Grand Rapids, Mich.: Eerdmans, 2007), 14.

6. Ibid., 15.

7. See also chapter 11, "The Worship Pastor as Caregiver," in the section titled "Worship gets to the heart of the matter."

faculties, our will and mind.[8] Our decision-making is deeply rooted in the want-ing and desiring parts of us.[9] This is why Jesus taught so much on the heart and its fruit (Luke 6:45; Matt. 5–7). We are gut- and heart-based creatures before we are head-based intellectuals. We default to rationalizing what we love and want ("it's only Diet Coke; it's not harmful"), not the other way around. Ashley Null has summarized this Augustinian and Reformational anthropology by saying, "What the heart loves, the will chooses, and the mind justifies."[10]

And while our affections are distinct from our emotions, our emotions play a significant role in expressing and determining our affections. If something feels good or brings us an intense sensation of a positive emotion like joy, we want more of it, and we pursue the means to obtain it. This is the essence of addiction and explains why it is so hard to break bad habits. We can rationalize all we want about health risks, social consequences, and the like, but cogent arguments rarely have power to override our "wanter."

Our emotions express our desires and enable us to know and experience truth more completely. I can choose, by intellectual assent, to love my wife, but my love for her is deepened and fulfilled when I don't just assent to it but I *feel* it. I can acknowledge conceptually that my sin offends God and violates our covenant relationship, but my understanding is more complete when tears are streaming down my face and my heart is aching in contrition. This is not to say that emo-tions understand more truth than our minds do or are better than intellectual understanding. They complement and complete one another. Our emotions help us know and experience truth more fully and deeply. Emotions help us see the truth in the best of light for what it really is. In the words of Jonathan Edwards,

8. Theologian Simeon Zahl has helpfully labeled this anthropological perspective "Affective Augustinianism." See his "The Drama of Agency: Affective Augustinianism and Galatians," in *Galatians and Christian Theology: Justification, the Gospel, and Ethics in Paul's Letter*, ed. Mark W. Elliott, et al. (Grand Rapids, Mich.: Baker, 2014), 335–52. It is a Christian tradition of thought, rooted in the Bible, elucidated by Augustine in response to Platonic/Aristotelian anthropology, carried into veins of medieval Christian tradition, championed in the Protestant Reformation (especially in the theology of Philip Melanchthon and Thomas Cranmer), and propelled forward in various traditions and figures including Puritanism, Methodism, and Jonathan Edwards. See also Ashley Null, "Thomas Cranmer and Tudor Evangelicalism," in *The Emergence of Evangelicalism: Exploring Historical Continuities*, ed. Kenneth J. Stewart and Michael A. G. Haykin (Nottingham: Apollos, 2008), 236; and Ashley Null, *Thomas Cranmer's Doctrine of Repentance: Renewing the Power to Love* (Oxford: Oxford University Press, 2000), 98–102, 130–31, 157–212.

9. This tradition was enlivened to me through James K. A. Smith's outstanding work, *Desiring the Kingdom: Worship, Worldview, and Cultural Formation* (Grand Rapids, Mich.: Baker, 2009), and much of this section is a summary of his introduction and first chapter. I have found this anthropological vision tightened by a more thoroughly Reformational outlook, especially in the ongoing work of Ashley Null and Simeon Zahl, mentioned above in n. 8.

10. Ashley Null, "Dr. Ashley Null on Thomas Cranmer," *Anglican Church League News*, September 2001, accessed June 12, 2015, http://acl.asn.au/resources/dr-ashley-null-on-thomas-cranmer/. See also Null, *Thomas Cranmer's Doctrine of Repentance*, 100–101.

God wants "to stir up the pure minds of the saints, and quicken their affections, by bringing the great things of religion to their remembrance, and *setting them before them in their proper colors*."[11]

If this is true, then the right formation of desire—and the right orientation of emotions—sits at the heart (pun intended) of real and lasting change in individuals. This is why the Reformers were fond of articulating Christian conversion in terms of the "renovation of the affections."[12] Emotional formation is a key component in how we effectively see disciples grow into mature believers in Christ.

Emotional Maturity and Worship

As we have said, emotional maturity isn't emotionless-ness. Rather, it is the right ordering of the emotions so that we feel the right feelings at the right times, rightly expressed in light of the truth. Jesus is the archetype of rightly ordered emotions, and he embodied this in several ways:

- Deep grief at the death of a loved one (John 11:35–36)
- Just anger at injustice (Matt. 21:12–13)
- Indignant woe toward self-righteousness (Matt. 23:13–39)
- Heavy sadness over sin (Luke 19:41–44)
- Anxious fear when facing difficulty (Mark 14:32–36)
- Peaceful resolve in a hope to come (John 14:25–27)
- Joyful merriment when partying with friends (Luke 7:34)

Worship is an emotionally charged event. It's full of evocative aesthetics, grand metanarratives, and physical-spiritual interplay.[13] Worship does something

---

11. Jonathan Edwards, *Religious Affections*, ed. John E. Smith (New Haven, Conn.: Yale University Press, 1959), 116, emphasis mine.

12. See especially Philip Melanchthon on "Sin," in his *Commonplaces: Loci Communes 1521*, tr. Christian Preus (St. Louis, Mo.: Concordia, 2014), 37–60; and Ashley Null's helpful explanation in "Tudor Evangelicalism," 238–46.

13. I wish we had more space to discuss how aesthetics play into our emotional (and therefore spiritual) formation. Suffice it to say that good aesthetics in worship—everything from music to architecture to symbol, to decorative "accessories" to rhetoric to storytelling to art—contribute to our emotional health. We don't experience the living and active Word of God in worship apart from aesthetics. Dan Siedell has pointed out to me that Nathan's confrontation of David through telling a *story*, effectively proclaiming the Word of God in the form of the law of accusation, created a context for the Word of God to pierce the heart through an *aesthetic* moment. As Siedell said, "The proclamation of Law and Gospel are aesthetic events" (from a tweet on March 15, 2014). Aesthetics also contribute to our eschatological orientation. As Jean-Jacques von Allmen masterfully said, "I think we must dare to say that liturgical expression must strive after beauty, since it is a process of nuptial preparation, and since the church of which [worship] is the epiphany is called to appear before its Lord 'in splendor, without spot or wrinkle or any such thing' (Eph. 5:27)." *Worship: Its Theology and Practice* (New York: Oxford, 1965), 103.

to and with our emotions, and it becomes a context where they are trained into health. Think of worship like a gym where our emotions get a chance to work out and train.[14]

When we plan and lead worship services, we hold the flock's feelings in our hands. The context we create can either haphazardly manipulate emotions or intentionally guide people toward "faithful feelings."[15] Worship leaders are emotional shepherds.

What Emotions Are and How They Work

One helpful way to understand emotions is to differentiate them from moods. We can think of a mood as an untethered feeling. When someone is in a "bad mood," they are in a general state of feeling sour. Emotion, on the other hand, is more like a mood with an object.[16] As Jeremy Begbie puts it, "I am not angry in the abstract, but angry about something or angry *at* someone."[17]

More precisely, Robert Roberts defines emotions as "concern-based construals," meaning that our emotions are tethered to concerns, things we care about.[18] This makes a lot of sense when we think about the situations where people tend to get the most emotional. Those concerned about justice for the poor often get fired up when politics are discussed. Those who have lost a loved one break down in tears at their remembrance. Our emotions are based in our concerns. But they are also *construals*, meaning "ways of perceiving." For instance, when I'm experiencing the emotion of joy in worship, it is (hopefully) because I am seeing the gospel as good. When I'm experiencing wonder in worship, it is (hopefully) because I am perceiving God as beautiful and awe inspiring. In this way, it is well said that emotions are "the eyes of our hearts."[19]

Putting all this together, then, emotional formation involves growing in how the eyes of our hearts can see things "Christianly" in our concerns—aligning our inner desires to God-honoring ends. If I want my brothers and sisters to be rightly concerned in worship (i.e., concerned in a Christian way) about the gravity

---

14. This is an allusion to and adaptation of Ambrose, who called the Psalms a "complete gymnasium for the soul."

15. I owe this helpful phrase to Matthew A. Elliott, *Faithful Feelings: Rethinking Emotion in the New Testament* (Grand Rapids, Mich.: Kregel, 2006); see also Jeremy S. Begbie, "Faithful Feelings: Music and Emotion in Worship," in *Resonant Witness: Conversations between Music and Theology*, ed. Jeremy S. Begbie and Steven R. Guthrie (Grand Rapids, Mich.: Eerdmans, 2011), 323–54.

16. Simeon Zahl, "On the Affective Salience of Doctrines," *Modern Theology* 31, no. 3 (July 2015): 440.

17. Begbie, "Faithful Feelings," 331.

18. Roberts, *Spiritual Emotions*, 11.

19. Adam Pelser, "Reasons of the Heart: Emotions in Apologetics," *Christian Research Journal* 38, no. 1 (2015): 34.

of their sin, I want them to see their sin not just as embarrassing, perhaps a sub-Christian emotion, but as offensive to God. Likewise, I want their experience of the gospel's joy to be because the eyes of their hearts see Christ's substitutionary sacrifice on the cross as inspiring.

Worship is a place where issues of ultimate human concern are addressed—sin, guilt, death, forgiveness, freedom, eternal life. When we come before our Maker in worship, we all bring these ultimate concerns to the table. Worship devoid of emotion is a dangerous thing because it can train us into believing that these concerns really aren't concerns. This is why emotionless worship is just as toxic to our faith as haphazardly emotional worship is.[20] If our human wiring is to feel what we are concerned about, then *not* feeling what we *should* be concerned about subconsciously trains us to believe that these ultimate concerns are either untrue or not real. Emotional shepherds must strive to create contexts where people can feel the right emotions at the right times. This tethering of feelings to their rightful concerns and objects is at the heart of faithful emotional shepherding in worship.

Music Is a Key Ingredient

In a previous chapter, we discussed music's unique power to move and shape us.[21] Martin Luther descriptively called music "a mistress and governess of . . . emotions."[22] One artist depicted the music-making process as "painting with emotion."[23] In Israel's worship, King David was well aware of the affective power of music, which is why when the temple was built and worship became established, he employed musicians from within the priesthood to expand the musical expression of Israel's liturgy (1 Chronicles 25). As one commentator put it, "Moses prescribed a liturgy without music and singing, but David, like a Mozart, transformed liturgy into opera."[24]

---

20. All worship encounters, not just the ones that *appear* to be emotional, are emotionally formative. Leaders in worship who, in the name of avoiding emotional manipulation, strip their services of emotionally charged music or expressive prayers and sermons must recognize that such services still shape people's emotions. In many instances, such deemotionalized worship trains worshipers to believe that godliness is equivalent to emotional constraint. The virtue of self-control is twisted in meaning and co-opted in support, resulting in worshipers who look more like the products of Greek stoicism or dispassionate Eastern mysticism than they do a robustly Christian *shalom*. A worship service which creates a cage around the emotions in the names of decency, orderliness, and self-control—all good, biblical ideas in and of themselves—is just as mal-formative as the emotionally unhinged, wildly charismatic free-for-alls that are so often uniquely vilified in these conversations.

21. See chapter 5, "The Worship Pastor as Prayer Leader."

22. Martin Luther, "Preface to Georg Rhau's Symphoniae Iucundae," *Luther's Works*, vol. 53, ed. Ulrich S. Leupold (Philadelphia: Fortress, 1965), 323. Luther used the Latin word *affectuum*.

23. From the online video, "Why We Create Music," from *Already Alive*, accessed June 11, 2015, http://vimeo.com/80072357.

24. Bruce Waltke and James Houston, *The Psalms as Christian Worship: A Historical Commentary*

The path to emotional maturity can be described as moving from what we *do* feel to what we *should* feel in a given situation. For instance, though fear is appropriate when facing death, a Christian whose emotions are matured will not feel hopelessly despondent and despairing, for their emotions have been trained that "to live is Christ, [but] to die is gain" (Phil. 1:21).

Music's ability to describe, mimic, and as a result engender feelings makes it uniquely suited as a vehicle to traverse the terrain toward emotional maturity.[25] Emotions can be trained through music's power to shift feeling from one state to another. Paul and Silas knew that though they were imprisoned, they should feel hopeful, not anguished, because the gospel led them to that hopefulness. So they sang, and their spirits were lifted (Acts 16:25). David helped shift Saul's emotions from hysteria to peace through playing the lyre (1 Sam. 16:23). When we grasp music's power to move a person's emotions from one state to another, we can then put the pieces together in helping people feel what they should feel at a given moment in worship.[26]

Important Considerations for Emotional Shepherding

Manipulation versus Shepherding

Inevitably, discussions like this one bring up the concern of manipulation. Are we coercing people to feel things they don't necessarily want to feel? While it is wrong to suggest that we are forcing someone to feel a certain way, it is true to say that we are advocating a right and wrong way to feel. This kind of advocacy is a part of intentional, pastoral leadership—shepherding—which is very different from manipulation. Manipulation implies that we are using people for our ends, while shepherding is about our intentions and the trust we have with people. As Brian Wren reminds us, "Without trust and trustworthiness, persuasion becomes manipulation."[27] Both a manipulator and a shepherd have a goal in mind for the people they lead. But a manipulator treats people as objects to force and cajole. A shepherd treats people as hearts to woo and to guide. A shepherd loves the people. A manipulator uses the people. A shepherd desires to persuade people in order to lead them to a destination that is good for them. A shepherd is not just getting people to feel things for feelings' sake, mere sensationalism or sentimentalism.

(Grand Rapids, Mich.: Eerdmans, 2010), 129.

25. See Begbie, "Faithful Feelings."

26. See the brief but helpful discussion of using music to mature the emotions in Scott Aniol, *Worship in Song: A Biblical Approach to Music and Worship* (Winona Lake, Ind.: BMH Books, 2009), 164–71.

27. Brian Wren, *Praying Twice: The Music and Words of Congregational Song* (Louisville: Westminster John Knox, 2000), 74.

Rather, a shepherd tries to help people's hearts to see the truths of the gospel, as Edwards said, "in their proper colors."

What Our Job Is and Is Not

The metaphor of a shepherd is helpful to parse what our job is and is not. A shepherd guides the flock to the stream, but he can't make one of the sheep actually drink. The sheep's inner desire—the instinct we call thirst—compels it to bend down and lap up water. The sheep does not think, "The shepherd is telling me to drink, and he is reminding me that it is good for me, so I will." No, the sheep's more primal urge kicks in, and it drinks. This is the way emotional shepherding works. Our job is to guide the people of God to various emotional "streams" along the way of worship, but we can't make them actually feel in a lasting, Christian, formative way. They do so only by a holy desire inside of them and outside of our control. The Bible tells us that it is the Holy Spirit in us who rightly desires and compels us, against the flesh, to hunger and thirst for righteousness (Gal. 5:16–25). So while emotional shepherds lead the people to contexts of faithful feeling, and while those contexts we create compel, evoke, and even provoke those feelings, the Spirit causes people to feel in a godly, soul-shaping way. We must always remember this division of labor.

Tethering Emotions to the Gospel's Story

So how do we do this? Guiding the flock toward faithful feelings is primarily a matter of tethering their emotions to the story of the gospel. We must be careful not to think of emotional formation in worship apart from the gospel. Truth is understood most deeply when it is apprehended not just intellectually but also emotionally, so if we want our people to be molded into the image of Christ, we must think about how to tether their emotions to the truths of His story.

Though it may be tempting, we cannot simply ritualize a series of emotionally charged practices. What do I mean? Just think about the countless worship services out there filled with highly emotionalized rituals: loud singing, dancing, shouting, and clapping. Those rituals in and of themselves won't aid long-term growth toward Christian maturity. And it would be erroneous to think that all we need to do is add new rituals that develop absent emotions. I have in mind here recent cries for more lamentation and contrition in worship. While these cries are necessary voices, the practices they advocate will prove ineffectual in forming people unless those practices are tethered to lamentation and contrition as part of the gospel's story of sin and salvation.

The gospel is the only thing that can fuel and form Christian growth and maturity in us, for it is Christ's love that compels us (2 Cor. 5:14). For a Christian, all true virtue, character, and emotional health is borne of grace alone through faith alone in Christ alone. This is why emotional experiences in worship that are not tethered to the gospel's story can actually be mal-formative.[28]

Taking People on the Gospel's Emotional Journey

The Gospel Story in Emotions

Previously, I summarized the gospel narrative of a worship service as the glory of God, the gravity of sin, and the grandeur of grace.[29] In light of this narrative, we need to ask: As believers journey through the gospel story, what do we hope they feel at various points? Let's start by exploring this visually. (See fig. 4.)

Figure 4

THE EMOTIONAL JOURNEY OF A WORSHIP SERVICE SHAPED ACCORDING TO THE GOSPEL

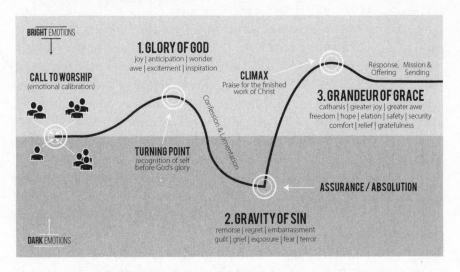

We can observe several things:

First, we are dealing with the full spectrum of emotions. Our hope is that a

---

28. Though I don't know whether Roberts would agree with how starkly I have painted this picture, there is certainly an overlap of thought here with his statement, "Emotions can be distinctively Christian only if they can be shaped by Christian concepts and the Christian narrative." *Spiritual Emotions*, 29.

29. See chapter 7, "The Worship Pastor as War General."

worship service carries the potential of guiding people through a (ritualized) journey that includes different feelings on the spectrum of human emotion. If worship deals with humanity's most fundamental human concerns, we should expect to encounter the broadest of emotional ranges—from the bright emotions to the dark ones.

Second, we're noting the kinds of emotions our people probably feel, but not all emotions are the best or the healthiest. For instance, Roberts points out that there are less and more formative ways to experience confession. If confession is merely regret, fear of punishment, or embarrassment, the eyes of the heart aren't seeing our sin in a way that can be formed by the gospel. By contrast, dismay at sin, guilt, and a grief whose object is the sorrow of God's own heart is a more Christian and formative way to feel in this moment.[30] Though we can't change people's hearts, part of our job at these given emotional moments is to pray and lead in ways that guide people toward the *right* emotion, the *right* way for their heart to see the truths about God and themselves.

Third, the gospel story dictates the emotions. When we enter into worship, our hope is to create a context where people can feel the joy, anticipation, wonder, awe, and excitement of gathering before the Ancient of Days in all His glorious, holy splendor. We imagine ourselves among the heavenly host shouting, "Holy, holy, holy!" (Isa. 6:3; Rev. 4:8). But such glory begins to make us uneasy, and a sense of inadequacy, even anxiety, creeps in. Like Isaiah, God's glory leads to confession, where the dark and lowly feelings of grief, remorse, fear, and contrition are present. Then in the middle of our confession, in an emotionally steep and powerful moment, God rushes in and offers the Word of Christ to us: "All is forgiven! It is finished!" The following moments are the emotional climax of the narrative—catharsis, greater joy, gratefulness, hope, safety, comfort.

Fourth, the lower the lows, the higher the highs. Emotionally, if we're aiming for a climactic reception of the gospel's declaration of Christ's finished work, some of the best preparation is to set confession and lamentation in an appropriately low place. Just as a light shines brightest on the darkest backdrop, and just as a mountain peak appears highest from the deepest point in the valley, so the climactic gospel can feel only as soaring as the confession is honest, dark, and deep.

Fifth, notice the beginning of the service. As emotional shepherds, we need to be aware that our sheep enter worship all over the emotional map. Some are nerve wracked after wrangling their kids all morning. Some are feeling guilty after a week of running from God. Some are bored and tired. As a worship leader, have you ever noticed that no matter what you do for the first five to ten minutes of

---

30. Roberts, *Spiritual Emotions*, 97–105.

the service (welcome the people, sing a song, read Scripture), they all seem pretty lost, distracted, and glazed over? It takes time to rally people emotionally, and we need to give space for that.[31]

Sixth, this emotional storyline is meant to fit all kinds of worship expressions. In the next chapter, we will address how this emotional shape can fit almost any worship context, whether a song-set-driven or a highly liturgical one, whether more preaching centric or sacramental. I'm not interested in dictating a one-size-fits-all approach to worship. My hope is that figure 4 can open our eyes to the gospel-shaped emotional contours already (or potentially) embedded in our worship services so that we can be shepherds of the story's corresponding emotions.

Making the Narrative Flow

In any context—from liturgical to free—the biggest killer of emotional experience is a break in flow.[32] My charismatic friends, who probably have the best command of the affective nature of worship's flow, often feel that liturgical worship is poor here. But I contend that liturgical worship can have a powerfully seamless emotional flow if it is led well. Emotional flow is far less about style and structure and far more about leadership, awareness, and intuition. It is a learned skill that is honed through practice.[33] Here are three ways continuous emotional flow can be guarded by a worship leader.

1. Careful Management of Transitions

An emotional shepherd concerned with worship's unbroken, undistracted narrative doesn't just think about worship's planned content. She thinks about the gaps in between. She begins to see the gaps as content too. If songs are sung back to back, the musical transitions are thought through and intentional. If transitions are verbal, the leader is very cognizant of how timing and delivery of their words in those moments affect the emotional movement between two points in the service.

---

31. This is why, in some traditions, people are asked to quiet their hearts (and mouths) and meditate during the Prelude, as a preparation for the worship service. Participating in and leading such services has blessed me. However, the downside in my experience has been that it (a) almost always sets a somber emotional affect (which may sometimes actually be appropriate) and (b) stifles communal interaction at the beginning of a service, which often catalyzes joy and togetherness on the front end.

32. We will expand on the concept of flow in worship beyond the emotional aspects in chapter 16, "The Worship Pastor as Tour Guide."

33. Interestingly, I wonder whether the rhetorical and performance arts—particularly acting—aren't uniquely suited as training mechanisms for worship leaders interested in honing the craft of emotional flow. Just my own anecdotal experience tells me that my training as an actor and singer in college has equipped me with some of the very tools I am about to mention.

2. Artful Use of Disposition, Countenance, Tone, and Cadence

In all moments of the service, whether in the planned content, the transitions, or even the spontaneous gaps, an emotional shepherd is aware of how their countenance and demeanor contribute to the desired affect. Furthermore, the tone, cadence, and expression of one's voice—whether singing or leading a liturgy—is immensely important in keeping emotional flow stable and appropriate. I have heard countless liturgists and Scripture readers slip into an odd orator's voice that sounds more appropriate for an emcee at a high-class event than a worship service. I have witnessed song leaders who introspectively look down, slouching in such an underwhelming fashion that the glorious truths they're singing about actually appear less glorious than they should. It should be said that disposition, countenance, tone, and cadence are tricky and highly context specific, depending on one's cultural mores and denominational practices. Study and mastery of them, though, is critical in contributing to a worship service's seamless emotional flow.

3. Masterful Employment of Music's Affective Qualities

From key selection to arrangement, from time signatures to BPMs, from chord movement to instrumentation, our many subtle and not-so-subtle musical choices make all the difference in the flow of the emotional experience. One of the most obvious agents of musical flow in modern worship contexts is the key/synth pad, embedded throughout the worship set—sometimes alone, sometimes overwhelmed by other sound, but always there. I have seen keys used very effectively as emotional glue to keep worshipers on the path.[34]

Where a song lies in a vocal range can also be an affective choice. I often set songs in higher keys in climactic moments of the worship service because I want the congregation's physical strain to reach those notes to match the intensity of the emotional moment. When a musical moment or a song lyric is intimate, stripping down instrumentation (for bands and orchestras) or decluttering your chord structures (for organists and pianists) is a powerfully affective move that aids in people feeling what is being sung. The best organists as well as the best modern worship leaders I know have a strong intuition about emotional moments

---

34. As an aside, I have seen the key pad receive its fair share of mockery in online forums. It has become a symbol of everything that is supposedly cliché about modern worship. Some even go so far as to tease that you can conjure the presence of the Holy Spirit in the room by swelling the keys. Though some might ignorantly put too much stock in the spiritualization of synthesized sound, I still believe it's important not to let the ignorance of some people obscure important wisdom—namely, that some traditions have an intuitive sense of emotional flow and how sustained sound in their contexts can aid in that.

in a worship service and what musical choices best serve those affects. These are healthy shepherding instincts.[35]

The End Game

The goal in all of this is that worshipers begin to experience what rightly ordered emotions feel like. Our desire in our flock's emotional formation is to help them learn to love the right things and to see the world in light of the gospel. We hope that because people have felt contrition in a moment of confession, they are better equipped to be truly, deeply, and appropriately sorrowful over their sin the other six days of the week. We hope that the relieving catharsis experienced by the gospel's proclamation trains the hearts of our people that the gospel truly *is* the most satisfying answer we will ever find to our deepest problems, quenching the urge to seek satisfaction elsewhere. The goal is that the emotions experienced in worship become part of the inner core of each Christian. Our desire is not only that worshipers *feel* joy, hope, and peace in worship but also that they *become* people of joy, hope, and peace outside of worship, which is ultimately achieved when combined with efforts outside the worship service.[36] For us, the call is clear: "Be shepherds of God's flock . . . not because you must, but because you are willing" (1 Peter 5:2).

O Desire of Nations, may Your Spirit be our longing
until the day You make all things new.

---

35. Musicologist Joshua Busman has noted the complexities of how one song's *arrangement* and *context* can greatly impact how it is received emotionally and theologically. Busman walks through a fascinating case study of the hit worship song, "God of this City." See his "'Yet to Come' or 'Still to be Done'? Evangelical Worship and the Power of 'Prophetic' Songs," in *Congregational Music-Making and Community in a Mediated Age*, ed. Anna Nekola and Tom Wagner (Farnham, England: Ashgate, 2015), 199–214.

36. I'm so thankful for this critical insight from my friend Dr. Ryan West, whose own studies in the philosophy of emotion have greatly influenced and aided my thinking in this chapter.

14

THE WORSHIP PASTOR AS LITURGICAL ARCHITECT

Christian worship is a "re-presentation" of the Gospel.
—Bryan Chapell, 2009[1]

When the narrative of the person and work of Jesus Christ permeates
worship consistently, worship itself becomes the message.
—Constance Cherry, 2010[2]

As a child, I loved drawing. The adults around me were always affirming my artistic abilities, and because of that I wanted to someday be an architect. I thought to myself, "People will pay me money to draw buildings all day!" I loved precision sketching, straight edges, tight angles, and neatly traced outlines. My mind was electrified as I visualized three-dimensional reality in two-dimensional space. In the language of that era, I thought architecture was pretty rad.

God rerouted that vocational direction on a student ministry retreat when I was fifteen years old. That morning, as I opened my Bible and read, I pondered the fact that Jesus' disciples left their nets in response to His call (Matt. 4:19–20). At the time, I thought of the "nets" as my own future career. My young heart heard God say, "Zac, you want to be an architect; I want you for pastoral ministry." That was a turning point for me.

Recently, though, I've come to a different perspective on that redirection experience, shifting from wanting to be an architect to a pastor. I don't see these two callings as mutually exclusive. For the worship pastor, the passions that drive

---

1. Bryan Chapell, *Christ-Centered Worship: Letting the Gospel Shape Our Practice* (Grand Rapids, Mich.: Baker, 2009), 116.

2. Constance Cherry, *The Worship Architect: A Blueprint for Designing Culturally Relevant and Biblically Faithful Services* (Grand Rapids, Mich.: Baker, 2010), 25.

service planning and leading are passions that also propel an architect. I loved that in architecture you can sketch something from your head and then see that drawing realized in life-sized, brick-and-mortar reality. An architect's job is, quite literally, to make dreams come true. But it's demanding work. You not only have to think about the forest, but you also have to keep in mind each individual tree. You have to obsess over the minutiae of plumbing, electricity, building codes, and construction phases, all the while never losing sight of the big picture of how it all fits together. Every detail is incredibly important, and yet the specifics cannot be considered independently from the master plan. I find that this commitment to navigate the worlds of small details and big vision is similar to the conviction that a pastorally minded worship leader needs. That's why I believe that a worship pastor is really a liturgical architect.[3]

Before we go further, let's make sure that we're all on the same page about the word *liturgy*. Whether you're a spontaneity-seeking Pentecostal or a structure-loving Anglican, you have a liturgy. Despite the fact that worship thinkers (including myself) commonly use the word *liturgical* to describe the more structured and historical worship forms, those that employ traditional readings, songs, and prayers, in the broad sense, if your service has elements and an order or flow, you have a liturgy. As worship planners and leaders, we're all liturgical architects.

Narrowing the Story Gap

Over the years, I have noticed that many worship leaders and pastors fail to give worship's structure adequate consideration. There are a host of opinions about what happens in worship (the elements) but far less thinking about the organization and sequence of events (the structure). Specifically, I believe we need to recover the understanding that worship is supposed to tell a story.

A very simple way to analyze your worship services is by identifying the typical components that make up a good story. Here are six possible sets of questions to aid in that identification process:

1. What is the story's backdrop and context?
2. How is the story set? How does the narrative begin?
3. Who are the main characters of the story? Who are the heroes and the villains?
4. What is the climax of the narrative, and how do the story's elements contribute to getting there?

---

3. Though others have previously utilized the architectural metaphor for worship planning and leading, the one who has taken it the farthest is Cherry, *The Worship Architect*.

5. How does the story end?
6. What is the point of the story? What message is being preached by the author?

You need to do two things with these questions. First, you need to ask honestly, "How does my church answer these questions in our worship services? What story do we tell?" When you ask these questions, it reveals what you value and what you think the church exists to do. Second, you need to ask, "How does God answer these questions? What story does He tell?" Our goal as worship pastors is to narrow the gap between the answers to the first and second sets of questions.

Christian Worship's One Story

The history of the church overwhelmingly testifies that God has one story to tell: salvation by grace through faith in Jesus Christ. And the many voices of the church over time have agreed that the Bible is not an anthology of disconnected stories compiled to enlighten us or systematize a value system. Rather, the Bible is one story from beginning to end that tells of the creation and fall of humanity and its redemption and consummation in and through the saving work of the Son of God. We call this story the gospel because even though it has good and evil elements and plot turns in it, in the end it is a message that announces good news for us.

The vast witness of the history of Christian worship across traditions agrees that the gospel is the story we should tell.[4] And a truly Christian worship service should tell this story. Any other story that defines your worship will be sub-Christian and in some cases anti-Christian. Bryan Chapell has detected a consistent pattern of this kind of storytelling across the scriptural depictions of worship in the Old and New Testaments.[5] In every era of biblical history, the worship of the people of God has attempted to tell the gospel story in some form. Robert Webber further encourages us that when we worship according to God's

---

4. After almost one hundred pages of historical survey, Bryan Chapell concludes, "Through the ages, the common pattern of the order of worship in the church reflects the pattern of the progress of the gospel in the heart. The gospel first affects the heart by enabling us to recognize who God is. When we truly understand the glory of his holiness, then we also recognize who we really are and confess our need of him. The gospel then assures us of the grace that he provides, and our hearts respond in both thanksgiving and humble petition for his aid so that we can give proper devotion to him. . . . The common liturgy of the church through the ages reflects this sequential flow of the gospel in our hearts." *Christ-Centered Worship*, 99.

5. Chapell traces the gospel story in these instances: Isaiah's encounter (Isa. 6:1–13); Sinai worship (Deut. 5); Solomon's temple dedication (2 Chron. 5–7); the pattern of offering in temple worship; Paul's pattern of "spiritual worship" (Rom. 11–15); and John's "eschatological worship" (Rev. 4–21). *Christ-Centered Worship*, 103–11.

narrative, we are enacting and embodying the very gospel being proclaimed.[6] As liturgical architects, when we invite people to worship through this story, we aren't merely asking them to observe the gospel structure we've built. We're inviting them to inhabit it.

Back in chapter 9, we saw that part of our job as a missionary is to analyze, understand, and contextualize the timeless worship practices of the Great Tradition. As we think, then, about historic Christian worship's gospel-shaped storyline, we will more easily see what those timeless practices are. Put another way, as we look at historic worship through the lens of the gospel, it becomes easier to separate time- and context-bound practices from the timeless ones. What follows is an attempt to filter out those timeless practices.

The Three Gs of the Gospel Story

There have been many helpful ways in which people have summarized worship's gospel-shaped narrative.[7] I would like to break it down into three broad structural components and show how they can work in a variety of contexts. We mentioned these in passing in chapters 7 and 13, but now we will fully describe them—the glory of God, the gravity of sin, and the grandeur of grace.

1. The Glory of God

Ordinarily, worship services should begin the way the Bible does, with the awe-inspiring glory of God on display. The story opens with the creative power of the Trinity—the Father speaking creation into being (Gen. 1:3) as the Spirit summons form from chaos (Gen. 1:2) in and through the Son, the Word of God (John 1:1–3). Similarly, worship begins with God's creative word, the Call to Worship. Into the formlessness and chaos of our broken lives, the Word of God through a psalm or scriptural call summons, "Wake up, sleeper, rise from the dead, and Christ will shine on you" (Eph. 5:14). With this call, we can enter into a time of seeing and savoring the glory of God by reading, singing, and praying about God's many attributes and mighty deeds. We want our people here to be overwhelmed by all the things that make God great—kindness, goodness, faithfulness, steadfastness, holiness, brilliance, immortality, creativity, omniscience, perfection, omnipotence, and on and on. We want worship to begin by putting God—who He is and what He has done—on center stage.

---

6. Robert E. Webber, *Ancient-Future Worship: Proclaiming and Enacting God's Narrative* (Grand Rapids, Mich.: Baker, 2008).

7. Cf., e.g., Mike Cosper, *Rhythms of Grace: How the Church's Worship Tells the Story of the Gospel* (Wheaton, Ill.: Crossway, 2013), 117–50; Stephen Miller, *Worship Leaders, We Are Not Rock Stars* (Chicago: Moody, 2013), 81–90.

2. The Gravity of Sin

The glory of God is the only proper context for human beings to understand themselves. In humanity's story, just as creation gave way to the fall, so God's perfections contrast with our imperfections. When encountering God's glory firsthand, Isaiah's instinctive response was, "Woe to me! . . . I am ruined! For I am a man of unclean lips, and I live among a people of unclean lips, and my eyes have seen the King, the LORD Almighty" (Isa. 6:5). For a good swath of evangelical worship, the reenactment of the fall through Confession of Sin is the missing piece of the biblical story's contour.

We can sing about God's glory, and we can revel in His grace. But neither can be understood fully and completely without a radical encounter with our own sin. The time of confession is the space in our worship where we come to terms with our offenses against the Holy One. It is also the place where we admit culpability in the world's evils and injustices. This time in our service when we come to grips with the gravity of sin, therefore, is both confession of our individual sin *and* lamentation over the world's brokenness, which we must own up to as participants in the sin of our forefather and foremother (Rom. 5:12). With Adam, Eve, and the rest of humanity, we stand naked and ashamed before God's all-seeing eye.

Confession is important because it sets the stage for the story's climax. Grace only appears as high as we are brought low. It is only as bright as the backdrop of sin we set it against. Whether we sing it, speak it, or silently pray it, we need confession. If the good news of Jesus seems dull and lifeless in our worship, we should stop to ask whether we've adequately "seen" our sin.

3. The Grandeur of Grace

After Genesis 3, the biblical story begins its steady ascent, with foreshadowed hints along the way, to redemption in Jesus Christ. The narrative of Scripture climaxes in the revelation of Jesus—most specifically Him on a cross—and the narrative of our worship should do the same. At the cross, we witness that day of final judgment, bending time, rending the heavens, and mending creation (Rom. 3:21–26; Gal. 2:15–21; 3:10–14).[8] Likewise in worship, we need that moment where we witness the God of the universe dying on a cross, bleeding unto death in exchange for our sin, pleading His life's merit in exchange for our unrighteousness. Our witnessing this cosmic scene makes it possible for us to then hear

---

8. "The 'now' of Jesus' death is the eschatological enactment of the future judgment." Jonathan A. Linebaugh, *God, Grace, and Righteousness in Wisdom of Solomon and Paul's Letter to the Romans: Texts in Conversation* (Leiden, The Netherlands: Brill, 2013), 146. For definitive treatments on the cross as final judgment in Paul, see Linebaugh's above work and his "Debating Diagonal Δικαιοσύνη: The Epistle of Enoch and Paul in Theological Conversation," *Early Christianity* 1, no. 1 (2010): 107–28.

and feel the words, "It is finished" (John 19:30). We can receive God's pardon, "Therefore, there is now no condemnation for those who are in Christ Jesus" (Rom. 8:1); "God made him who had no sin to be sin for us, so that in him we might become the righteousness of God" (2 Cor. 5:21).

We as worship leaders must find a way to declare God's Word of grace to His people, and then we need to celebrate Christ's work in the gospel in its totality—life, death, resurrection, ascension, second coming, and the new heavens and new earth. This part of the service should feel like cosmic catharsis. It is the moment in the story when the hero arrives on the scene, vanquishes His foes (sin, death, and the devil), and claims His glorious and rightful throne around which we join heaven, crying, "Worthy is the Lamb, who was slain, to receive power and wealth and wisdom and strength and honor and glory and praise!" (Rev. 5:12). While not all will agree with me, I am becoming increasingly convinced that worship's climax in the gospel happens through what some traditions call "absolution," that moment when God declares through a pastor, "In Christ, your sins are forgiven."[9]

4. Response

Many worship thinkers and liturgical theologians rightly point out that at this point in the story, we must talk about our responsive elements. This is where we typically think about things like intercessory prayers, ministry times, offering—as in responding to the gospel by a recommitment to give ourselves to God and live for him—and sending, a final blessing to the people as we are sent out on mission into the world. But in worship, we must never mistake or confuse our response to the gospel as part of its story. The only contribution we make to worship is our sin. The only thing we bring to the service is our need. Our response is not the gospel. It is the fruit of the gospel. Gospel-shaped worship is God's story through and through, and the only two places we find ourselves in that narrative is first *in sin* and then *in Christ*. There is no room for triumphal boasting (Rom. 3:27).

Unfortunately, so much of worship today feels like heavy doses of response with very little gospel narrative. We can't assume that the gospel is implied in the hearts of our people as we approach worship. If the root of sin is unbelief—forgetting the gospel—then this story in worship must be as overt as possible.[10]

---

9. See the discussion of absolution in chapter 11 under "Delivering the Cure." Cf. James R. Thomson, "A Plea for the Absolution in the Reformed Churches," *Church Service Society Annual* 19 (1949): 33–40.

10. "Every sin since the beginning of the world has been unbelief and ignorance of Christ, since the promise concerning the Seed of the woman was given right after the fall of Adam (Gen. 3:15), which was made known throughout the houses of the fathers until the fullness of time (cf. Gal. 4:4)." Martin Luther, *Solus Decalogus Est Aeternus: Martin Luther's Complete Antinomian Theses and Disputations*, ed. and trans. Holger Sonntag (Minneapolis: Cygnus, 2008), 111. "What greater rebellion against God, what greater wickedness, what greater contempt of God is there than not believing his promise? For what is this but

Therefore, as we look at this structure through various lenses, we will focus on the gospel's narrative, understanding that our response is to be appropriately woven in but never dominant nor primary.[11]

Implementing This Structure in Every Tradition

What we have just walked through with the three Gs is a simple, gospel-shaped liturgy. I believe this structure is flexible enough for any tradition to incorporate yet true to the biblical witness and the Spirit's work in worship across Christian history. For worship pastors serving in more liturgical traditions, this structure may already be present. Your job will simply be to discern it as it is embedded in your liturgy and think through how to increase the effectiveness of communicating these primary parts of the story. The challenge for liturgical traditions is always to ensure that the story is not lost in the details but that the details serve the story.

For worship pastors in nonliturgical traditions, there may be more ground to plow, yet I'm convinced that the practices and elements of worship prized and cherished in your traditions don't have to be sacrificed to engage in a gospel-shaped worship service. Elements such as Confession of Sin don't have to look and feel liturgical for those moments to be true to the biblical story. You can engage in what David Gungor has referred to as a "ninja liturgy,"[12] with the gospel story embedded in a song set or carried out over an entire service, as we'll see.

Various Forms of Gospel-Structured Worship

If we take the emotional storyline developed in chapter 13 as our visual map, we arrive at the basic narrative structure for worship illustrated in figure 5.

Keep in mind that this diagram is more illustrative of the story's shape and less descriptive of actual time spent. We may find, depending on the service and our tradition's worship elements, that the three broad sections are shorter or longer than visualized. We're not looking for equal thirds. We're looking for the fullness of the story. As we look at the ways the biblical story is told in worship across

---

to make God a liar or to doubt that he is truthful? . . . Therefore God has rightly included all things, not under anger or lust, but under unbelief." Martin Luther, "The Freedom of a Christian," in *Three Treatises* (Minneapolis: Fortress: 1970), 285.

11. For more theological reasoning behind this idea, see the discussion on the Old Adam in chapter 6, "The Worship Pastor as Theological Dietician."

12. I have heard David Gungor use this term on more than one occasion, including in a small symposium he and I attended at Calvin College in May 2014.

various traditions, we find two models with several variations. The first model we can call the "Big Story Model," and the second I refer to as the "Retelling Model." In the Big Story Model, the gospel structure is displayed in one expansive arc throughout the service. In the Retelling Model, the gospel structure is recapitulated more than once in the worship service.

Let's illustrate how these models might look across a few traditions.

Figure 5

GOSPEL-STRUCTURED WORSHIP

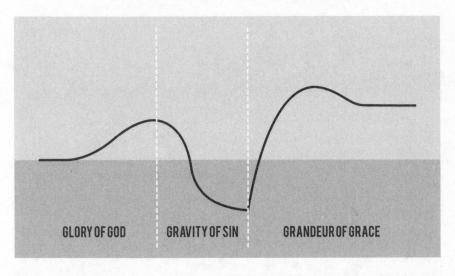

Big Story Model 1: The Worship Set into the Sermon

The Worship Set into the Sermon model is probably the most common service structure in many evangelical churches today: a block of songs that runs into a sermon. (See fig. 6.) In this model, the worship set is the primary vehicle for driving the gospel story, and the sermon, while hopefully preaching the gospel, is part of the response to the narrative. As we plan, we structure our song set around the contours of the gospel story, weaving prayers, transitions, and possibly readings throughout the set, perhaps sitting atop a musical bed, the way a movie is supported by a soundtrack. The following two models are variations on this theme, but we'll outline them both because they have been very influential across broad cross sections of Western Christian worship.

Figure 6

BIG STORY MODEL 1: THE WORSHIP SET INTO THE SERMON

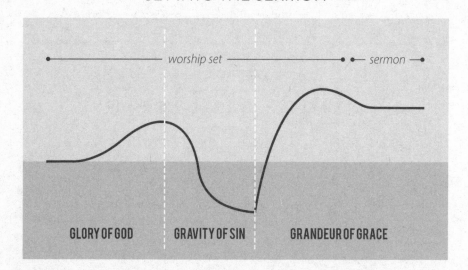

Figure 7

BIG STORY MODEL 2: PRAISE AND WORSHIP "TEMPLE" PROGRESSION

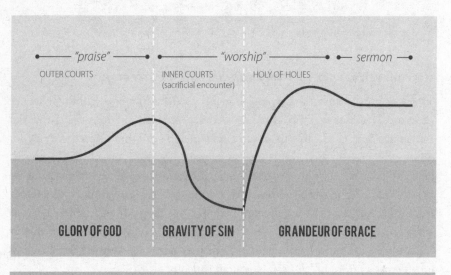

Big Story Model 2: Praise and Worship "Temple" Progression

Forged in the musical fires of the 1960s Gaither-influenced testimonial songs and the '70s and '80s Jesus People/Calvary Chapel movement, and merged with developing Pentecostal teaching, the Praise and Worship model has influenced many churches' worship structures, from evangelical to mainline Protestant and even into sectors of Roman Catholicism.[13] Important for this model is the metaphor of temple worship depicted in the Old Testament and the distinction between praise and worship.[14] (See fig. 7.) Praise is jubilant, expectant, and preparatory; it is in response to what God has *done*. Worship is intimate, adoring, and tender; it is in response to who God *is*.[15] It is from this worship structure that many of us have received the standard song progression beginning with fast, upbeat songs moving into slower ones.

Most descriptions of worship structure from advocates of Praise and Worship won't sound gospel shaped, but contour can be added, especially if we begin to think of how an ancient Israelite would have physically experienced the progression of the temple architecturally. The outer court (i.e., the "great court," 2 Chron. 4:9 ESV), the place where the people assembled (Jer. 19:14; 26:2), was the context of jubilant, thankful praise (Ps. 100:4). The inner court (1 Kings 6:36), where the priests ministered (2 Chron. 4:9), was the place of more focused and personal worship on the way to intimacy with God.

Many who cherish the Praise and Worship model need to remember here that within the inner court, before the intimacy of the Holy of Holies could take place, stood a necessary gospel encounter of sin and grace at the altar of burnt offering in front of the temple (2 Chron. 15:8; 2 Kings 16:14). At that sacrificial moment, an acknowledgment of sin and the gracious provision of a substitute punishment bearer would have been clearly visible (Leviticus 1). If the Praise and Worship model is a true temple model, the confession and a clear proclamation of the Lamb of God who takes away the sins of the world are natural additions. Those who worship in the Praise and Worship/temple tradition can easily expand through songs and prayer into a more thorough gospel storytelling.

---

13. See Robert Webber's helpful summary of the Praise and Worship tradition in, "Enter His Courts with Praise: A New Style of Worship Is Sweeping the Church," *Reformed Worship*, June 1991, accessed July 29, 2015, http://www.reformedworship.org/article/june-1991/enter-his-courts-praise-new-style-worship-sweeping-church.

14. See for example Judson Cornwall, *Let Us Worship* (Gainesville, Fla.: Bridge-Logos, 1983), 155–64.

15. Ibid., 158–59.

Figure 8

BIG STORY MODEL 3: VINEYARD CHARISMATIC

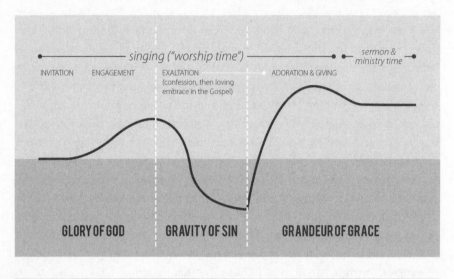

Figure 9

RETELLING MODEL 1: HISTORIC
LITURGICAL (WORD AND TABLE)

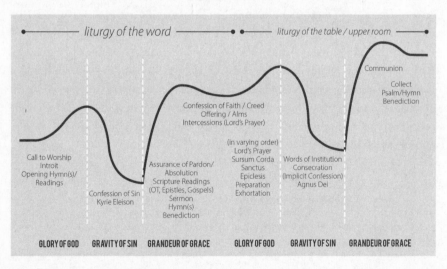

Big Story Model 3: Vineyard Charismatic

John Wimber, founder of the Vineyard movement of churches, identified a pattern of worship whose goal was intimacy with God. Many evangelical churches today, along with much of the most influential and broadly circulated modern worship music, have been knowingly and unknowingly impacted by Wimber's vision. There are obvious similarities of worship's goals and progression with the previous model, which makes sense given the Vineyard's history as an offshoot of the Calvary Chapel movement.[16] (See fig. 8.) Wimber articulated five phases to the "worship time," the singing portion of the service, as a description of the way the human heart progresses through an encounter with God: (1) Invitation / Call to Worship, (2) Engagement / Jubilation, (3) Intimate Exaltation / Expression, (4) Intimate Adoration / Visitation, and (5) Giving.[17] Though admittedly a stretch, one can detect and foster, especially if we see the often missing piece of Confession of Sin within phase three's notion of intimacy, a more overt gospel shape if both confession and words of grace become more explicitly led through appropriate prayers, songs, and scriptural statements.[18] Often in this charismatic model, before or after preaching, there is a ministry time when people's needs are prayed for and the gifts of the Spirit may be revealed.

Retelling Model 1: Historic Liturgical (Word and Table)[19]

Broadly speaking, historic Christian liturgies break down into two retellings of the gospel, commonly articulated as (1) the Liturgy of the Word, and (2) the Liturgy of the Table / Upper Room. (See fig. 9.) Some historic liturgical traditions do not celebrate the Eucharist every week, but this liturgical diagram depicts worship in these traditions when the Eucharist is included. This two-part structure is present in some of the earliest accounts we have of Christian worship.[20]

---

16. See Charles E. Fromm, "Textual Communities and New Song in the Multimedia Age: The Routinization of Charisma in the Jesus Movement," (PhD diss., Fuller Theological Seminary, 2006).

17. I have attempted to combine several mildly conflicting articulations of the five phases. Perhaps they conflict because either the categories were so fluid, Wimber's own teaching evolved over time, or varying Vineyard and charismatic traditions "tweaked" the articulation. Cf. John Wimber, "Worship: Intimacy with God," in *Thoughts on Worship*, ed. John Wimber (Anaheim: Vineyard Music Group, 1996), 4–7; Don Williams, "Charismatic Worship," in *Exploring the Worship Spectrum: 6 Views*, ed. Paul A. Basden (Grand Rapids, Mich.: Zondervan, 2004), 143–44; Lester Ruth, *Loving God Intimately: Worshiping with the Anaheim Vineyard Fellowship, 1980* (Grand Rapids, Mich.: Eerdmans, forthcoming).

18. One of the ironies of Vineyard-influenced charismatic worship is that Wimber was quite aware of confession's role in corporate worship. In one of his most clear articulations of his philosophy of worship, he explicitly named confession as one of the three central "ways described in the Old and New Testaments" that we worship God. "Worship," 3.

19. The following is a condensation of Chapell's liturgical comparisons in *Christ-Centered Worship*, 74, 83.

20. See Robert Webber's comments on Justin Martyr's *First Apology* (150 A.D.) in *Ancient-Future Worship*, 93–94.

Some worship scholars argue that the Liturgy of the Word complements the Liturgy of the Table. The former tells the gospel in a linear structure; the latter tells the story though nonlinear symbols.[21] For the sake of simplicity, I have depicted the Liturgy of the Table in a more linear fashion. That said, I would add that the narrative of historic liturgical worship is complex and varied (even more so than I have presented here). My hope with this diagram is to help liturgical architects in these traditions more clearly see how the broad sections of the gospel story align with their liturgy's narrative. Discerning the overall shape can help make sense of the parts so that leaders in worship can more intentionally guide the story along. This can guard against dilution of the big story amid the complexity of the many details.

What I've identified as the "gravity of sin" section in the Liturgy of the Table is more implicit than explicit. My rationale is that as a worshiper receives the Words of Institution, light is shed on his sin. Most Words of Institution begin, "On the night He was betrayed, Jesus took bread." In this statement we can hear more than a mere recounting of Judas' transgression, we hear an accusation of our own culpability: "*You* are Christ's betrayer; *you* are God's enemy" (Rom. 5:10). This accusation furthermore sets us up to hear the Consecration, the setting apart of the elements, as a setting them apart *from me* for holy use. Here is where I begin to hear seeds of the gospel, for I am being set apart as well. The fact that the *Agnus Dei* is present at this point in many liturgies tells me that Christians of the past have sensed their sin at this moment in the liturgy. I indicate this with the label "(Implicit Confession)," and it happens somewhere on the journey from Institution to Communion.[22]

Retelling Model 2: Reformational and Charismatic

First, we should note that the Reformational and Charismatic model is a blending of liturgical and charismatic sensibilities in that it seeks to progress through the liturgical gospel story, weaving historic liturgical moments into a more seamless song set. (See fig. 10.) There is an attempt at the front end, not unlike the charismatic versions, to give the liturgy a greater flow. Second, in distinction

---

21. E.g., Chapell, *Christ-Centered Worship*, 99.

22. It's very interesting to note the way reformer Thomas Cranmer intentionally edited this moment in the liturgy in his crowning 1552 Prayer Book. The Medieval Roman rite he received contained a lot of elements (prayers, liturgical actions, etc.) between the Words of Institution and the actual reception of the elements. Cranmer desired to narrow the gap between Institution and reception particularly because of the way he understood the radical grace of the gospel. The gospel, freely given, requires *no* action on our part, merely reception. So for Cranmer, it was appropriate that we as "enemies" receive grace before any attempt at a meritorious act. In an age when the right kind of penitence made one fit for earning divine grace, Cranmer wanted to show that grace was *freely* given to the unjust, ungodly, and undeserving.

from the Big Story "Worship Set into the Sermon" model, this model views the sermon itself as a new experience of the gospel progression. Here we have a more Reformational understanding of what a sermon is and what it does. The sermon is the preaching of the Word of God in such a way as to expose the human condition and then offer the Cure. Traditions that espouse this philosophy of preaching may tend to be more sacramental as well, and the service might have four or more cycles or symbolic encounters with this gospel story. Though the depictions of baptism and the Lord's Supper are smaller in the diagram, that is not an indication of their significance.

Figure 10

RETELLING MODEL 2: REFORMATIONAL AND CHARISMATIC

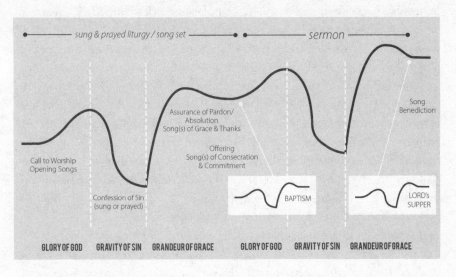

These models aren't meant to be exhaustive but illustrative. My hope is that they open up our liturgical imaginations to reenvision worship in our own context. For instance, if you are familiar with Robert Webber's well-known explanation of the fourfold pattern of worship, it could fit into either a Big Story or Retelling model.[23] Much will depend on how sacramentally oriented your tradition is and

23. See Robert Webber, *Worship Old and New*, rev. ed. (Grand Rapids, Mich.: Zondervan, 1994),

what kind of philosophy of preaching your church espouses. The main point in sharing these models is to encourage worship leaders to structure worship so it is faithful to the gospel story for the nourishment of God's people.[24]

The Christian Year: A Gospel Superstructure to Weekly Worship

I want to briefly mention one added benefit of more liturgical traditions. In many of these traditions there is a flow throughout the calendar year that follows the Christian calendar as part of their worship cycle. Not only do these traditions retell the gospel story each week in gathered worship, they are also enacting the story over the course of a year. Those skeptical of the church year's biblical warrant should consider the precedent set by God in establishing an annual cycle for Israel's worship through special days and seasons—Passover, Feast of Firstfruits, Pentecost, Feast of Trumpets, Day of Atonement, Feast of Tabernacles, and so on. Remember that Jesus both celebrated these worship cycles Himself and then went on to explicitly teach that He was their fulfillment (John 5–10). If anything, Jesus wasn't abolishing the annual cycle of worship; He was encouraging its reinterpretation around *His* story.[25]

The historic Christian calendar is also helpful for understanding how Christians who have come before us have fleshed out Christ's reinterpretation of annual worship. (See fig. 11.) With the cycle moving through the life and ministry of Christ—from heralding (Advent) to birth (Christmas) to childhood (Epiphany) to temptation in the wilderness (Lent) to passion and crucifixion (Holy Week, Maundy Thursday, Good Friday) to resurrection and ascension (Easter) to His sending of His Spirit (Pentecost)—we can detect many of the same contours to the gospel story that we have been outlining.

Not every tradition and context will be open to celebrating the Christian year. But for those that are, worship leaders can draw from a rich trove of resources that communicate the gospel story to their congregations. I believe there is great

---

149–94. His fourfold pattern (Acts of Entrance, Service of the Word, Service of the Table, Sending) could be seen in a Big Story model, especially in the instances when the "Service of the Table" is viewed more simply as a time of thanksgiving rather than the Eucharist itself. The pattern could be seen in a Retelling model not unlike the Historic Liturgical one if Communion is viewed as a recapitulation of the gospel story.

24. Refer back to chapter 6, "The Worship Pastor as Theological Dietician." The "Structure" section of "How Worship Theologizes" is a reminder of what is at stake if our worship is *not* shaped according to the gospel. When this structure is absent, we run the risk of implicitly teaching our congregations that we don't necessarily need Jesus to approach God rightly.

25. For a more thorough outline of the biblical rationale for the church year, see my blog post, "Is the Christian Calendar a Biblical Idea?": http://www.zachicks.com/blog/2012/3/6/is-the-christian-calendar-a-biblical-idea.html.

benefit in adding this dimension of telling the Bible's story to your worship planning. The church calendar serves as a "gospel superstructure" that reinforces the weekly rhythms of worship.[26]

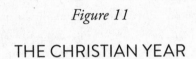

Figure 11

THE CHRISTIAN YEAR

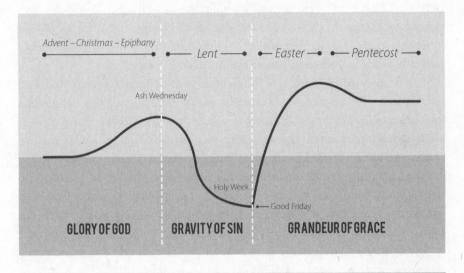

Ruts of Righteousness

In Psalm 23:3, David testifies, "He leads me in paths of righteousness" (ESV). Commentators point out that these paths are really ruts—grooves worn into the earth by months and years of travel. Walking in these grooves is easier because over time the foot learns to feel them, and we remain in the ruts even when the storms arise and the night is dark. The repetition of the gospel story works like a well-worn path. The story's contours become "ruts of righteousness" that wear grooves into our souls so that in the stormy moments of sin, in the dark nights of doubt, and in the painful confusion of grief, our feet find solid earth in the path of the faithful.

I remember when I first experienced the power of these "gospel ruts." Having grown up in a broadly evangelical worship tradition, I had recently joined a

26. For an introduction to the Christian year, see Robert Webber, *Ancient-Future Time: Forming Spirituality through the Christian Year* (Grand Rapids, Mich.: Baker, 2004).

liturgical Presbyterian church that practiced a weekly gospel-shaped liturgy. One week, I fell into one of those habitual sins and had a clear sense of my guilt before God. The "old me" would have sought to respond to that moment by doing penance—engaging in various disciplines to punish myself and show God I was serious about sin. But this time, I was led in another direction. My soul fell into a well-worn groove, one I had learned through our weekly worship liturgy: confession. I began to confess my sin to God, using the language I had recently begun appropriating in worship: "I've sinned against You . . . in thought, word, and deed . . . I haven't loved You with my whole heart . . . I am truly sorry . . . have mercy on me." And I heard God's Word, spoken to my heart, "As far as the east is from the west, so far have I removed your transgression from you, to remember your sins no more. There is therefore now no condemnation."

In that moment, I experienced the freedom of grace and the love of God, and I was grateful and empowered. I saw how worship had formed a gospel-shaped spirituality in my life. And those rhythms are a saving grace to me still to this day. These ruts of righteousness are the ways that I, my wife, and my children relate to one another when we have hurt or wronged another member of the family. We stop, confess, pray, and remember our forgiveness in Christ. We find that worship's ruts bring not only healing to our lives individually but reconciliation to our family as a community. Worship's gospel centrality is the ground zero of true and lasting justice and reconciliation.

When we plan and lead worship services that repetitively walk through the "same old story," we participate in God's formation of Christ in our people. If the gospel really is the power of God in the lives of our flock (Rom. 1:16), then we know the best thing we can give them is the story of Jesus—nothing more, nothing less.

This type of formation is effective in proportion to how embodied and emotionally invested worshipers are when they engage in worship. The more that our whole being is engaged in the service, the more we stand to gain in our formation in Christ. The story must be felt physically and emotionally, not just cognitively. This is why as liturgical architects we desire our people not to just *observe* worship by going through its motions, but to *inhabit* the ups and downs of the gospel story in its structure. In the next chapter, we will turn to three things—flow, ambiance, and leadership—that aid in helping people move from a cognitive observation to an invested inhabitation of worship's narrative.

Father, as Architect and Builder of the coming city, and Son, as Cornerstone of the house of God, send the Spirit to inhabit our worship's structure until we are all built up into the fullness of Christ.

15

THE WORSHIP PASTOR
AS CURATOR

A good curator makes it look easy. In fact, she will be invisible and not even noticed.

—*Mark Pierson, 2010*[1]

Cultural analysts tell us that today we live in a curated reality. The life we experience each day is highly mediated and customized. We experience reality through filters that are specific and personal. And technology has all but guaranteed that this curated life is here to stay. We may all have smartphones, but not one of us will have all the same apps arranged in all the same ways. We might all be on Facebook, but we don't all see the same thing. Facebook's algorithms curate our experience, gathering data about what we like and the things we click on, then giving similar items to us (ads, links, etc.) in greater frequency. We might all use Google to search the internet, but no one's search results will be exactly the same. Google gathers information about us and curates our search results based on what it thinks we want to see.

But this is just the tip of the iceberg. We curate ourselves. Through social media channels, we handpick what we do and don't want others to see—and what we do and don't want *ourselves* to see. If I don't like a certain person or perspective, I just take them off my feed. I can create the world I like and avoid what I do not like. I can even create the person I want others to see when they encounter me. But if I'm honest, the social media me is not the real me. It's the curated me.

Before curating was a buzzword for the authenticity crisis of our postmodern age, it was (and still is) a vocational calling. An obvious place where a curator does her work is an art museum. Here we recognize that the art curator functions as a go-between. She is not the architect of the space, nor does she lead tours. Her role falls in between those who own the space and those who view the art; she stands

---

1. Mark Pierson, *The Art of Curating Worship: Reshaping the Role of Worship Leader* (Minneapolis: Sparkhouse, 2010), 44.

in the middle as a mediator and is indispensable to the museum goer's experience. A curator's job is to work with materials—art pieces, frames, display cases, signage, accessories—making critical choices about both *what* to present and *how* to present it. She thinks through how those materials should be put together and arranged because she knows that a museum goer's experience of art is about much more than the art itself.

The curator, if she is good at her work, doesn't just rely on her own set of values and opinions. She considers everything—from the architect's vision for the museum space to the artist's intentions for a painting to the museum goer's experience viewing the art. A curator is skilled in the art of making fine distinctions about the details of the materials (e.g., the thickness and texture of a single wood frame) while keeping in mind the vision of all the other parties involved.

I believe that a church worship leader does the same thing. Worship pastors are curators.[2] Starting with the architecture of a service, a worship curator creatively fills that space with the right elements arranged in the right way. A curator brings a variety of perspectives to bear on the selection and presentation of worship's materials. This includes selecting music,[3] choosing prayers, arranging readings, connecting these elements with the preaching, incorporating the sacraments, and thinking through transitions. In what follows I want to model and illustrate what curating might look like through the various lenses we've examined in this book, hopefully stirring up your pastoral imagination as you curate in your own context. Each of the pastoral perspectives we've talked about can be a curating grid through which you sift the materials of worship. What you'll discover is that sometimes those perspectives work quite well alongside each other, while other times they must be held in tension.

Material 1: Music

Most worship pastors spend more time with music than with any of worship's other materials. And this shouldn't be surprising. Music is powerful, and it must

---

2. The term *curator* has been floating around for several years in conversations about the worship leader's role. It appears to more formally have entered the discussion with Pierson, *The Art of Curating Worship*, and Jonny Baker, *Curating Worship* (New York: Seabury, 2010). Pierson claims to have coined the term (p. 28), which may very well be the case.

3. Michael Farley helpfully points out that, in discussions like these, it would be better if we didn't treat music as a discrete element of worship but rather a sub-category. Perhaps music might be more rightly understood as a "mode or manner of accomplishing the biblical elements of worship." In a day and age where music is so readily equated with worship, this is worth pondering. See Michael A. Farley, "Daniel Block: *For the Glory of God: Recovering a Biblical Theology of Worship:* A Liturgical Studies Response," *Biblical Worship Section of the Evangelical Theological Society*, San Diego, November 20, 2014, accessed November 5, 2015, https://etsworship.wordpress.com/.

be stewarded with care. As a corporate mystic, a worship pastor keeps in mind music's biblical role in aiding the church's experience of the presence of God.[4] Music is not simply an aesthetic experience but a spiritual one, and we pray, both before and during the service, that our people don't *merely* sing and *merely* listen but truly and deeply experience the presence of God. Corporate mystics are quick to remind skeptical congregations that God actually visits His people as they sing. As a church lover, the worship pastor favors music that encourages participation of the many over performance of the few. Music's role is predominantly seen as a handmaiden to congregational singing.

As a doxological philosopher, a worship pastor thinks critically about musical style, knowing that "the medium is the message," that musical style indirectly but powerfully communicates aesthetic and cultural values.[5] We're not content with certain musical expressions, either, because "we've always done it that way" or because we're simply imitating what is popular in culture. We philosophize about our instrumentation and forms, and we have informed answers to all of the "whys" of our musical choices. "Hip," "relevant," and "attracts the young folks" are insufficient reasons. Worship pastors refuse shallow answers to deep questions.

As prayer leaders, we cherish music's ability to center and unify congregational singing as sung prayer. We allow Scripture's rich teaching to shape the diversity and power of our congregation's sung and spoken prayer, aiming to employ all the various kinds of prayer in the worship life of the flock—praise, adoration, thanksgiving, confession, petition, intercession, and supplication. We select songs with these functions of prayer in mind. Pastoral prayer leaders compare their congregation's corporate prayer life in worship to the breadth of prayer modeled in Scripture—the Psalms, the Lord's Prayer (Matt. 6:9–13), the biblical canticles (i.e., other songs outside the Psalms), Jesus' High Priestly Prayer (John 17), the great prayers of Old Testament history (e.g., Neh. 1:5–11; 9:6–37), and the prayers of the New Testament epistles.

A theological dietician recognizes how music forms a church's ecclesiology—their sense of connectedness to the broader church across time and space. If we want our churches to recognize their connection to historic Christianity, we are open to historic songs and styles that may aid in this vision. If we want

---

4. See the biblical argumentation for God's presence in music in chapter 2, "The Worship Pastor as Corporate Mystic."

5. If the concept of musical style communicating cultural values is new or foreign, I recommend (though I strongly disagree with most of the rest of the book) T. David Gordon's chapter on "Contemporaneity as a Value," in *Why Johnny Can't Sing Hymns: How Pop Culture Rewrote the Hymnal* (Phillipsburg, N.J.: Presbyterian and Reformed, 2010), 103–28. The author makes a convincing case for one particular value—namely novelty—that can sneak into contemporary musical styles.

our churches to see our cross-cultural identity, we open our churches to global musical expressions and different instrumentation and arrangements in addition to our own indigenous ones. I have found that exposing a congregation to a wider variety of musical styles beyond their favorite genres has the added benefit of creating a more flexible and generous worship culture, warding off idolatries associated with consumerism and selfishness that so often plague a church's musical appetites.

Similarly, caregivers think of music, among other things, as a means of hospitality. A worship pastor listens to his or her congregation's musical heart language—the sounds and styles that are comfortable and engaging for the diverse makeup of the flock. While worship pastors aren't jukeboxes or DJs, taking requests and pandering to people's self-absorbed desires, a caregiver still pays attention to the people so that the music selected and played hospitably engages the church's varying sensibilities.

Here we find one of the pastoral tensions I mentioned: while a theological dietician desires to stretch a congregation in musical style, a caregiver does so in a measured and sensitive manner. If your church is ripe for stylistic growth, a great way to begin culture change is to engage styles that are a degree off from something familiar. If your congregation's context is rock, consider adding blues or gospel. If your church's expression is classical, find choral and organ works that incorporate more contemporary classical styles or elements of world music.

War generals remind their congregations that joining in singing is entering into spiritual battle. We select songs and psalms with lyrics that highlight worship's warlike characteristics. We are also ever mindful of how our fellow musicians may be subject to the enemy's targeting, keeping watch over their vulnerabilities.

Worship pastors also think like missionaries when processing music's contextualization to their culture. We are listening to the sounds of our city and region and winsomely incorporating elements of our own context's musical language. In South Florida, I quickly discovered that the abundance of Caribbean and Latin music, along with electronic dance music (EDM), signaled the need for more rhythmic congregational accompaniment. Even our traditional hymns often took on more rhythmic characteristics. Still (exposing yet another tension), while we listen to culture, we remain on guard as watchful prophets against the careless appropriation of our culture's idolatries, wisely aware of the deeper meanings embedded in cultural musical practices.

As curators, we see how every decision we make is pastoral rather than purely pragmatic. We don't select music merely because it's popular. A host of pastoral factors flood into our minds and hearts as we make these formative choices for our people.

Material 2: Prayers

Worship is filled with prayer, and whether our prayers are extemporaneous or prescribed by a liturgical tradition, as curators we have a responsibility to ensure that our church's corporate prayer is deep and rich. As a disciple maker, the worship pastor is aware of the fact that worship dramatically shapes the prayer lives of the disciples in the pews. Perhaps you've noticed that the expressions of prayer spoken in worship are picked up and appropriated into the prayers of your people. Part of the reason "Christian-ese" exists as a linguistic anomaly is because the way we pray before one another is contagious. Worship pastors understand this dynamic and seek to make the language of their prayers thoughtful and shaped by Scripture. A shallow public prayer practice will lead to shallow private prayer in the congregation. But the reverse is true as well. Robust public prayers nourish a congregation's imagination for their own personal prayers.

The worship pastor as theological dietician recognizes that worship's prayers are great places to incorporate the various names and attributes of God found in Scripture. We use our prayers as an opportunity to fill our flocks' minds and hearts with the wonder of who God is and what He has done, refusing to settle for the anemic and repetitive defaults of prayer.[6] For instance, we might replace a prayer of need that begins, "Dear God," or "Father," with "O Provider of every good and perfect gift." Along these lines, as caregivers we recognize that praying for the hurts and needs of the congregation in worship is one of the most powerful ways we administer pastoral care to the flock, so we make room for supplication and intercession for God's guidance and healing in the lives of our people. Simple prayers that acknowledge various categories of care—the sick, the lonely, the lost, the depressed, the disabled, the grieving—go a long way in making the service a place where the Spirit can pour out healing grace. Some traditions even host special services of prayer for the hurting or offer extended ministry times right in the middle of a worship service.

As morticians we know that prayer is a key place to hold the end before the people of God, adding to our prayers and lamentations the *maranatha* cry of longing for the day when Christ will come again and make all things new. As war generals we remember that prayer in the Spirit is among the chief offensive strategies against the work of the enemy (Eph. 6:18). As watchful prophets, we allow the language of our prayers to be filled with quotations of and allusions to

---

6. Very helpful in expanding our imaginative vocabulary here is Debra Rienstra and Ron Rienstra's *Worship Words: Discipling Language for Faithful Ministry* (Grand Rapids, Mich.: Baker, 2009). I have also found the Anglican Collects, short prayers embedded at various points in the Book of Common Prayer, especially rich and instructive here. In particular the Collects penned by Thomas Cranmer are a goldmine for study and appropriation. See especially C. Frederick Barbee and Paul F. M. Zahl, *The Collects of Thomas Cranmer* (Grand Rapids, Mich.: Eerdmans, 1999).

Scripture, powerfully wielding the Word over the flock. Even if our prayers are extemporaneous, we are so filled with the Scriptures that they take on psalmlike qualities and expressions. Our prayers sound like the Bible.

As missionaries, those of us in liturgical traditions recognize the liabilities of set prayers inherited from other times, places, and cultures. As we use those prayers, we are sensitive to the ways their language and expressions may be inaccessible to our context. We're willing to either educate our flocks or amend the language when possible so that we might contextualize our tradition for our church.

In any tradition, as missionaries we are leading our congregations in prayer for the world, igniting missional fire in the hearts of our people. In worship, we bring to our people an awareness of the outreach and missionary efforts of our church by petitioning God's grace and favor and seeking His aid in our missional work. We also keep the needs of our cities and country before our people—our government, our public servants, and our community's good endeavors. These along with our prayers for the countries of the world and current events help to aim our congregation's hearts outward.

As emotional shepherds, we model what faithful feelings look like when brought before the Lord. We aim our prayers in all kinds of emotional directions, knowing that some in our flock are despondent and need to cry out to God and lay their fears on the table, while others are experiencing seasons of rest and blessing from the Lord and need to be led to the joy of remembering that all prosperity comes from His hand. In confession, we give deep, rich language to the emotions that make up the complexities of true contrition—godly sorrow, hatred of and anger toward sin, and a desperate but hopeful clinging to the mercies of our gracious God.

Material 3: Readings

One of the painful ironies of the evangelical worship landscape today is that while evangelicals are historically committed to Scripture, we read so little of it in our worship services. Often, people in nonevangelical liturgical traditions—Roman Catholicism, Eastern Orthodoxy, and portions of mainline Protestantism—end up hearing far more of the Word of God read in their public services. Worship pastors who are watchful prophets are not content with the biblical illiteracy of our churches today, and they are advocates for both the preaching and the reading of the Scriptures in worship. People want to hear a word from God in worship, and there is no more sure way to make that happen than to read the Scriptures aloud. When the Bible is read aloud, God speaks in an audible voice.[7]

7.   Martin Luther: "Let the man who would hear God speak, read Holy Scripture," *What Luther Says: An Anthology*, vol. 2, ed. Ewald M. Plass (St. Louis: Concordia, 1959), 62.

As theological dieticians, we strategize about how the whole counsel of God might be heard in worship over an extended period of time, and we think long term about the scriptural diet our congregations will receive as we plan the readings in our services. This is what is so wonderful about the traditions that use lectionaries. Oftentimes the theological diet has already been thought and prayed through by the faithful men and women who compiled the reading lists.

As missionaries, we think about how to contextualize the rich traditions of nonscriptural liturgical readings that have been part of Christian worship for centuries. Perhaps we set portions of old Christian liturgies (e.g., historic litanies, responsive readings, etc.) to new music, rendering the readings more accessible and affectively charged. But more centrally, we make sure that our congregations are confessing the core of our faith in the historic creeds of the church (e.g., Apostles', Nicene, Athanasian).

Worship pastors who are emotional shepherds care greatly about *how* readings are read, knowing that the affective dimensions of inflection, tone, drama, and cadence, which are certainly context specific, either help or hinder a congregation's apprehension and appropriation of the readings.

Material 4: Preaching and Sacraments

Worship pastors care about all parts of the worship service, developing a rich understanding as doxological philosophers about how each and every element contributes to the formative experience of the people of God. Because we care about the whole of worship, we are highly supportive of preaching and the practices of the sacraments of the Lord's Supper and baptism. As church lovers, we recognize that the other pastors with whom we serve, who are engaged in these ministries of the Word, aren't enemies robbing time from the things we are planning and doing. We don't view preaching and sacraments as competing with the other elements that we may have more direct control over.

As corporate mystics, we believe in the ministry of Word and sacrament, not wanting our people to believe that God's presence is sensed and felt only during singing. As disciple makers, we remind our congregations that we are participants in a sermon as we offer up the worship of our ears, being formed by God in the moment of preaching. We passionately believe that as we witness baptism and partake of Holy Communion, the faith of our flock is being strengthened, nourished, bolstered, and renewed. As emotional shepherds, we think of strategic ways to appropriately support the affective tone of baptism and the Lord's Supper by selecting music that emotionally fits the occasion.

Many have noted the powerful role music can play in exploring the many dimensions of the Lord's Supper. Some have thought of the table like a funeral, where with sober hearts we recall and mourn Christ's death. But we remember that Christ instituted Communion as a revelation of future joy (Matt. 22:2; Mark 14:25; 1 Cor. 11:26; Rev. 19:9). Communion is a foretaste of the feast to end all feasts, the greatest party the world will ever know. Therefore, as morticians, we not only highlight Christ's death but also set the joy of the Second Coming before our people in the Eucharist. The music we select before, during, and after the celebration of the Lord's Supper can greatly aid in our congregation's understanding of the future that awaits us. Communion becomes a moment of theologizing where we, as theological dieticians, expand our people's understanding of who they are as part of the church in God's cosmic plan of grace and redemption. When Communion feels joyful, the church more clearly sees her destiny.

As curators thinking about preaching and sacraments, I recognize that most of us won't have much control over the content and presentation of these materials of the service. Normally, worship leaders are not preparing sermons or administering baptism and Communion. Still, we have a significant role to play in shaping what happens *around* these things. We can either create a worship context where preaching and sacraments are seen in unity with the rest of worship, or where they are a distinct and separate experience. A curator thinks about the whole experience and seeks to support, supplant, and surround all of worship's elements with a sense of unity and wholeness.

Material 5: Transitional Content

Worship pastors in all traditions recognize that transitions in worship aren't filler used to smooth out our production of an event. Just as an art museum curator thinks about a museum goer's experience in the hallways between exhibits, so we see transitions as bona fide content that is as important as music, prayers, and other elements. We don't neglect transitions.[8]

I have found transitions to be strategic places where we can simply but effectively educate the flock. For instance, as an emotional shepherd, I choose my words when I ask our people to be seated for confession—instead of simply telling people to be seated, I invite them to "bow their bodies" as they sit. Or instead

---

8. Pierson helpfully calls the curator's role of managing transitions "aggregation"—bringing together seemingly disconnected things—though he places aggregation on a much larger scale to include how we bring together elements and happenings of the larger culture and community (*The Art of Curating Worship*, 33ff). Having discussed culture and community in chapter 9, I will narrow the discussion of curation here to transitions in worship, but I appreciate just how far Pierson has imaginatively extended the metaphor of curator. It's worth mentioning as well that underneath this discussion of transitions are the sociological realities of how "the medium is the message" and "context is content." See Pierson, *The Art of Curating Worship*, 30.

of just asking people to stand in worship, we might say, "Weekly worship is a celebration of Christ's resurrection, and so we stand to sing and praise as a visible sign that Christ has risen and we will one day rise with him!" Embedded in these short transitions are theological insights that the worship pastor communicates as mortician and theological dietician.

During the offering, we want our congregations to engage in more than giving their money. We want the time to be a rich opportunity where they respond to the gospel by offering their *whole selves* as living sacrifices (Rom. 12:1). I sometimes transition into a time of offering by saying, "Let's respond to the gospel now by giving of our tithes and offerings, which is just another way of saying, 'Jesus, take *all* of me.'"

When we begin worship as many of us do with a welcome, it becomes a moment as a doxological philosopher to briefly frame what worship is and does. I will sometimes say, "Good morning, church. God has gathered us together for a great, cosmic purpose that He might give Himself to us yet again by showing us just how much we need Jesus and then offering His very presence to us. We aren't here to just go through the motions. We're here to encounter the living God!" Here the corporate mystic comes out too. If you want to be strategic with your welcome, think through some of the five to ten most important things about worship that you want your congregation to grow in over the next few months, and come up with a plan over time to briefly highlight these in a minute or less.

If your congregation engages in a time of fellowship or greeting in the worship service, the transition to the greeting time can become a moment where we as missionaries and watchful prophets might say, "Because God has reconciled us to Himself through Jesus, we can be reconciled to one another. As we greet one another, we're embodying this reconciliation in a small way so that God can make us agents of reconciliation in the world, until He comes again." Again, pastorally using transitions is attempting to fill our worship with rich meaning from top to bottom. When we think through transitions pastorally, we give purpose to worship's seemingly purposeless acts.

Other Materials

Some worship services have additional components that might not fall within the primary categories but are nevertheless real and present for us as worship pastors. Many of these components come under the category of body life. Here we think of elements like testimonies, mission reports, ministry spotlights, and (so often dreaded) announcements. If we're honest, it's these elements that drive us crazy, eating so much time and often disrupting flow and disintegrating a worship-ful atmosphere. A church lover recognizes their value as acts of worship. These moments often fall under the horizontal dimension of worship—the edification of one another (Eph. 5:19; Col. 3:16). Even announcements can be delivered in such a way that they become less like commercials and more like an invitation to praise God for what He is doing in our community. As theological dieticians, we believe that ministry and mission spotlights are a means to help the church more fully understand who she is as a connected, ministering, and missional body. These building materials greatly aid in developing a church's ecclesiology. As corporate mystics, we think long and hard about where these types of elements go because we are sensitive to how people's experience of God's presence among us may be distracted when these things are placed in the wrong spot and/or led poorly.

As watchful prophets, though, we're mindful of the ways that agendas can creep in to these elements of worship and crowd out what worship is centrally for. Ministry leaders may want more air time for their spotlights simply to increase numbers at their events. Organizers may want an extended commercial for their ministry gathering, and missionaries may (understandably) need to raise significant support. These desires can shade and color the way these ministry leaders communicate with the church. Announcements especially have a way of getting out of hand.

All these things need to be carefully overseen and faithfully guarded. Curating these things involves speaking up about what these elements are and what they are not. Worship is not a social club, nor is it a platform for people's public service announcements. Just because worship is the one time the entire body is gathered does not mean that the church's communicative burden must fall here. Instead, we need to guide these elements toward being worshipful acts that glorify God, display the Spirit's power, and edify the body. We must remember that worship is primarily the church's encounter with the awe-inspiring presence of the Holy One. It is this vision that must drive the scope and trajectory of these elements.

As we said at the beginning of the chapter, a curator operates as a go-between, vetting worship's materials so that the various pastoral perspectives can come to bear on how elements are selected and presented. The curator begins when the architect's work is finished, filling the space with carefully chosen and thoughtfully placed materials. Once the space is filled, the curator passes the baton to the tour guide, where all the pastoral preparation can hopefully be applied in a faithful and formative way for the people of God. But before we get to the service, let us pray one more time.

O Only Wise God, You alone know best what Your people need.
Be Thou our Wisdom as we curate worship's elements. Amen.

16

THE WORSHIP PASTOR
AS TOUR GUIDE

The experience of public worship, like the experience of museums or baseball games, is infinitely richer when one is guided by perceptive and instructive docents.

—*John Witvliet, 2010*[1]

In the last two chapters, we discussed worship's structure and materials, observing that when we arrange worship's elements in an order that tells the Bible's big story—the gospel of Jesus Christ—we create a spiritually formative, historically rooted, and biblically faithful worship service for the people of God. We recognized that we need the minds of both architects and curators, deftly navigating between the zoomed-out big picture of worship's structure and the zoomed-in details of worship's elements. We turn now to what must be done when those jobs are complete. It's one thing for the architect to design a space and for a curator to gather all the ideal materials and organize their presentation in a holistic and healthy way. It's quite another to lead a group of people through that space.

This is where the worship pastor moves into the role of a tour guide. Aware of the nuances of the building, the thought behind the construction, and the purposes of the materials, tour guides are skilled in the art of making all those things seen, heard, and felt by the people.

As worship's tour guides, we can think in three broad categories—flow, ambiance, and leadership. We might view these categories as modes of influence or tools of persuasion. We desperately want our people invested and engaged in worship's story, and these tools are tangible aids toward that end. As in the previous chapter, we're going to explore how we use these tools in a pastoral way by applying to them the book's various pastoral perspectives.

---

1. John Witvliet, "The Worship: How Can Art Serve the Corporate Worship of the Church?" in *For the Beauty of the Church: Casting a Vision for the Arts*, ed. W. David O. Taylor (Grand Rapids, Mich.: Baker, 2010), 194, n.9.

Tool 1: Flow

When structure is theologically rather than pragmatically driven, the service can sometimes run the risk of coming across as clunky and disconnected. I have been in worship services (and led a few myself) where the leaders tried so hard to tell the story rightly that they gave very little attention to how the story was actually being experienced. If worship is indeed a narrative rather than a haphazard potpourri of elements, it should be experienced like a story—smoothly, continuously, and seamlessly. Many great worship thinkers call this "flow." A great key to flow lies in understanding and guiding your worship service's emotional journey, as we discussed in chapter 13. However, we can explore a few more things.

The Spirit's Presence as the Service's Flow

Part of leading a worship service's flow as a corporate mystic involves keeping the awareness of God's real, abiding presence before His worshipers. As all of the elements of worship pass by, the one constant—the True Flow—is the presence of the Holy Spirit Himself. Simply and naturally mentioning God's presence at key moments goes a long way toward helping worshipers know that He is truly with us. This practice also goes hand in hand with our impulse as a watchful prophet to guard the flock against seemingly innocuous but nevertheless idolatrous distractions. Our frenetic age of push notifications, multimedia stimuli, and perpetual entertainment has created generations of highly distracted people whose short attention spans make it difficult for them to focus and remain attentive to the presence of God among us.

We need to find loving, strategic ways to point out distractions to our people. Perhaps we open a service with the statement, "Brothers and sisters, it's so hard for us to focus ourselves on what is at hand. We all have busy lives and various devices to remind us just how busy we are. Let's not forget that God wants to richly bless us with His presence today, so we call on the Holy Spirit to give us focus and ears of faith to hear His voice." We might also weave similar thoughts into a corporate confession, praying, "O tender Father, always speaking to us by Your Spirit, forgive us for all the ways we let the noise of life crowd out our ability to hear Your voice. Forgive us for reading our status updates more than Your Word. Forgive us for the ways we tend to be more attentive in worship to the buzzing in our pockets and purses, or the gurgle in our stomachs, than to the fact that You're here in a special way to bless and nourish us. By all these actions and more, we're showing in these moments that we love these things more than You. Have mercy on us, Lord, and help us to worship You."

Worship as Unceasing Prayer and Unending Battle

As a prayer leader, we want the worship service to come across as one long prayer—a continuous conversation between the Trinity and His precious adopted sons and daughters. Leading worship with a prayerful heart and attitude and encouraging the other leaders in worship to embody the same go a long way in aiding flow. Additionally, coaching the various leaders in worship about the prayerful atmosphere and tone of worship is also critical. Sometimes the most disruptive moments in a service are simply when someone else is coming up to lead a prayer, song, or reading. They are either too loud or too soft, too quick or too slow, too excited or too somber compared with the tone of what happened previously. Transitioning a prayerful tone from one person to another is like passing a baton in an Olympic race. It must be handed off with a synchronization of rhythm and pace if the transition is to be successful.

As war generals, we're quick to remind the people of God that when we're engaged in battle, there is no time to pause, lose focus, or veer off course. Reminding our flocks that we are engaged in spiritual warfare as we worship is a powerful way to encourage a solidarity of focus, and this focus is a great catalyst for good flow.

Technologies as Aids for Flow

Among the chief enemies of flow are the limitless distractions that abound in worship. Some things like crying children, disruptive people in the congregation, power outages, and so on are simply out of our control. But because we care about a service's flow, we work hard to identify and minimize the potential unnecessary distractions that *are* within our control. As a worship leader, I've often said that half my job is simply attempting to eliminate distractions for the people of God.

The question of the use of media and technology in worship is again pastoral rather than purely pragmatic. If we use print media (orders of worship, hymnals), how do we help our congregants manage those worship aids well so that worship flows as a participative story rather than a Sunday matinee? We don't want our orders of worship functioning as a playbill so that worshipers become spectators. We want our print media to contribute to people's experience of the story. Perhaps, then, we think more critically about layout, headings, and font sizes to highlight the story's importance. Bulletins laid out poorly and in a bland, nondescript manner often do more harm than good in people's experience of a worship service.

If we use screens, are we diligent to avoid typos, bad grammar or punctuation, and distracting or unfitting backgrounds? If the fonts are too big or too small, how do people's visual experience of the things displayed distract from their engagement? Those who are running lyric slides in our worship services need to feel the gravity of their role in helping or hindering the flow of a worship service. There is nothing more difficult for singing congregations than perpetually slow slide movement. Likewise, if our church utilizes lighting and projection design with color and/or movement, we need to press beyond questions of whether these elements make things look "cool" to whether their displays, actions, and transitions aid in worship's movements and moments. This is where we as theological dieticians and doxological philosophers can spend some time educating our technology teams about worship's story and the accompanying moods and affects we are after.

But nowhere does technology run the risk of being disruptive to flow more than in sound. For traditional churches and spaces, acoustics matter greatly to flow. Good organists, pianists, and choir directors are especially sensitive to their acoustical surroundings. Too quick a tempo on an energetic hymn in a highly reverberant space can throw a congregation's timing off and make the music sound like mush. Too slow a tempo in a dampened space can suffocate the life and energy out of a congregation's hymn singing.

In settings where modern sound equipment is utilized, proper training and skills for sound engineers can't be stressed enough. Poor EQ, lack of compression and gating, inactive mixing (just setting the board and letting it go), mistimed cues for turning a microphone on, feedback, either too loud or too soft an overall volume—these and more are incredible speed bumps to worship's flow. On the other hand, attentive engineers who are tuned in to the rhythms of worship's story will understand their critical role in helping shepherd a congregation through a worship experience.

Sense of Timing and Rehearsing for Worship

Flow, finally, comes down to transitions and an intuitive sense of timing about the way one element moves into another. Too much pause feels like a lull. Too quick a shift feels like a jolt. Silence, which is important in worship, should always be intentional. Developing sensibilities for these things comes from experience and processing a host of factors, including the types of technologies and entertainment our congregations are accustomed to. Whether we like it or not, the production that goes into TV shows, commercials, film cutting, and the like have greatly shaped the way modern people feel transitions.[2] Because the goal of flow is preservation of worship's narrative experience, we're always connecting dots and

---

2. Some may say at this point (and I sympathize) that these "cultural liturgies" we imbibe from the world of film production need to be *challenged* by "counter-liturgies" rather than *accommodated* in worship. Let me simply say here that in a given moment in the life of a church, even *this* choice—i.e., whether to challenge or accommodate—is a *pastoral* one. It's one thing for a counter-liturgy to be acknowledged as *good* for a congregation (a *watchful prophet's* observation). It's quite another to determine whether that

smoothing what comes before with what comes after—musically, conceptually, and verbally.

For all these reasons and more, I do believe that worship services, as far as they are planned, require rehearsal. When it comes to music, I often spend an inordinate amount of time working on and reiterating musical transitions compared to the songs themselves. I likewise have continued the basic habit of writing out certain verbal transitions and practicing them before worship.[3] When it comes to other elements, especially if other people are leading them (i.e., readers, leaders in prayer), I've found rehearsing when to walk up and begin to speak is crucial to the stability and continuity of flow. Nothing breaks flow like an awkward transition.[4]

Tool 2: Ambiance

Discussions of flow naturally lead into considerations of ambiance. Sociologists and artists alike tell us that ambiance is everything. Ambiance tends to be much more felt than observed, but our job as worship pastors involves tuning in to how worship's ambiance shapes people's experience of the gospel story.

Architecture

We need to think about the architecture of our worship space, whether a living room or a cathedral, and the accessories that occupy it. While most of our church architecture is fixed and immovable, we need to be aware of the impact that our space has on our people's perception of God and worship.[5] As worship pastors, we need to ask what our worship spaces are saying to our people.

For instance, I once served in a church with a high ceiling and massive walls of dark brick. The worship space communicated awe and majesty, maybe even fear. This wasn't necessarily a bad thing, but as a theological dietician I became aware that God's transcendence is so much more naturally felt than His immanence in

---

counter-liturgy is good *now* (a *caregiver's* observation). See James K. A. Smith, *Desiring the Kingdom: Worship, Worldview, and Cultural Formation* (Grand Rapids, Mich.: Baker, 2009).

3. For a helpful, brief tutorial on verbal transitions, see Paul Ryan, "Consider Those 'In Between' Words: Spoken Transitions in Worship," *Reformed Worship* (March 2006), accessed August 7, 2015, http://www .reformedworship.org/article/march-2006/consider-those-between-words-spoken-transitions-worship.

4. Below, we will discuss shared leadership and empowering others, but it is worth noting Mark Pierson's insight here about how pastoring other worship leaders intersects with faithful management of transitions. As Pierson points out, managing transitions involves not only managing elements, but *people*: "[In curated worship,] communities have the expectation of participation by a variety of people leading different segments of worship, and stationed responses in the service are commonplace. In these communities, the curator's job involves managing the segues between all these people and elements." Mark Pierson, *The Art of Curating Worship: Reshaping the Role of Worship Leader* (Minneapolis: Sparkhouse, 2010), 44.

5. Here we note interesting new exceptions to fixed and immovable architecture: technologies of immersive and atmospheric projection that can virtually "change the walls."

a space like this, and I knew that worship's elements and presentation needed to compensate. Similarly but on the other end of the spectrum, houses of worship mirrored after theaters and stadiums come with liabilities as well. Watchful prophets are aware that such venues drag in a host of potentially idolatrous cultural dispositions—an "entertain me" attitude, passive observation rather than active participation, and an expectation of feeling comfortable and being "waited on." Worship leaders thinking pastorally will find strategic ways to confront and address these potentially hazardous counter-messages spoken by their worship space.

Design

When we think as caregivers, we become aware of how comforting or discomforting, how hospitable or unwelcoming, the design of our worship spaces can be. Our pastoral instincts here cause us to seek discomfort only where appropriate, for example when God's law confronts our sin, and to root out the unnecessary irritants that take away from what worship should be. As missionaries, we're aware of the difference between worship spaces that feel purposefully ancient and historic and those that are simply dated, many times caused by accessories like banners, color schemes, and choices of metal and wood. Dated worship spaces can be unnecessarily off-putting to outsiders, and they can communicate that our church has nothing relevant to say. Just as with worship's elements and structure, so too the design of our spaces should be appropriately contextualized to our culture.

Accessories

A doxological philosopher thinks long and hard about how worship's accessories communicate what we value in worship. For instance, I have been in some churches where Communion is highly valued and seen in the magnificent, artistic tables placed front and center. The positioning, materials, and craftsmanship of worship's primary furniture (e.g., the pulpit, baptismal font or baptistery, and the Lord's Supper table) speak volumes to worship's philosophical values. The kinds of art we display and utilize, whether physically mounted or digitally projected, help our congregations understand what it means to "worship the LORD in the beauty of holiness" (Ps. 96:9 KJV). Everything from the type of bread selected for Communion to the size and positioning of the cross up front either adds to or takes away from people's experience of the story we are trying to tell in worship.

Lighting and Visuals

Lighting and visuals are a big part of being an emotional shepherd in our day. Many sociologists and anthropologists tell us that we are shifting from being a dominantly literary culture to a visual one. What we see often shades how we feel (just ask Hollywood). Whether we greet our postliterate age with great joy or grave concern, we must reckon with it, especially as missionaries seeking to contextualize worship in this present age. Graphic designers, photographers, interior decorators, film producers, and lighting specialists can offer great wisdom about how lighting and visuals affect the psychology of the modern worshiper.

Artists as Experts in Ambiance

Here we come to our final consideration about ambiance. As church lovers and disciple makers, we have a passion to catalyze the gifts of the church and equip the saints for the work of the ministry (Eph. 4:12). And as artist chaplains, we know that the gifts of artists are especially germane to this discussion. Artists have a keen awareness of and sensitivity to how architecture, props, visuals, and other accouterments speak in a given setting. We might say that culture's artists are fluent in the language of ambiance. Our congregants and community members who are regularly involved in the arts can help translate what our worship spaces are saying to our people, and they can help us say the right things as we work in partnership with them.

Tool 3: Leadership

Flow and ambiance are important for the experience of a service, but meaningful, formative worship often simply comes down to a worship pastor's leadership in the moment. I have seen great worship leaders overcome many obstacles of flow and ambiance simply because they knew how to lead well. Our desire to be excellent up-front leaders comes from our heart as church lovers. We lead well because we have a passion for Christ's bride and long for worship to be a place where she experiences a greater sense of her union and communion with her Bridegroom. We believe in worship's formative power, and we lead out of that conviction so that our church "will grow to become in every respect the mature body of him who is the head, that is, Christ" (Eph. 4:15).

Leading through Disposition

As an emotional shepherd, we know that our mannerisms, postures, countenance, and vocal inflections all either help or hinder our people in experiencing God's presence. We're sensitive to our context in this regard. If we are overly dramatic for our context, despite our best arguments for being authentic, we end up being more of a distraction than an aid. If we are overly subdued for our context, we likewise aren't leading well.

For leadership situations where the congregation is more subdued in worship and needs to grow in physical and emotional expressiveness, a helpful way of thinking about our leadership disposition is to first discern the average expressiveness of our congregation and then strive to be a few steps ahead of where they are. A stiff, forlorn congregation doesn't need their leader to be flipping cartwheels. They need an example of a joyful countenance and uplifted posture, to start. For highly expressive congregations, chances are their area of growth is in learning how to be reverent, quiet, and introspective. The situations we set up in worship (i.e., confession, lamentation, meditation, etc.) along with the appropriate accompanying physical disposition aid well in our congregation's expressive maturity. Ultimately, our goal is to tastefully and appropriately mirror to our congregations the kinds of affective dispositions we hope they have in a given moment in the worship service.

Leading through Prayerful Education

As a doxological philosopher and theological dietician, part of our job is to lead in such a way that educates our people about what worship is and does. Worship should never feel like a classroom, but we can in creative ways naturally weave doctrine and philosophy into our statements, transitions, prayers, and songs. Yet as corporate mystics, we're sensitive to the ways that overexplaining and a hyper-cognitive approach to worship actually quench a congregation's ability to sense and experience God's presence.

I've been in many worship settings where a commitment to explain everything in worship effectively killed any sense that worship was anything more than a head exercise where people could walk away saying, "Fascinating!", "Interesting!", or "Stimulating!" These are not the expressions of one who has encountered the living God. For instance, I could more didactically instruct my congregation before confession, saying, "We confess our sins because God is holy, and His perfection exposes all our imperfections." That's okay. However, I'm convinced it's better to weave such teaching into a worshipful moment rather than pause for instruction. I could instead, after songs and readings of God's greatness, pray very similar words directly to God: "O God, You are holy; we are not. You are beautiful; we are marred in ugliness. You are righteous; we are unrighteous. What can we do in this moment but confess to You our sin?" Or at the end of worship, instead of more overtly instructing, "This is the moment when, reinvigorated by God's gospel, we go forth into the world as witnesses and missionaries," I could offer a direct commission from God: "God says, 'I have shown you again the riches and glories of Christ, so now go and bear witness to what you have tasted and seen!'" We see in these moments that when we combine our call to educate with our call to be prayer leaders and missionaries, we become much more effective in forming our congregation's theology of worship.

Leading with Backbone

A war general knows that there are times in a worship service to be bold and forceful. Too often, our view of leading with a worshipful attitude is one dimensional, bending toward a default mode of wistful sentimentality. There are times and places for a tender disposition that exhibits intimacy between God and His people, but worship leaders also need to exhibit backbone—a Christ-empowered confidence in worship's war against the enemy. Leadership of this type offers the people a different picture of our great Worship Leader, Jesus—a picture that a mortician offers of the end, where Christ comes to judge and to conquer in mighty triumph.

I often find that the time to exhibit this kind of strength is at the beginning of a service as a means to rally and center the troops, and then at the end of the service when we as missionaries and watchful prophets are commissioning and sending Christ's soldiers to the field for the battle of witness and deeds of love and mercy. For me, this kind of strength looks like a strong and forceful countenance accompanying bold singing, prayer, and declarative statements. I've seen other worship leaders effectively shout declarations from Scripture about God's character and deeds during the musical turns and pauses between verses, choruses, and bridges.

Leading by Empowering Other Leaders

As disciple makers, we also need to consider how others around us are leading the service. All the above considerations need to be taken into account as we coach and work alongside the other pastors, musicians, readers, and liturgists who assist up front in worship. Concern for this kind of collaborative training comes from a desire to see those leaders grow as disciples of Christ and to see our congregation properly shepherded in worship. I can't tell you how many experiences I've had leading worship when another leader has unintentionally undermined some aspect of worship simply because they were poorly equipped to lead in that given moment.

Along these lines, I encourage worship pastors to consider a more communal leadership model with a diversity of voices and faces in worship leadership. For example, I have found great value in our congregation hearing the prayers and song leadership of a woman in complement to my prayers and singing. Congregants will often comment about how the other leader's unique perspective or leadership angle spoke to a different place in their heart. Likewise—and especially important in multicultural contexts—it is critical that the faces and voices of our worship leadership reflect the ethnic diversity of our congregation and city. The same is true for cultivating a diversity of ages up front. This diversity visually says something to the congregation about the nature of the church and allows every kind of person in the congregation to find a point of identification in a worship service. Diversity of leadership up front allows a congregation to see themselves worshiping.[6]

Our Sacred Trust

The gravity of a tour guide's job is directly proportional to the value of what they are presenting. We all know that there is a vast difference between a real estate agent showing a one-bedroom, one-bath condo in a run-down part of Wichita and an expert guide leading a tour through the Notre Dame Cathedral in Paris. When we think of the value of the gospel, then, we have ventured into the territory of life and death, of ultimate things. As worship pastors, we have a sacred trust, a commission from the Father, to join the work of the Spirit in showing off the beauties and excellencies of the Son. There is nothing more precious than this call. As we plan worship services and as we lead them, we are inviting a lost and wandering people to know, feel, taste, see, and hear what matters most—Jesus Christ, the hope of the world.

O Holy Spirit, help us to feel the weight and value of our call, and then fill us up to lead with love and grace, all for the sake of Christ. Amen.

---

6. For more on diversity and multicultural leadership, see Sandra Maria Van Opstal, *The Next Worship: Glorifying God in a Diverse World* (Downers Grove, Ill.: InterVarsity, 2016), especially chapter 4.

THE WORSHIP PASTOR AS FAILURE

Up to the hills where Christ is gone
To plead for all His saints
Presenting at His Father's throne
Our songs and our complaints.
                    —*Isaac Watts, 1719*[1]

With tongue only slightly in cheek as I say this, I hate books like these . . . books that make broad, sweeping claims about who we are and what we should be . . . books that appear to be helpful manuals for faithful practice but really are overwhelming descriptions of impossibility. If you've skimmed, selected several chapters, or read all of this book, I imagine that many of you have had the same experience reading this as I have had in writing it—droplets of inspiration and encouragement surrounded by a flood of, "How in the world am I supposed to do all of this?"

To be honest, *The Worship Pastor* depicts someone who doesn't exist (well, almost . . . we'll get to that). The worship pastor described in this book is a mythological superhuman, supremely gifted in all arenas, unchangeably wise in every endeavor, inexhaustibly supplied with endless energy. (And here all this time you thought you were reading a nonfiction book!) Ironically, one of my fears in writing this book has been that my own congregation and co-pastors might read it and discover what a poor job I'm doing.

The Worship Pastor stands as an impossibly high benchmark. It probably feels less like a window into what our ministry practice could look like and more like a mirror reflecting back to us all of the things we aren't. Although it might first come to us as something inspirational and attainable, in practice, its suggestions, admonishments, and encouragements can ultimately feel like an unbearable weight. We might shore up a few weak spots through some concerted time and

---

1. Isaac Watts, "Lord, in the Morning Thou Shalt Hear" (1719). Public Domain.

effort only to find other balls dropped behind us. So how are we supposed to do this? Unfortunately, the news gets worse before it gets better.

What We Should Be

I've purposefully downplayed something throughout this book that probably should have had more prominence. It's what many medieval Christians called the "interior life" of a pastor. Pastors have a high call, and one perpetual temptation we all face is to get busy "doing stuff" for God while neglecting the faithful cultivation of a personal, intimate relationship with God. Gregory the Great's accusation of pastoral carelessness feels very true of me: "They take it as a pleasure to be weighed down by such activities . . . they disregard those interior matters which they ought to be teaching others."[2] Even if you and I were to be busied up in our jobs with all the stuff outlined in this book, doing all of this would only burn us out in an endless cycle of doing to the neglect of being. So alongside the work of the worship pastor we have outlined here, we need to add the faithful practices of Bible reading, meditation, prayer, fasting, silence, Sabbath, and so on. Worship pastor, your job is even more demanding than you thought.

Add to these demands the qualifications for church leadership that God outlines in the Scriptures. Stephen Miller, distilling J. Oswald Sanders, summarizes 1 Timothy 3:1–13 and Titus 1:5–9 well:[3]

- *Social qualifications.* Above reproach, with a good reputation among believers; dignified; displays a holy and joyful life; respected by others.
- *Moral qualifications.* Not arrogant; not greedy or a lover of money; not in ministry for dishonest gain; above reproach; not a slanderer or liar; faithful to their spouse; temperate (having self-control).
- *Mental qualifications.* Able to teach sound doctrine and rebuke false teachers; hold the mystery of the faith (have a good grasp of the gospel); have a well-ordered mind, which results in a well-ordered life.
- *Disposition (personality) qualifications.* Genial, considerate, and gentle. Self-controlled and disciplined. Given to hospitality. Not quick-tempered, violent, or quarrelsome; not a drunk.
- *Domestic qualifications.* Singularly committed to their spouse (not flirtatious); able to manage family well; has spiritual aspiration in leading family.

---

2. Gregory the Great, *The Book of Pastoral Rule*, II.7, 68; quoted in Andrew Purves, *Pastoral Theology in the Classical Tradition* (Louisville: Westminster John Knox, 2001), 71.

3. What follows, with just a few changes, is the outline in Stephen Miller, *Worship Leaders, We Are Not Rock Stars* (Chicago: Moody, 2013), 62–63. Miller is summarizing J. Oswald Sanders, *Spiritual Leadership* (Chicago: Moody, 2007), 39–46.

- *Maturity.* Not a new convert; able to teach; tested—has had opportunities to serve in less prominent tasks that have developed both natural and spiritual gifts; faithful; sober-minded; holy; upright.

Unless we're formal pastors, elders, or deacons, the collar might loosen up a bit on these qualifications. Still, given the burden of this book—namely, that worship leaders, like it or not, inherently function in a *pastoral* role—we should take this outline for church leadership seriously. The worship pastor's call is no joke.

"Who May Ascend the Hill of the Lord?"

If one of the ways the Bible describes worship is ascent to God (Psalms 120–134), then Psalm 24 sums up the question and answer that we all must consider:

> Who may ascend the mountain of the LORD?
>   Who may stand in his holy place?
> The one who has clean hands and a pure heart,
>   who does not trust in an idol
>   or swear by a false god.
>
> —*Psalm 24:3–4*

Clean hands? Pure heart? No idols? Do you feel the crushing weight of this like I do? Does the burden of the worship pastor's call feel similar to God demanding that you carry a refrigerator uphill, two miles, in the snow . . . in other words, impossible? Who may ascend that hill? Who is worthy to be a worship leader? Not you. Not me. Worship pastor, give it up. We aren't worthy. We are failures.

But, guess what? That's *exactly* where God wants us.

Failure as the Starting Place of Ministry

So much of our pristine, modern Christianity is literally hell-bent on telling us that ministry must start with success. A person could hear *The Worship Pastor*'s call as, "Just do these things, and you will be a successful worship leader." But the Scriptures offer us a different starting path to success.

I've read Psalm 51 many, many times. And every time I do, my sense of failure resonates with David's deep, soulful, eloquent confession: "Have mercy on me . . . blot out my transgressions . . . my sin is always before me . . . against you, you only, have I sinned . . . I was sinful at birth." Still, whenever I hit verse 13, it feels out of place: "Then I will teach transgressors your ways, so that sinners will turn back to you." This statement seems to me to be what philosophers call a *non sequitur*—it just does not follow. It never made sense to me that "teaching transgressors" is something that immediately follows an abject recognition of failure. I thought such ministry was reserved for the people who were on their spiritual A-game—you know, those *successful* Christians, *successful* ministry leaders. How could David, in exposing what is arguably the darkest sin of his life, move from confession to thoughts of ministry?

But the "then" is unbelievably critical: "*Then* I will teach transgressors your ways." It's the recognition that we are first lacking, first deficient, first needy, first inadequate, and *that* gets us ready for the surprising "then." As odd as it sounds, worship pastor, the more you come to grips with your need and inadequacy, the more ready you are to *then* be a worship pastor. Failure is the great (and perpetual) starting place of all successful ministry.

Failure as the Starting Place for Worship

For the same reason, failure is the great and perpetual starting place for worship too. The worship of God begins only when the worship of ourselves ends, and acknowledgment of our failure hastens that ending. I imagine this is why hymn writer Joseph Hart (1712–68) included this verse in one of my favorite call to worship songs:

> Let not conscience make you linger,
> Nor of fitness fondly dream;
> All the fitness He requireth
> is to feel your need of Him.[4]

What does God require of His worshipers? What is our entry ticket into worship? What's the password? It's "I need you, God." As C. FitzSimons Allison said, "Restlessness, uneasiness, and dissatisfaction with ourselves is the only qualification for worship."[5] We can properly look up only when we are flat on our backs. Failure leads to a life-giving shift in posture, a change from looking downward and inward to looking outward and upward. And then the very hill that we know we can't ascend becomes the mountain on which our hope lies:

> I lift up my eyes to the mountains—
> where does my help come from?

---

4. Joseph Hart, "Come Ye Sinners, Poor and Needy" (1759). Public Domain.
5. C. FitzSimons Allison, *Fear, Love, and Worship* (New York: Seabury, 1962), 27.

My help comes from the LORD.
                    —*Psalm 121:1–2*

It is atop that same mountain that the angel took a despondent apostle John when he was weeping over the unworthiness of the whole world. And as their eyes ascended the hill, an elder cried, "Do not weep! See, the Lion of the tribe of Judah, the Root of David, has triumphed. He is able." And John turned, lifting up his eyes to the mountains, and saw "a Lamb, looking as though it had been slain" (Rev. 5:5–6). Atop the hill we could never ascend, the hill of Calvary, hangs the Lamb of God who takes away the sins of the world—the One with clean hands and a pure heart.

Who may ascend the hill of the Lord? The Lamb answers, "I."

And suddenly, our failure is swallowed up in worship.

The Successful Worship Pastor

Remember when I said that the worship pastor described in this book doesn't really exist? We now know the good news: He *does* exist. We've named Him before, but let's end by naming Him again. Our one true Worship Leader, Jesus Christ, is the worship pastor every church (and every human) longs for. Jesus is the one true Church Lover whose self-sacrificial love for her knew no bounds (Eph. 5:25–27). Jesus is the one true Corporate Mystic, the highway between heaven and earth on which God travels to meet us (John 14:5–11). Jesus is the one true Doxological Philosopher, the definition of good, right, holy, acceptable worship (John 4:21–26).

Jesus is the one true Disciple Maker, calling us from dead to joyful obedience in His way (Matt. 4:19). Jesus is the one true Prayer Leader, teaching us to pray (Matt. 6:9–13) and purifying our misguided prayers before the Father (Rom. 8:34). Jesus is the one true Theological Dietician, feeding His people with the best theology money can't buy—His very body and blood (John 6:54). Jesus is the one true War General, the Warrior Lamb who leads us into battle against sin, the flesh, and the devil (Rev. 17:14). Jesus is the one true Watchful Prophet, the very Word of God (John 1:1). Jesus is the one true Missionary, sent by the Father from heaven to earth to redeem a lost world (Gal. 4:4).

Jesus is the one true Artist Chaplain, both the inspiration of all creativity (Col. 1:16) and Answer to every artist's deepest question (Rom. 3:21–26). Jesus is the one true Caregiver, binding our wounds, grief, and sorrows (Isa. 53:4–5). Jesus is the one true Mortician, the one in whom we all died (Rom. 6:1–4) and the one who will come to raise us anew on that great and glorious day (Rev. 22:20). Jesus is the one true Emotional Shepherd, for He is the desire of nations (Hag. 2:7). Jesus is the one true Liturgical Architect, the cornerstone of God's house (1 Peter 2:4–7) and the framework of His worship (Heb. 11:10). Jesus is the one true Curator, the very Wisdom of God (1 Cor. 1:24). Jesus is the one true Tour Guide, leading us straight into the Most Holy Place by His blood (Heb. 10:19–22).

We are qualified, worthy, and able because Jesus is qualified, worthy, and able. This is a freeing, inspiring, faith-producing, worship-engendering word to every failed worship pastor. It means we're free to take a stab at this thing called worship pastoring, even in the deep awareness that we are not adequate to the task. We're free to soar; we're free to crash and burn. We're free to strive; we're free to rest. The burden is lifted, and the pressure's off.

> Now may the God of peace, who through the blood of the eternal covenant brought back from the dead our Lord Jesus, that great Shepherd of the sheep, equip you with everything good for doing his will, and may he work in us what is pleasing to him, through Jesus Christ, to whom be glory for ever and ever. Amen.
>
> *—Hebrews 13:20–21*

SCRIPTURE INDEX

SUBJECT INDEX